# Stolen

## What Readers Are Saying About Will Astrike

## and the Frank Bass Series

Meet Buffalo Robe Bass, the Crocodile Dundee of Wyoming Territory. But wait…his lady friend, Sally Bloom, is every bit his match. This sleuthing pair brings the Old West back to life, keeps you guessing until the last page, and leaves you hoping that Bass and Bloom and company will soon ride again. –Margaret Coel, New York Times bestselling author of *Winter's Child.*

… As a writer who lives in Wyoming and writes about the West, I can honestly say he nails it: lock, stock, and barrel. Speaking of new heroes, when you think Will Astrike, think early Elmore Leonard. - Gregory Zeigler - Author of The Jake Goddard and Susan Brand Thrillers

I loved the whole book. Characters, plot, and descriptions were all excellent. I especially enjoyed the language-- the expressions, idioms, and pace were outstanding. It put you back to the 1880s and how people talked, dressed, and acted. Will read the next book. Thanks, Deputy Marshall Bass, for letting me ride.

… the book was well written, the characters fun, and the story interesting. I have read all of Louis Lamour's books, many two or three times and Will Astrike might be just as good a writer.

# Stolen

This was a great read with outstanding characters and lots of action. 'Would highly recommend this book to all those that enjoy a great Western story.

Book two of the Frank Bass series by Will Astrike. This story was full of mystery and drama. 'Enjoyed every page. Thank you.

An excellent read. Keeps you tapping the Kindle. The characters are exciting and believable. I am anxious to read more of Ezra Lacy's adventures. All of you cowboys and cowgirls will enjoy this book. So, "Giddy Up."

... I still think Will Astrike may be the best Western author since Louie L'Amour. I look forward to his next book. A most wonderful read. Gotta love following Deputy Marshall Bass and Sally around and the messes they get themselves into!

Frank Bass series book Three by Will Astrike. I love the character of Frank Bass. The legendary Marshall of the West. This has been a great series and I've enjoyed reading each book. This story's legacy of the young man who wants to clear his father's name is a good one also.
Another great read. Excellent characters, plot, and description of surroundings. But my favorite thing is the dialog. The idioms and meanings of the day are right online. I had never heard of "consists" used as a noun. Keep 'em coming.

# Stolen

Robert F. Thompson

*5.0 out of 5 stars* **Another winner...**
Reviewed in the United States on May 26, 2023
Verified Purchase

I enjoyed the read... fast-paced...I learned a thing or two about how people lived and survived back then...The descriptions of the city of Austin, the bars, hotels, were great...The characters? AWESOME!!!!...I was never a huge fan of Western novels, but Will Astrike has made me a Frank Bass fan for life...can't wait for Book 6?

Verified Purchase
**I have read Mr. Astride's Frank Bass series also...This one was really good...the colorful characters...the historical figures of the West came alive...The Texas Rangers...The Indian Nations...The Civil War...Custer...Crook...I will read anything else by Mr. Astrike...**

Deborah Sue Lacy

*5.0 out of 5 stars* **Great writing**
Reviewed in the United States on December 3, 2023
Verified Purchase

**You, sir, are an awesome writer, and the story of Amos Getting was the BEST Western I've read in my 75 years, of which the last 65 have been as an avid reader.**

# Stolen

Other Books

By

Award-Winning Author

## Will Astrike

The Knack

The Skills of Ezra Lacy

Legacy

Stolen

*Amos Getting*
A Life on the American Frontier

Slaughter

The Regulator

Rustling

*Winner of the 2024 International Impact Award for Historical

Fiction*

# STOLEN

# By Will Astrike

www.westernauthor.net

# Stolen

Prologue

The acreage that would become the XIT Ranch in
Texas was purchased in 1879 and immediately became the
largest landhold in the United States. It was also the most
expansive working ranch in the world, comprising over
three million acres, all fenced. It stretched across ten
counties of Northwest Texas, and its western fence line ran
for two-hundred miles along the border with New Mexico
and crossed ten counties in the Texas Panhandle.

Investors Charles and John Farwell of Chicago
purchased the land. The price they agreed on with the
Governor of Texas, Oran M. Roberts, would be the amount
needed to build the grandest State Capitol in Austin. The
final cost for construction was three million, two hundred
thousand dollars, and change, making the price per acre just
over a dollar. The giant property was split into seven cattle
ranching divisions, and Colonel B. H. Campbell was named
general manager, with Berry Nations hired on as range
boss.

During Campbell's tenure as manager, certain ranch
areas were used as rendezvous and hideouts by various
miscreants and villains. These outlaws were mostly from
New Mexico Territory to the west and Oklahoma Indian

# Stolen

territory to the north. In 1887, the Farwell brothers sought out a man to do what Campbell was unable to do: clean up the reputation of XIT and make it a safe place to live, work, and conduct business. The brothers found their man in a thirty-five-year-old attorney and legislator, Avery L. Matlock.

Avery Lenoir Matlock earned a reputation as a no-nonsense prosecutor when he worked as county attorney for Montague County, Texas. He had successfully prosecuted and won convictions of several marauding gang members and cattle thieves during his appointment from 1875 through 1878. He was elected to the Texas House of Representatives in 1881 and the Texas Senate in 1883. Matlock was a small man of five feet and seven inches, with a large, neatly trimmed mustache and dark brown hair that matched the color of his eyes. He dressed neatly in four-button suits; the jackets always buttoned at the collar. He managed to maintain the striking visage of a man waiting to spring a trap. He was quick to smile, though always on his guard.

Because of his success and well-documented belief in justice and honesty, he was persuaded to join the XIT with the title of Legal Investigator and General Manager.

# Stolen

And in the process, he became a target for every cut-throat and miscreant in the territory.

The XIT division headquarters for cattle was located in Buffalo Springs, a small crossroads about thirty miles south of the Oklahoma border. As there were no schools, churches, markets, or post office and railroad in Buffalo Springs, on November 15, 1887, Avery, his wife Alice, and their three children moved to Hartley, Texas.

Hartley sat along the recently completed mainline for the El Paso and South Western Railroad. The tracks connected Hartley with Amarillo, sixty miles to the southeast, and Texline, fifty miles to the northwest. Texline lay about a thirty-minute horseback ride to the XIT northern headquarters of the cattle division of the ranch. There was also a telegraph terminal in Texline, making communication with the other offices more convenient.

*6:00 p.m. December 24, 1887*
*Matlock House,*
*Hartley, Texas*

Hartley, Texas, is at the extreme northern end of the Llano Estacado. It's surrounded by plains, low ridgelines, and shallow gullies. The horizon stretches for miles in any direction with nothing to interrupt the view. When there's rain, the prairie provides decent grazing. But in the late summer and early fall, the winds and heat keep anything from taking root and growing.

Late December brings cold nights and occasional snow to the panhandle of northwestern Texas. It had been an ordinary day at the Matlock home of chores, of course, animals to be tended, firewood brought in, and tins of lamp oil needing filling. Theirs was a two-story house, but there were no stoves on the second floor for the sleeping quarters. Instead, vents in the second-story floors were opened to allow the heat generated by several stoves downstairs to rise and warm the upper floor.

It was Christmas Eve day, and with several inches of fresh snow on the ground, the two older children—Ruth, twelve, and Susan, eight—had built a snow fort in the front yard and peppered each other—and the neighbor boys—with snowballs and childish taunts. The air was crisp and scented with wood smoke, and the deep blue December sky was so clear that Ruth could see Eddie Cathcart's barn three miles distant. A humble snowman from the day before listed slightly and had lost his pipe.

Ruth was the tomboy of the family. She loved riding, shooting, her foreman teaching her, and any kind of

# Stolen

competition she could devise to dare the boys at school. She rarely wore dresses, preferring always her jeans, flannel shirt, sheepskin jacket, and woolen gloves (never mittens). Rather than a woolen hat that covered the ears, she chose a narrow-brimmed, grey-felt Resistol hat with a red band and half a pheasant plume sticking out of it.

Susan had been sickly as a baby, and even though she was thriving now, she was still small for her age. Susan enjoyed dressing up and having her blonde hair curled. She had tried to convince her mother, Alice, that she was old enough for rouge, but she never succeeded.

The baby, Edward, was eight months old, taking solid food and sleeping through the night.

Avery Matlock's job allowed him home for two weeks a month. Otherwise, he would stay at ranch headquarters in Buffalo Springs. During those times, he would see to the wealth of paperwork generated for his position by the courts. But now and then, especially if there were tip-offs, he would make time to ride the fences with the new range boss, A.G. Boyce, and some hand-picked riders for protection. While on the trail, he would take notes and draw rough maps for future reference. If they came upon a band of outlaws, his procedure was always the same.

# Stolen

Under the protection—and ready weapons—of his riders, he would advise the lawbreakers that he was making a list of their descriptions, which he would hand over to the ranch foreman. He'd announce that he would not disturb the local law enforcement agencies. The courts were overcrowded anyway. If they chose to remain or later return, they would be hanged on the spot for criminal trespass. It only took one or two occasions for posse men to act on the threat before word got around that the XIT was off-limits.

Tonight, he was at home and participating in all matters with his family. He played the shadow game with the girls, sang carols with neighbors, and decorated the tree with keepsakes and handmade ornaments. At dinner, he said grace at the family table and fed the baby by the fire in his rocker. When the children were asleep, he joined Alice in placing carefully wrapped presents beneath the tree in the front parlor at the window. By 11:00 p.m., he and Alice were asleep, and the house was quiet.

# Stolen

In a sheltered ravine called Lone Rock Coulee, one-quarter mile west of the Matlock house, a group of hard-looking men stood their horses while they smoked and passed around a pint of tequila. They were all members of Vicente Silva's White Caps Gang. Jose Chavez y Chavez was in charge tonight. With him were gang members Eugenio Alarid and Julian Trujillo, killers with eighteen murders and maimings credited to them, though most in the know said that number was low. They were the gang's most valuable assassins. Then, there was Octavio Romero and a Cherokee warrior named Crawford Goldsby, sometimes known as Cherokee Bill Guerrero. Bill had just returned from completing his portion of the night's mission. Using his bow, he had eliminated both the family dogs as they were yelping at his approach near the barn. The dogs fell in the shadows with very little noise. As he returned, it was time for the other four to complete the action. Cherokee Bill would stay in position with the animals, and at the appropriate time, he would walk the horses to an agreed-upon spot closer to the house.

# Stolen

The four men approached the back door at a low trot, staying in the shadows of the building as much as possible. They all hugged the walls of the house as they stood silently on the back stoop. The moon was full and provided enough light for the terrible work they planned to do, and it also gave them the shadows needed to remain undetected.

Using a glazer's tool, Jose Chavez y Chavez, both his father's and mother's surnames were Chavez, etched a large arc in the glass of the back door and, with surgical tape, attached a five-foot twine to the outside of the glass arc. He gently tapped the etching using the same glazer's tool until the glass broke free. The glass arc fell inside, but the twine held, and the glass did not hit the floor.

The four men moved quickly now. They all put white hoods with eye cutouts over their heads and tucked them into their shirt collars, making them more difficult for a victim to remove. They had memorized the layout of the house, knowing that it would be considerably darker inside. The Matlocks habitually kept a small lamp lit all night for the children's sake in the upstairs hall, but it usually died out before dawn.

Romero went first to the parent's bedroom, where he heard Avery and Alice Matlock still sleeping soundly.

# Stolen

His job was to make sure the parents did not interfere. The other three went into the children's room. All three children were sleeping, but the baby was beginning to stir. Chavez signaled to Trujilo to silence the infant while he and Alarid covered the mouths of the sleeping girls with a chloroform-soaked bandanna. Each struggled as they were roused by the cloth, but in short order, each was unconscious. The baby began making short gasping noises, and Trulilo, who was large and violent but also mentally deficient, remembered only that the baby was not to be stolen. There were no provisions in the plan made for caring for an infant. Surprised and confused by the sounds, he forgot about his chloroform rag and used his knife to cut the baby's throat.

The others were on the move, with each carrying a little girl across his shoulder. Seeing the others emerge from the children's room, Romero left his position to signal Cherokee Bill. As quietly as they could, the stairs and flooring creaking under their weight, they slipped back downstairs and out the back door. Cherokee Bill stood on the drive on the north side of the house, holding five horses as far from the barn as he could be. Any closer to the barn, and the men feared their horses would scent the animals in the barn and begin calling to them. Within several minutes,

# Stolen

they were far enough from the house to spur their horses into a low gallop. Like wayward calves at branding time, the girls had been tied across the laps of two men. The sky was starting to lighten as the five horses cleared the western water tank bed and drove for the coulees beyond.

# Stolen

*5:15 a.m. December 25, 1887*

*Matlock House*

*Hartley, Texas*

"Dear, dear, wake up, dear. Merry Christmas, Avery. I'm going to get the baby. The girls are probably already downstairs. Why don't you put on your robe and go down and check?"

"Good Lord, Alice, it's still dark outside . . . Merry Christmas."

Alice was already putting on a dressing gown and heading to the hallway. Avery sat on the side of the bed, trying to make out the time on his watch, but the house was still too dark to see. As he reached for his robe, he heard the most horrifying scream he could imagine echoing down the hall. It was followed by a pitiful wailing and the sight of his wife in extreme panic, scrabbling down the hall, calling for him and sobbing at the same time.

"My God, Avery. My sweet Lord. They're gone, dear God, the girls are gone, and Eddie's covered in blood."

Her face was twisted in fear and disbelief, and she crumbled to the floor, nearly frozen in confusion and grief.

# Stolen

When she looked up, her expression seemed a plea for Avery to explain.

Avery Matlock's eyes were wide open, and he fumbled for a match to re-light the hall lamp. He carried it, trembling, into the children's room, noticing immediately the empty beds of his two daughters. He went to the baby's crib and saw blood smeared all over little Eddie's face and neck. Parts of the bedding were wet with blood. He was suddenly flooded with hope when the baby, reaching up for him, opened his mouth and began to cry. Matlock saw a jagged cut along the baby's upper chest and neck, but it appeared shallow, and thank dear God, the baby was breathing deeply enough to cry. He lifted his son from the crib and took him out to his mother, who remained slumped on the floor, her head in her hands, sobbing.

"Alice, Alice, my love, look. Look, dear. Eddie is alive. He has a cut, but he's still alive. We have to get the doctor out here. Please, Alice, look at me, sweetheart, look at me. Eddie is alive, but he needs a doctor. I want you to take him and bandage his chest as best you can. I'm going to send Emilio to town for the doctor."

Avery handed the baby to Alice, who cradled him gently in her arms, and the two of them went downstairs,

# Stolen

Alice to the kitchen for water and bandages, and Avery out to the bunkhouse to roust out Emilio.

"Emilio! For the love of God, Emilio! Emilio, where are you?"

"Si Señor, what is it, Mr. Avery, sir?" Emilio was still half in sleep as he listened to Matlock, but as the desperation of what happened sank in, he was quick to bridle a horse and go without taking time for a saddle.

Avery went back inside and found Alice on a kitchen chair holding the baby, rocking him gently and humming. Her eyes were closed, but he could still see the puffy redness around them. Avery was still in a daze himself, with no clear idea as to what had happened during the night. Somehow, his girls were taken, and his baby's throat was cut, but he had no idea who could possibly want to do such an unspeakable thing. Eddie was alert and active. He moved his head and made the same small grunting noises he usually did, though, at times, his movement caused pain, and he cried out. He saw that the baby had taken Alice's mind temporarily away from the girls, so he decided to go outside and wait for Doc.

Avery stood outside in his robe and slippers, oblivious to the winter weather. He felt the sun coming up as it warmed his right side, and the light seemed to draw

# Stolen

things closer into perspective. He would have to see the Marshal, certainly, though he knew he had little to offer. Matlock had no idea who the District Marshal was. He'd met the sheriff of Hartley naturally, and he seemed a capable fellow, but his jurisdiction ended at the city limits. He was pulled from his thoughts by his foreman, Curtis Lane, an aging cowboy, though solid and reliable. Salt and pepper hair. An experienced man.

"Yes, Curtis, what is it?"

"You oughta see this, sir."

Matlock stepped down from the porch and followed Lane to an area well to the far northern side of the house.

"I believe they gathered here, sir, away from the second-floor windows. Looks like four, maybe five ponies, all unshod. You can see they headed out to the west, yonder Mr. Matlock."

"Dear God, Indians, do you suppose?"

"Not likely. They don't steal people so much anymore. Too much trouble carin' for them. An 'sides, Injuns would'a gone for your horses."

At that time, one of the day workers came running up, "Mr. Matlock? There're two dead dogs lyin' just outside the barn, sir. Arrows in both of 'em."

# Stolen

"Jesus Lord." Then, looking at Lane, "Not Indians, huh?"

"I still don't believe so, sir. 'Gotta figure they knew who they were looking for and where in the house to find 'em. 'Means somehow, they know the layout of the house. 'Spect there's a rat in the bunkhouse."

"Hell. Well, you're probably right now that I think of it. 'You have any suspicions?"

"No sir, I know all five of the fellas myself. Worked with all of 'em before. Do you remember any of 'em been inside the house, upstairs an' all?"

"Not that I can recall. Alice might've had someone in for repairs, but she's in no condition to ask right now. I want you and two others to ride out 'follow those tracks as far as you can. See if you can find out if they changed direction out beyond view. Don't take any chances, Curtis, but if you see an opportunity and you feel you have an advantage, I'd be very grateful. Take whoever you— is that Doc's buggy?" Matlock's eyesight was not as reliable as he could wish.

"Believe it is, sir."

Matlock nodded, dashed down the drive, and began filling the doctor in on what happened. Lane headed toward

# Stolen

the barn. He decided on the two hands to take: Clifford Bale, a good tracker, and Elmer Wold, a stoic young man with plenty of experience in gun work.

Doctor Harrow B. Conklin was a middle-aged man with prematurely gray hair and a full beard. He wore a black frock coat, with a silver satin vest, and black pinstriped trousers. He was tall and heavyset but nothing near overweight, and when he wore his derby hat and smoked a cigar, he looked like a retired prizefighter. Both men went into the kitchen, where Alice was still holding Eddie, rocking as she was doing when Avery went out front. The baby was crying and restless now. Obviously, the wound on his neck was causing a pain he had never experienced before.

"Now, now, Alice, let me have a look at little Eddie here." Conklin was as soothing as he knew how to be. He recognized the shock that Alice had suffered and knew he'd need to help her, too.

"Why, this isn't so bad, Alice. The cut is a long one, true, but very shallow. You've done an excellent job of cleaning it, too, Alice. Say, I don't think he'll need more than two or three stitches to close this up, back here under his left ear. He'll have a scar, though. Something to brag about on the schoolyard in a few years."

# Stolen

Alice smiled weakly, and her tears began again. Conklin thought they might be tears of relief. "Alice, I'm going to use a light anesthetic on Eddie's chest and neck so he won't be able to feel the stitches, but I'll need you to hold him close. Can you do that for me?"

Alice nodded and turned her face away when the doctor used the curved needle.

"There now. I'm going to wrap his throat in sterile gauze and cotton as a bandage. I'll leave a supply with you so you can change it at least twice a day. Oh. And only sponge baths for the next ten days. Now I have something for you too, Alice. It will help calm you. Nothing too strong, but it may make you drowsy. Avery? A glass of water, please."

Avery had been watching the whole process while standing behind Alice with his hands on her shoulders. He handed the glass to Conklin, who added a white powder and mixed it with his finger.

"Drink as much of this as you can, Alice, and then stretch out on the divan. I'll have a nurse come by to help with Eddie in an hour or so. Avery? Will you be kind enough to bring the baby's crib down so he can sleep next to Alice?"

# Stolen

"We have a bassinet in the dining room. The crib will need cleaning."

"That'll be fine."

The opiate Conklin used on the baby's wound was effective. He had already drifted off to sleep. Once Alice and the baby were moved to the parlor, Avery and Doc Conklin walked back out to the doctor's buggy.

"What in the hell happened here, Avery?"

"Don't really know, Doc. Someone came in last night, took the girls, and did that to Eddie. No idea who or why?"

"Jesus Christ. On Christmas, too . . . fucking bastards."

Avery had forgotten the holiday. With Eddie and Alice tended to, his primary thoughts, now, were to find his daughters. He had no idea how to begin.

# Stolen

Chapter 1

*10:15 a.m. December 25, 1887*

*The Matlock Home*

*Hartley, Texas*

The local sheriff arrived at the Matlock house and knocked on the front door. He noticed some activity around the barn but saw no one through the windows in the house. He knocked a second time, and Avery Matlock answered.

"Gabe, come in, come in. Thanks for coming out on Christmas." Avery was pale and stooped-shouldered, looking as though he carried the weight of the world.

Gabe Viligry was the recently elected Sheriff of Hartly Township. A handsome man in his late twenties, he was slim and a few inches taller than Avery. His hair was black with curls at the collar, and his fur-lined jacket held a five-point star pinned on the left shoulder. His sidearm was a Colt .44 Peacemaker, and he stood hat-in-hand as he talked with Matlock.

"My God, of course, Avery, of course. Doc said the baby's throat was cut?"

"Yes, but not deeply, thank our sweet Lord. He's doing ok now. The Doc took good care of him."

# Stolen

"Do you have any idea who would do something like this or why?"

"Absolutely none, Gabe. There've been no recent threats. We haven't noticed any strangers about the property. And there was no note left behind indicating a ransom demand. I know you have a jurisdictional issue, so I was hoping you could tell me who to see about this.

"Sure, I can. What you're looking for is a Federal Marshal. The Marshals are a no-nonsense lot, experienced and tough. They'll track a man all over the territory for as long as it takes. Outlaws know it, too. They don't want to tangle with a Federal Marshal, believe me. 'Course now that I said that, I need to say that the Marshals for our district, brothers Jim and Andy Roff, were killed somewhere out in the Territories. They haven't replaced 'em yet. Right now, the closest Marshal is up in Liberal, Oklahoma territory. Frank Dalton's his name. Has a good reputation for tracking. Man used to be tough as nails. Don't know so much now. 'Problem is he drinks a lot.

There is a guy in El Paso 'has the southeastern district. I never met him, but he's supposed to be the best. Hell, 'even wrote books about him. You might try askin' him. He's got a big district to cover, so he might not be able to help, but he'd be the guy I'd want. If you can talk to him, that is. Names Bass, Frank Bass."

Avery nodded as he listened and said, "Oh yes, forgot to mention. At seven this morning, I asked Curtis Lane to take a couple of boys and follow the tracks that led from the side of the house as far across the prairie as he was able to see them. 'Course, I cautioned him not to endanger himself in any way but to take whatever amount of time was necessary. He's still out, and I'm starting to worry about him. He may have come upon those vermin suddenly and took the worst of it."

From inside the house, Avery heard Alice in a short scream and then, in unmistakable grief, called for her husband. Avery dashed upstairs to find Alice standing outside the children's room, holding a piece of paper. Tears traced down her cheeks as she handed the letter to Avery. He read aloud.

*Mr. Avery Matlock,*

*As you are reading this, you are aware that I have taken your two daughters, Ruth and Susan. Please rest assured that they are well and being treated kindly. They are warm and well-fed. I know this is a shock for you, so I will be brief.*

# Stolen

*I require $25,000 from you by noon on Monday, January 2, for the safe return of your children. If you do not pay for any reason, I'm afraid your worst nightmare will become real. If you agree to my demand, place an ad in the Amarillo Herald that says simply, "Yes, I agree." I have people who will notify me of your answer. At that time, you will receive additional instructions via wire.*

*Please do not doubt my sincerity, Mr. Matlock. I have done this before and have been quite successful.*

*I imagine the Sheriff was your first thought. 'Understandable but pointless. We will not communicate again until I have the money. Once I am satisfied with the payment, you will be advised on where to retrieve your children.*

"I have to show this to Gabe Viligry, Alice. We will certainly pay my love, just as this devil demands."

"Do we have the money, Avery?"

"Not now, but we will shortly. I'm putting together a plan with Gabe. He's referred me to someone who might be able to help. I have to go back down and show this to him."

Avery went back downstairs to talk again with Gabe Viligry. He handed Gabe the letter, saying, "This was somewhere in the bedroom. It was so dark, and we were so focused on the baby that we didn't see it."

Gabe took a few minutes to read and digest what was said in the ransom demand.

"Can you make the payment?"

"Yes."

"That's my advice then. We don't know who the writer is or where the girls are. I believe you're gonna need some real professional help with this, Avery. I'll do everything I can, of course, but you oughta send a wire to the guy in El Paso."

"I will, and thank you. I want to wait for Curtis Lane to return. He might have something to add."

"Boy, Avery, I wish you'd a let me do that. I know it was early, and I know how desperate you musta been, but 'seems to me these people ain't got the morals of a snake. What kinda man cuts the throat of a baby? Anyway, I believe you're workin' against some pretty bad outlaws, and I'm afraid your man might not be up to it. I believe I'll ride out on their trail myself, 'see if I can find your people."

# Stolen

"Thanks, Gabe. I know you're right, but Lane's the most experienced man I got. I believe he'll be all right."

"All the same . . . those tracks start over yonder?"

"Yes, by the side of the house."

"I'm gonna ride out ninety minutes. If I don't see anything, I'll head back. Look for me about one. Then I think I'll get some good men together. This could turn into a long trail, so we'll need provisions. I'll try to get movin' by tomorrow noon. We'll start tracking yonder by the tanks. Hopefully, I'll find your people today, but if not, we won't stop till we do."

Viligry mounted his small roan horse and headed out in the direction of the tracks. The snow was heavy in places and thin in others, and it started to melt as the sun got higher. Gabe knew that horses make tracks in wet sod as well as snow, so he had no problem following the trail as it led away from the house. In fifteen minutes, he was out of sight.

Avery went back inside to check on Alice and the baby. Alice had changed the bandaging, and now both had fallen asleep. He walked into the kitchen, poured himself a tall whiskey, and took it outside to add snow. The back porch was in full sun, and it was warm enough to see steam floating above the roof as it heated.

# Stolen

Avery looked around his place. He had three acres around the house. He was not a rancher, but he kept a few horses and a milk cow for the family's use. He'd considered buying a mule in case he decided to till an acre or so but thought better of it. His duties at XLT kept him too busy to do any kind of farming. There were six hands in the bunkhouse, including Curtis Lane, all XLT cowboys assigned to take care of his place when he was away. He remembered what Curtis said about having a rat in the bunkhouse, and he thought it might be true. Still, there were many people who may have had access to the house and the rooms upstairs. The freighters that moved their furniture came to mind. Then, there was a carpenter Alice hired to make changes in the children's room just after they arrived.

How do you tell? How do you know the bad people from the good? Again, he thought of Curtis saying they'd need some help. Gabe knew it, too. A hard-nosed, professional lawman with experience dealing with outlaws was required. What did Gabe say his name was? Bass, like the fish. In El Paso.

# Stolen

Chapter 2

*8:45 a.m. December 25, 1887*
*Front Room, Main House*
*TwainHeart Ranch*
*El Paso, Texas.*

"Merry Christmas, my love. Help me to sit in the chair by the fire, will you, dear?" Sally was ending the eighth month of her term and found maneuvering from one sitting position to another required assistance. Bass enjoyed caring for her. She had saved his life on more than one occasion, nursing his various wounds, sitting with him, and changing bandages and all so that he was more than happy to be whatever she needed at any given time.

"Ah, much better. Now I can see the front yard down to the Rio, how pretty it looks, all covered with snow, and the steam off the Rio. And our tree, where did you ever find a fir tree around here?"

"There's a thicket on Theo's place. We both took trees from it. Along the river south of the house."

"It looks beautiful." Bass refreshed her coffee and moved the matching chair from the other side of the fireplace to sit next to her.

# Stolen

"And all the ornaments from your sister. It's all so pretty, goddamnit, now I'm too warm. Help me up again, please I'll sit on the divan. Thank you." After a pause, "You know, Frederick, this is our first Christmas together as a couple . . . oh, and our last too. Next year, Anne will be with us. Do you still think it wise and proper that we not marry? I know we've talked about it many times . . . ."

"Just last night, in fact."

"Yes, yes, just so. I'm still in a quandary over it, though."

"A what?"

"What?

"Yes. You're in somethin 'er other."

"Oh. Yes, dear, a 'quandary.' Um . . . it means 'uncertain'."

"Ah. I thought it mighta had somthin' to do with bein' big like you are."

Sally's face became churlish. "Yes, Frederick. I am big, and I will be big until I can push this little devil out of me. Quite a painful thing that I am not looking forward to a'tall, I can tell you."

"I completely understand, Sal, and I'll be—"

"Frederick, you do not understand anything I'm going through right now." After a pause, Sally's face softened, "Oh, I am sorry, dear, you're being wonderful. And understanding. Hand me that package there, in the red wrapping."

Bass lifted the large package and set it on the sofa next to her.

"What can it be? A mirror. It's beautiful, Frederick."

"It's to replace the small one on the wall above that little desk you sit at night when you comb your hair."

"It's very thoughtful, dear. Now. That one there, the small one in the blue paper. You open that one. It's for you."

"Gloves! Just perfect. What are they made of?"

"Lambskin, dear. They're not work gloves, now, they're for dress-up."

"They feel real soft. How did you know my size? Oh, right, right. Of course. Here, open this next."

"Goodness, it's lovely, a new blanket for Glory. Where did you find it?"

"Sheffield's, in town. It's a Navajo weave. Colorful, huh?"

"Perfect, she'll love it. Of course, I won't be riding her for several weeks yet to come. Will I?"

# Stolen

"Now, don't worry. This blanket's gonna wait for you to saddle that little horse of yours. Nesta's girls have been exercising her, well you know that, but they'll keep usin' the blanket from her rack 'til you're ready."

"Thank you, dear. Hopefully, it won't be long."

They each settled back into their quiet morning, sipping coffee, watching the light flurries of snow drift on the chilled breeze above the yard, admiring their tree, listening to the crackle of the fire, and generally just appreciating the simple things they had together.

Soon, Bass would have to do his barn chores, which involved everything from turning out the horses into the corral to mucking the stalls, feeding the chickens, and making sure the animals were fed and watered. He usually took a turn around the herd, but the cattle were all hearty breeds, and there were enough swales and coulees for them to find refuge from the wind. He usually took a wagon or two of baled fodder out to the animals, and he knew Paulo would, too. But for now, he was happy with his thoughts and his coffee.

The previous year, he didn't recognize the Christmas tide at all. His first wife, Moon in the Winter Sky, and his infant son had both succumbed to typhus the month before and for several months thereafter, he threw

# Stolen

himself into his work and his whiskey in pretty much even parts. It was then, in his solitude, that he first started seeing the 'vignettes,' as he called them. Small scenes that played in his head, mostly involving the men he'd killed.

As a Cavalry Scout with General Crook, then as a very young Ranger with Captain McNelly's Special Force, and now as a US Deputy Marshal for the District of El Paso, the number dead by his hand had swelled. He tried to remember each one's face, thinking that by remembering, he was somehow forgiven. There were so many over those seventeen years that, try as he might, there were some whose faces he just couldn't see. He remembered the places, the battles, and even the sounds, but their faces were lost to him. Those were the ones that came for him most often—the faceless apparitions.

Then, he met Sally Bloom in Wyoming. Her niece had been brutally assaulted, and Sally, knowing only his reputation at the time, came to him pleading for his help and to take her to Torrington, Wyoming, a three-day ride. During those three days, she became his salvation. His world. And now, in a month or so, the mother of his child. He was nearly thirty-five, and for the first time in a long time, almost half his life, he was at peace.

# Stolen

Bass stood and told Sally he was going to begin his daily chores, so he would have time to clean up before their guests arrived. She nodded, though her mind was in the kitchen timing the meal she would serve. They were expecting old friends Paulo and Chinesta Armendez and new but equally close friends Theo and Marianna Treece. Both couples were neighbors who were invited to an early dinner on Christmas Day.

Bass's first stop was the grain bin, where he filled a canvas bag with seeds and mullet for the chicken coop. They kept about ten laying hens and one rooster, Caesar, though he planned to allow for more hens in the spring. Next, he grabbed his manure fork and began on the first of six stalls. One was empty due to the loss of an older gelding named Buck over the summer, but the other stalls needed cleaning and fresh straw. There was his favorite, Emma, a tall mare, sixteen hands, that he got as a filly when he was with the Rangers. She'd be ten or eleven now but still spry and alert. She'd been trained in Fort Smith by an old Comanche, so she understood the 'stand' command and the release 'go.'

Next to her was Glory, Sally's quarter horse mare, small and chestnut color with a blond mane; she was trained as a cowpony by the man who originally owned her.

# Stolen

Sally bought her in Cheyenne before the journey that brought Bass—Sally called him Frederick—and Sally together. Glory was a sweet-natured little horse and faster than anything on four legs over the short haul.

Next to her was Susie, the mule that Bass had usurped from the Cavalry when he left. She was tall, red, strong, and used mostly for any heavy work that needed to be done around the ranch. Across the aisle was Jake, an Appaloosa stallion younger than Emma and a few inches shorter at the withers. Bass had plans to stud Jake when he found the time. Next to Jake was Dominoe, a black and white Pinto'd American Saddlebred that Bass was given by a White Mountain Apache friend he'd scouted with. Dominoe could be a bit rank, and Bass only exercised him when he felt like a workout. Still, he was a handsome gelding with speed and stamina equal to Emma.

Next, he went out to the lean-to in the corral where the two draft horses were kept. Bass called it a lean-to, but actually, it was a fully-enclosed structure butted up to the barn. Bass had plans to extend the barn or even build another, but those notions were way down the list in importance.

The two draft horses, Butch and Melody, were brother and sister and pulled in synchrony with each other.

# Stolen

Melody favored her left side, and Butch favored his right. When the two were hitched accordingly, they pulled equally in left and right turns. Bass cleaned the lean-to just as the stalls. And after loading all the feedbags with oats and a little barley, he filled the water troughs for all seven animals. Before going back into the house, he checked the number of mineral licks he had on hand and planned to take a few out to the range tomorrow, along with seven or eight bales of hay and alfalfa.

He walked back into the mud room, where he stripped down and grabbed two five-gallon buckets of hot water from the kitchen stove. He needed a good scrub, and the tub was in the crapper downstairs. Ordinarily, Sally would join him, but right now, the two of them together wouldn't fit.

At three o'clock, they were both dressed as festively as their wardrobes would allow. Sally wore a green and red maternity dress decorated with Elves and Santas with white satin at the hems. Bass wore a brown cowhide vest and his good white shirt.

They watched Theo Treece and his wife Marianna ride up the drive in a covered buggy. Marianna had a woolen throw over her lap, and Theo, a Professor of Physics and Mathematics at age twenty-one, wore a

# Stolen

sheepskin jacket and gloves against the light snow. They had become close friends with Bass and Sally. During the summer months, Bass helped Theo vindicate his deceased father, a Cavalry Major and Commander of Fort Selden in the New Mexico Territory, whom villains had accused of robbing a gold shipment while it was in his charge. Bass had exposed the true offenders and found the hidden gold in the process. Theo was awarded a finder's fee, which he shared with Bass and Sally, and purchased a small ranch on the Rio Grande, south of TwainHeart. Theo gave up his teaching position at Purdue University, and together, the families began a side business, T&F Feed and Grain Supply, in El Paso. To date, business has been booming.

Behind Theo and Marianna, by thirty minutes, came Bass's oldest friends, Paulo and Chinesta Armendez. Bass and Paulo had been Rangers together, but Paulo quit to take care of his wife and family. They had twin girls, Idris and Isabella, who kept their parents busy enough for four adults. Paulo share-cropped a fair amount of Bass's land, and they also jointly owned around eighty head of Hereford and Angus beef cattle, hearty breeds capable of withstanding the winters of El Paso. Bass also owned two bulls and a giant black Shire horse named Sir William, or

# Stolen

Willy, as Bass liked to call him. He'd inherited Willy when he bought the ranch and intended to stud him.

Now, as all six sat at the dining table, the remains of two geese still on the carving board, the point of several conversations eventually came around to Sally's pregnancy and impending delivery.

Paulo suggested, "Theo, I imagine you and Marianna will be swelling the numbers of your house soon enough, hey?"

"We've talked, of course, but pretty much agree that we need to wait for a while to see how business pans out. Much as we love the house and the land, it's hard work and plenty, too, just to keep up with it. I don't know how you and Frank manage all that you do and grow a herd to boot."

"Hell, Theo, Frank don't account for hardly any of it. He just sits down to his fancy office sippin' coffee and chattin' up folks that happen to straggle in . . . any real law work to be done he turns over to Bart or me. Yessir, been that way most his life, I'd say."

Bass, who sat at the head of the table, had been talking with Nesta and Marianna about what his carpenter friend, Silas Pratt, had done to the baby's room upstairs when he heard his name and lifted his head.

# Stolen

"Beg pardon, but my ears are burnin'. You gents been unloadin' on me while I was in polite conversation with the ladies? I'm listenin' now. Go ahead with your jawin'."

Theo spoke up, "Oh, it was nothing, Frank. Paulo was just remarking on how able you are to manage this spread, help out at the grainery, and still keep El Paso's streets safe and free of outlaws and bandits and such. Pretty miraculous if you ask me."

"Well, Theo, I am a pretty miraculous man, and you both need to remember it, especially Paulo, who's barely got sense to drink when he's thirsty. And as for you, while I have great respect for your capacity for book learnin', I'm always surprised that I have to keep remindin' you to quit tryin' to milk the bull."

There was laughter around the table. Even Marianna, who was not yet fluent in English, got the joke and enjoyed watching her husband's face turn a bit red.

Sally emerged from the kitchen with two mince pies she'd made and handed them to be placed on the table. With Bass's assistance, she took her seat, poured wine for herself, and passed the bottle to the ladies. The men sipped iced whiskey except for Theo, who preferred a neat brandy.

# Stolen

The cloth was pulled, and everyone sat in the great room enjoying the fire and telling stories of Christmases past. Some of them true, some not so. The twins were arguing over the pie in the kitchen when Chinesta suggested it was time to go. The afternoon had flown by quickly, and evening chores still waited at home. Theo and Marianna took their leave as well, and by seven o'clock, the house belonged again to Bass and Sally.

"You know, Sal, if someone had told me last Christmas that I'd be enjoying life so much this Christmas, I believe I'd a spit in his eye."

"I know, dear. This time last year, I was at home preparing year-end statements for two businesses. In March, I was on a riverboat bound for New Orleans. And by myself. Meeting you in Wyoming changed my life for the better, far the better. Damnit, I'm still hungry! Would you fetch what's left of the pie for me?"

And, of course, he did.

# Stolen

Chapter Three

*1:10 p.m., December 25, 1887*
*Village of Narvaez*
*Northern Llano Estacado,*
*New Mexico Territory*

One Cherokee and four Mexican outlaws carrying two stolen White girls reined up at the small rancho of Alexandro Dominguez to rest their horses, eat, and drink. They had a long way to travel and would not be expected for several days, assuming their captives were cooperative. They were met as they approached the lean-to by Dominguez.

"How are you, my fine friends? Was your journey fruitful? I have a warm fire in the hearth and plenty of food and drink."

Alejandro Dominguez was a frail-looking man with copper-colored skin that looked like parchment. He was Mexican but had some Indian blood that gave his face a square-jawed look, a prominent forehead, and a flat nose. He was dressed in soiled white linen, his trousers frayed at the cuffs and held in place with green suspenders. Dominguez supplemented the meager income he gleaned

# Stolen

from his property by accommodating Señor Silva's men whenever they crossed the Llano. As long as he kept silent, he could live comfortably on the fees Silva paid. Jose Chavez answered him.

"We're fine, old man. Take these two niñas into the house and feed them. Watch them close. If they escape, it will mean your head."

Cherokee Bill was assigned to care for the horses and watch their backtrail. As an Indian, he was only tolerated by the primarily Mexican gang. Chavez, Alarid, Romero, and Trujilo walked into the small adobe dwelling and sat at the only table in the sparsely furnished hut. Chavez asked Dominguez to keep watch on the little girls. He would need to take great care of the prize from their mission. Chavez knew any damage to either girl would cause Señor Silva great distress, and in distress, Silva always turned to 'El Chalequero' Francisco Guerrero.

Guerrero was known as the worst serial killer in the history of Mexico. He was proven to have killed at least twenty prostitutes by slitting their throats and half again as many Norte Americanos, Apache, and Comanche warriors. Physically, he was more than formidable. He stood six and a half feet tall, and weighed, it was approximated, two hundred fifty pounds. He was of Spanish and Bolivian

# Stolen

descent, an explosive mixture of violence and intelligence that made him even more frightening. He had a full black beard that covered his mouth, and his hair grew to his shoulders in the back and down nearly to his eyes in front. Of course, this was all by design to make it impossible to read the man's mood or temperament. His hands were abnormally large and strong, capable of cracking a man's arm or leg like a tree branch. He wore expensive clothing, custom made to his peculiar size, in fine fabrics and exotic leathers, and always a vest, hence the nickname 'El Chalequero.'

Everyone stayed out of Guerrero's way, just as everyone tried to keep on Vicente Silva's good side. Silva had made a lifelong friend of Guerrero in 1880 when he was arrested for the murder of a prostitute in Nogales. Several jailers in that state were on Silva's payroll, and at Silva's request, they facilitated an escape for Guerrero to the city of Las Vegas in New Mexico Territory. Vicente Silva was a respected businessman in Las Vegas. He owned several shops in the town and two full blocks along the north and east sides of the City Plaza. He sat on the city council and was influential in local politics. Silva saw the asset value in a man of Guerrero's size and talents and made him into a solid citizen, gainfully employed, in Las

# Stolen

Vegas. The fact that El Chalequero would occasionally dispatch some of Señor Silva's detractors was never made public. 'Little wonder that Chavez was anxious to please Vicente Silva.

The talk at the table ranged from the dry tortillas to the spicy frijoles and about the ride remaining for them. They also discussed how to handle the niñas when they woke up.

"We must treat them good, muchachos. See to their needs. They will wake this afternoon, so we must not to frighten them. The niñas will be scared already. Each of us, including you, Trujilo, must be their friend."
Dominguez walked into the room along with Cherokee Bill. Chavez looked up and said,

"*Viejo, necesitamos mantas, si?*"

"*Por las niñas, bien.*"

"*Descanseramos acqui durante tres horas. Tequila, por favor.*"

"*Tequila si, Señor.*"

Chavez turned back to the others, "And you, Cherokee. Did you check for followers?"

The Cherokee brave did not look at Chavez. He was watching the fire in the hearth.

"I check."

# Stolen

"Are we followed?" Again, Cherokee Bill did not turn to Chavez.

"No longer."

Chavez grinned, displaying one silver tooth and a collection of tobacco stains in his smile.

"So. Drink, eat, sleep. We will go this afternoon and travel at night. Those who follow they will not expect this. The Llano is cold at night. And dark. Las niñas will be frightened. We must be their friends."

More food and tequila was brought to the table. And the conversation, always in English, Silva's orders, revolved around their mission and how smoothly it went.

"Even the Cherokee Injun did a good job, eh Bill?"

Sitting on the floor by the fire, Cherokee Bill only turned and scowled. He had left his people because the healer in his Wikiup said his soul was so evil that he must be turned out. He could never go back to his people. All Cherokee would shun him.

As much as the men in the shack disliked Cherokee Bill, he disliked the Mexicans more. He stayed for the money and the protection of the White Caps Gang. There were bounties on him in most of the Indian territory. He could not travel there safely.

# Stolen

"And you, Trujilo, even you did well. Tell me, how did you keep the baby so quiet?"

Trujillo smiled at the compliment, made the cut-throat gesture, and said, "From his white ear to his white ear."

He was nodding and smiling, proud of his work, until Chavez said, "Hombre, you cut the throat of a *bebe inocente*?" Trujillo stopped smiling and looked into the leader's eyes. Chavez was horrified. Though he himself had murdered, and more in his time, he had never assaulted an *inocente*, the Cordero de Dios. Trujillo began to sweat as the room became deathly still. Chavez finally tilted his head and spat out, "Salvaje Barbaro."

And in one quick movement, 'drew his pistol and shot Trujilo between the eyes. The sharp bang startled everyone in the room, and as the echo faded, Alarid heard one of the girls cry out. He jumped to his feet and went into the room where the girls had been laid down. In a moment, he returned, nodding to the group that they were both still asleep.

Jose Chavez called Dominguez to the table. "Señor. I am sorry for the murder I have done in your house, but the man did a terrible thing and deserved to die. Please accept

# Stolen

my apology, and please bury him where he will not be found."

Dominguez nodded rapidly, his eyes wide, holding his poor straw hat before him, and he scurried out to find a shovel.

"*Mis amigos*, this fool has done more than he knew. A dead *bebe* is a terrible thing, and the Gringos will be enraged to see it. But when the *bebe* dies of his throat cut? The Gringos will stop at nothing to run us to the ground. If we are caught, we will be slaughtered, not simply hanged, make no doubt. This rabbit brain has given them another reason to hunt us down and kill us. We will keep our plan and leave later this day. It will be harder to track us at night." He swallowed his tequila and slumped in his chair.

# Stolen

Chapter 4

*1:50 p.m., December 25, 1887*
*Dominguez Rancho*
*Village of Narvaez*
*New Mexico Territory*

Curtis Lane and two riders, Cliff Bale and Elmer Wold, came upon the Dominguez place as they topped a large coulee a mile southwest of Narvaez. It was the first dwelling they'd seen since leaving the Matlock place five hours earlier. Smoke wafted from the chimney of the small adobe, but there was no sign of any movement anywhere else around the structure. Cliff Bale had done well in his tracking, but their trail was so obvious that Cliff mentioned to Curtis, "They don't care if we follow, Curtis. Ain't tryin' to hide nothin' when they could've back at that shallow creek we crossed. There's still just five of 'em. Maybe they met some compadres at that shack and passed the girls on to them?"

"Coulda', but I don't think so. We know there's at least five horses leadin' here. Woulda taken more than two or three to steal the chil'ren." Then Curtis turned to Elmer Wold. "Elmer? You swing wide around the barn in that coulee and check what's in there. We'll wait here. Don't do no more'n that, now."

Elmer backed his pony down the side of the small ravine they were hiding in and rode off about half a mile past the barn. He poked his head up over the edge of the ravine and saw no one out back, so he tied off his horse to a large stone, took his rifle, and ran to the back wall of the barn, staying as low as he could.

The sun was bright, and the snow that drifted up to the barn wall was starting to melt to the point his footing was questionable. He tried to peek through a crack between the wall planking but couldn't see enough. Keeping as low as he could, he stole around the far side of the barn from the shack and took a quick look around the corner. He counted five horses and a swayback mule, all facing inward. There was a donkey in a small corral on the other side. He decided he'd seen enough and retraced his steps to his horse.

Elmer rode back below the same coulee to report what he'd seen. When he got to within a hundred feet, he noticed the horses had been separated, and as he rode up the slope, he spotted two bodies lying face up in the snow, arrows in each man's chest.

# Stolen

Both had been scalped. Elmer's eyes wouldn't close. Beads of sweat erupted from his forehead and neck as he turned his head left and right. The snow was blinding with the sun overhead, but he kept searching anyway. After what seemed like hours but, in fact, was just seconds, Elmer Wold spurred his horse into a gallop heading back to the east. He'd gotten no more than twenty strides when he felt the arrowhead plunge into the center of his back. Even through his winter clothing, the single arrow went enough. His arms fell limp to his sides. His legs were numb, and could not hold him in the saddle. His pony stopped running when he no longer received the urging from his rider, and Elmer toppled from the saddle into the snow.

He was still alive, but he could not move. He saw the Indian, bow in hand, draw another arrow and send it into Elmer's side. The young man did not feel the arrow but knew it would be fatal. He saw the Indian approach closer, a steel blade gleaming in the sun, and saw only the movement of his head as the Indian yanked his hair up and cut a swath of skin from his scalp. He watched the Indian walk away, leaving him to bleed out into the snow.

# Stolen

*Noon December 25, 1887*
*Northern Llano Estacado, Texas*

Gabe Viligry had been riding across the high plains for a
bit more than the ninety minutes he allowed with Avery
Matlock. He'd been following the tracks of the original five
horses and the tracks of another three that had come after
the first set. Certain these were the tracks of the men that
included Curtis Lane, he was hopeful to see the three ride
over the deep gulley that stretched before him at any
moment. He took the field glasses from his saddlebag and
scanned the horizon, searching for a trace, a dark speck
against the snow, but after several minutes with no luck, he
turned his mount's head back to the east and spurred
toward home. He began to think of the men he would ask to
come with him tomorrow as he rode.

# Stolen

*4:00 p.m. December 25, 1887*

*Dominguez Rancho*

*Narvaez, New Mexico Territory*

Jose Chavez y Chavez opened the door to the small room where the two little girls had slept. Just entering the room was enough to startle Ruth awake. In her most indignant and furious tone, she said, "Who are you, Mister? What the hell do you want with us?" Her voice waivered just a bit when she swore, and she tried to conceal the fear that overwhelmed her.

"Please, Señorita, my name is Jose, and I will assure you we mean you and your sister no harm. We are taking you both to a place where talks will be made with your parents for your return home. My compadres and I are simple banditos. We are just as hopeful for your safe and ah . . . how is it said . . . *rapido* return. I am telling you this so that you will know I speak truthful."

Ruth answered back, "I hope you realize that my father is an important man and will stop at nothing to get us back."

"Señorita, that is what I am wanting most. You will see. This will end soon, and you will be home with your parents. But, Señorita, I must ask that you and you sister . .

54

# Stolen

. ah . . . comper— er—cop—cooperate with us. We do not wish to tie you, but if we must, we will."

"Hah! You can try. We will need warm clothes. Neither of us is dressed for winter."

Susie had snuggled up next to her big sister, a blanket pulled up to her chin. Her eyes were wide with fear and confusion, but as long as Ruth did not cry, neither would she.

"Oh, *si* Señorita, we have thought to bring these fine clothes for you both. I'm afraid our journey is to be a long one." Chavez set a large valise in front of the girls. "But you both will be treated with respect and mercy. There will be meat for you before there is any for my men." As he turned to leave, he said, "You will have privacy now to put on these fine clothes. We want to leave in a hurry, but you both must eat some of our food, too. Thank you, Señoritas." Chavez bowed as formally as he could think to and left the room.

"Ruthie? What's happening? Why do I feel so funny? And why are we with that Mexican?"

"Well, as near as I can figure, Suz, we've been kidnapped. These men came to our house and took us while we slept. I think what they want to do is have Daddy pay them to get us back."

# Stolen

"But it's Christmas? I want to be with Mommy and Daddy and open presents and sing songs."

"I know you do, sis. Me too. But for right now, we're caught up a creek without a paddle. Don't worry, Suz, Daddy will come get us soon. 'Til then, we just have to do what the Mexican says. Here, put these on."

The clothing they were given was for boys of a similar age. There were trapdoor long johns and thick woolen socks, boots that were too big, and brand-new Levi-Strauss coveralls that were so stiff it hurt to move. Thick flannel shirts, knitted scarves, and sheepskin jackets rounded out the winter gear. Just as the girls were finished dressing, Jose Chavez knocked on the door.

"*Oh, Señoritas, que hermosa.* We are all ready to leave. You, your name is Ruth, yes? You will ride with me. And Susan? You will ride with Eugenio. Tonight, we will ride to a line shack abandoned many years ago. It is only thirty miles away, but because we must travel at night, we cannot go *rapido*. At the line shack, we will have food, warmth, and time to sleep." Jose was smiling broadly as if this was a family campout or picnic. "So, ladies, let us go."

The three walked into the main room and saw the other men who had taken them. They were all dirty, unshaven, and smelled of garlic and liquor. Trujillo's blood

# Stolen

was still on the floor, and both girls looked at it, becoming squeamish.

"What is that?" Jose kicked himself for not having the old man clean up.

"Oh, that was a chicken that Mr. Dominguez cooked for us. He did not have time to clean."

Everyone walked out the backdoor to the horses. The jingle and tramp of deep-roweled spurs and heavy boots was frightening. Both girls had only limited experience on horseback, and the strange sights and sounds were intimidating. Ruth turned back for a last look at the blood and then noticed five horses for four men.

# Stolen

Chapter 5


*2:00 p.m. December 25, 1887*
*Front Porch*
*Matlock House*
*Hartley, Texas*

"I didn't see nary a trace of 'em, Avery. Plenty a' tracks out there to follow, all headin' west. I counted five horses, followed by three more. That 'bout what Curtis figured?"

Gabe Viligry had returned from his ninety-minute scout.

"I remember him saying four or five, yes."

'Saw two animals heavier than the others; must been the ones with the girls. I noticed one, though, that lagged twice. Prob'ly one of 'em checkin' their backtrail."

"How can you tell all that from just some footprints in the sod?"

"Trackin' takes some learnin' how. And experience." Gabe Viligry took off his hat, slapped it against his leg, and said almost apologetically, "Too late today; be dark in a few hours. But tomorrow mornin', Avery, I'm gonna take a few men out toward Narvaez in the territory. If your boys are out there, we'll find 'em, sure."

# Stolen

Viligry didn't say it, but Avery understood it wasn't likely his men were still alive.

"Thank you, Gabe. I suppose it goes without saying how badly I feel having asked Curtis to run those savages down. Wish I could take it back." Avery Matlock was looking west. Into the sun. Into the wind. Into the land that had swallowed his children.

"I believe I'll travel to El Paso tomorrow. Talk to this Marshal Bass." Avery Matlock's voice cracked, and his eyes began to fill.

"That trip will be a long one, Avery, and time ain't on your side. A wire would sure be quicker."

"I know you're right, but I must see this man myself and make him understand. That's not possible through a wire. I know, sure as I'm standing, the good Lord will return my children to me. Perhaps Marshal Bass can lend Him a hand."

# Stolen

*6:15 a.m. December 26, 1887*
*El Paso and South Western RR.*
*Mail Terminal*
*Hartley, Texas*

The township of Hartley, Texas, did not have a freight or passenger terminal. It was not on the 'local' designation. It did have a mail sub-station for dispatching and receiving mail, and it also had a telegraph office. When a passenger presented himself for transit, as Matlock often did, a signal lamp was lit, indicating to the engineer of the oncoming train that he needed to make a brief stop. As often as not, accommodation could be found in a passenger coach, especially at that early hour. Avery waited in the telegraph office, his eyes gazing northward.

The long blast of a steam whistle meant the southbound engineer saw the red indicator lamp and reduced throttle to begin braking. Avery had only a small valise with a few things for a night or two, if necessary, so there was no steam lost in the stop.

Avery began his trip at 6:30 a.m. and traveled for nearly thirteen hours before arriving in El Paso. The cities and villages along the way included Brownfield, where he changed trains after a forty-minute wait; Seagraves; Hobbs, where there was time for lunch; Carlsbad; and finally, El Paso. It was after 7:30 p.m. when he stepped off the platform and made for the nearest lit establishment, which turned out to be Hannigan's Irish Clover Saloon.

Matlock was not a drinking man, but neither was he a tea totaler, so he ordered an Irish whiskey and asked the barman about hotels nearby.

"Well, boyo, the best room you'll find in town is the Vendome Hotel, bein' three blocks down this road outside. What brings you to our fair city, then?"

"I need to speak with the Marshal, Marshal Frank Bass."

"Ach, you're a reporter then, or one a' them book writers from back east. I can tell you now, as I know the lad, he don't want to see ya."

"I'm not a reporter or writer. I'm from up north, Hartley, to be exact. My ah . . . my daughters have been kidnapped by outlaws. Marshall Bass has the best reputation for tracking in Texas, and I'm here to ask for his help."

The bartender's big red face flushed even darker. "Kidnapped. And wee lassies, too? The Marshal is the best manhunter in Texas, sure, maybe the country, I'll say. He also has a soft heart, boyo, and I wish you luck wid him.

# Stolen

His office is on St. Louis Street, which means you go right from the hotel to Santa Fe Street and right on St. Louis to the corner of Mesa Road. But a good stretch a' the legs, it is. His office is upstairs of the sheriff. Another taste? On the house, fer luck?"

"I believe I will. Thank you . . . ah, I don't have your name?"

"Patrick Hannigan. Himself will know me as Paddy. I'll have one with you. To your lassies' safe return."

Matlock checked into the Vendome at 10:00 p.m. and asked to be roused by seven. He slept fitfully, waking twice in a sweat from terrible dreams. Naturally, he focused on his daughters and how they were being treated. The worst always presents itself first at night and leaves little room for hope and light. He also knew he was responsible for Curtis and his men, and again, not knowing their condition allowed only the blackest conclusion.

# Stolen

Boone Waverly, Mike 'Patch' Patchelski, and Deacon Allen Ramsfeld sat in Gabe Viligry's office drinking coffee and eating the biscuits that Annie Ramsfeld had sent with her husband. Waverly was a middle-aged rancher whose wife had died the year before. He'd been an officer with General JEB Stuart in the war of the rebellion and served as a Cavalry Scout and mapmaker for General Miles Nelson during the Nez Percé campaign in Montana. He was the oldest member of the posse and the one with the most experience. He was tall, straight, and clean-shaven, with a military bearing and an officer's respect for orders and command.

Mike Patchelski was a gunsmith, single, and a year or so younger than Waverly. He had no military training but was known as an honest man and fair tradesman. He was also an excellent marksman.

Ramsfeld was younger, still with a wife and a congregation that he'd assumed at the death of the previous minister a year before. He was devout but not a stickler, recognizing that frontier life was different from life in the eastern cities. He'd also served the Confederacy in the War, first as a flag bearer and then as a Corporal in Colonel Hobby's Eighth Infantry. He was heavyset with long light brown hair and mutton-chop sideburns. All three men had responded to Viligry's call for volunteers.

Viligry opened the door, letting a blast of cold air and snow flurries in, and went to the stove to warm his hands.

"I appreciate you boys volunteering on short notice, 'specially at Christmas. Matlock and his wife are awfully good folks. Can't imagine the sorrow that's laid out on them right now." He then turned to Ramsfeld.

"Preacher, these other boys here are bachelors, but you got a wife 't home."

"Gabriel, the Lord has chosen not to bless my house with children but instead has given me the kind people of Hartley. I would be a sorry shepherd indeed if 'didn't try to return my lambs to the flock."

"I understand, Reverend, but there's likely to be some shootin' on our trip, maybe even some killin'. Are you gonna be okay with that?"

"Well, I was okay with it at Chicamaugua, and I was okay with it at Second Manassas. Believe killin' vermin is

# Stolen

all part of the Lord's plan. Make sure your aim is true, Gabriel. Don't worry about mine."

"Okay then, Patch, I know you like that squirrel gun a' yours, and you're welcome to take it, but please take one a these Henry repeaters, too." Viligry threw Patchelski a weapon from the rack on the wall.

"Say, I can hit damn near anything I can see with this piece. An' you seen me do it too, Gabe."

"Yes, I have, Patch. Take the Henry just the same. Okay, y'all raise your right hand. Do you solemnly swear to uphold and enforce the laws of the state of Texas?"

After the 'I dos,' Gabe tossed them each a badge.

"You're all on the payroll now, and that means I'm the boss. We're gonna pick up their trail at the western tanks. 'Seen 'em there yesterday. Be no turnin' back. Nobody's gettin' homesick. We're gonna follow those tracks 'til we get those children and kill every one a' the devils who took 'em."

Viligry paused and looked as deeply into the hearts of his three men as he could. Then he said, "Mount up." The four men used their own horses and gear, and Viligry brought a mule to carry supplies, a tent, water, and grain.

65

# Stolen

As they headed west on the tank road, Viligry said, "My guess is, since they headed west, they're makin' for Narvaez. Nothin' else out that way. 'Solid forty-mile ride. Figure a couple breaks for the horses and be there by two o'clock."

# Stolen

*1:30 p.m., December 26, 1887*
*One mile west of the Texas Border*
*Llano Estacado*
*New Mexico Territory.*

Gabe Viligry's posse was in view of the small village of Narvaez when Reverend Ramsfeld spotted a dark figure in the snow at the bottom of a deep coulee.

The sheriff called to Ramsfeld, "Go have a look, Reverend. We'll wait for you here."

Allen Ramsfeld handed off the leader for the mule and approached the figure slowly against the possibility of a trap. As he got closer, he recognized the shape as a human form with two arrows in the body and a bloody open scrape to the bone on top of the head.

He said a very quick prayer and called back, "It's a dead body. 'Killed by arrows, and he's been scalped. Could be one of the three hands that you mentioned."

Viligry rode over to the body to see what he might find out when Patch called out from a position ahead and to the left.

"Two more over here, Gabe. Couple arrows each, both been scalped."

# Stolen

Ramsfeld asked, "Can you tell anything from the arrows?"

"Cherokee markings and colors. Comanche tips."

Gabe Viligry thought for a moment. "We'll bury 'em here. Most likely the three men from Matlock's ranch, poor souls."

Three graves were dug in the cold, wet sod, and rocks were piled on top to thwart local critters. Viligry removed wallets and valuables that he would give to the next of kin when they returned. After the Reverend read scripture, the four mounted and regained the trail. It took them to a small adobe and sod hut with a lean-to instead of a barn and a donkey standing well inside, away from the wind.

"First stop, boys. Believe this is where the outlaws spent the night."

The four men dismounted and took their weapons out as they slowly walked about the hut. After only a few steps, a small Mexican man jumped from a doorway and charged the group, slashing about with a machete.

"*Diablos Blancos. Los matare a todos.*" The man flailed wildly and smelled of mezcal.

They easily sidestepped his efforts, and eventually, the old man fell to the ground, exhausted and sick.

# Stolen

"Let's take the poor son of a bitch inside—oh, excuse me, Reverend."

"Think nothin' of it, son. Let's get the bastard inside and see what we can find out."

# Stolen

*7:00 a.m., December 27, 1887*
*Vendome Hotel*
*El Paso, Texas*

He was awake before the 7:00 a.m. knock on his door. He had already used the privy in the back and was washing up at the basin in his room. He dressed in the same suit of clothes as the previous day. The jacket and vest rested on the silent butler near the window, and his trousers lay flattened between the mattresses to restore the creases. Alice had always done his bow tie. It was a small morning ritual before going off to work.

But Alice was in Hartely with the baby, and he had long forgotten the magic of the bowtie. He decided to go without and buttoned his shirt with the stiff collar to his chin. He walked downstairs, smelled the heartening aroma of coffee, and decided to sit in the lobby with a cup and maybe one of those biscuits on the counter. He did not buy a paper. It would only slow his progress, so he stepped out onto the boardwalk and followed Hannigan's directions to the corner of St. Louis and Mesa. He walked into the sheriff's office to find Bart Mariany sitting at his desk, reading a newspaper and twirling his mustache.

"Sheriff?"

# Stolen

"Yes, sir. Bart Mariany, how can I help you?"

"I'm looking for Marshal Frank Bass. Is he in?"

"He ain't at the moment. He's tendin' a small business he has on Franklin Street down near the train station. He'll be back in an hour or so. Usually is. Is there something I can help you 'bout?"

"Well, I'm here to see the Marshal about helping me. My two daughters were kidnapped Christmas morning, and I really have nowhere else to turn."

"By God. Lord in heaven. That was in this morning's report. It's a telegraph wire alerting law enforcement to be on the lookout. I am so sorry. . . your name's Matlock, right from up to Hartley?"

"Yes, that's right."

"Let me get you some coffee. Would you like a sweetener, Mr. Matlock?"

"Whiskey?"

"Uh-huh."

"No thanks, 'bit early."

Mariany handed Matlock a cup and sat back at his desk. "This happened on Christmas?"

"Yes. Before sunrise. We have an eight-month-old baby who sleeps in the same room as the girls. They cut his throat. I guess to keep him from crying."

# Stolen

Mariany's eyes widened in disgust and outrage. "My God! Cut a baby's throat?"

"He's all right, though. They did a poor job of it. It must have been too dark to do it right. Thank the Lord."

"And your wife? How is she holding up?"

"As well as can be expected, though I suspect she's avoiding thoughts of our daughters by focusing on the baby. She didn't want me to come down, but I convinced her that we needed real help, and El Paso was where we'd find it."

"I understand, Mr. Matlock, and I'm so very sorry for your situation."

"Thank you, Sherriff."

"And you're right, too. Frank Bass is the best in Texas, maybe anywhere, I reckon. Best tracker, 'most honest, and most reliable. A family man, as well, or soon to be, his wife is due next month, I think."

"They're a wondrous gift from God. Children are. How old is he?"

"Frank? Oh, lessee, I'm forty-eight, and he's some younger. I had a birthday not long ago. Oh hell, I'd guess thirty-four or thirty-five."

"What else can you tell me about him?"

# Stolen

"Well, he was a Texas Ranger as a kid. He was prob'ly twenty or twenty-one. 'Know he was with them for some time. After that, he was a scout for General Crook in Arizona. 'Ts where he learned his trackin' skills from the White Mountain Apache he scouted with. That's where I met him. I was an Injun fighter at the time. Kinda adviser to the General, you'd say. He left the army when they caught Geronimo. Said he'd done enough." Bart leaned back in his chair. "Tried ranchin' for a year or two but couldn't settle into it. About three years ago, he joined the Marshal's Service. And here he is today."

"Thank you, Sheriff. That's all very reassuring. I think I'll take a stroll about town if you don't mind. I'll come back in an hour or two."

"Why yes, yes, of course, Mr. Matlock. When he gets back, I'll tell him you stopped by."

"Very good. Goodbye now."

Avery Matlock stepped outside and took a deep breath of cold, damp air. He coughed reflexively as his lungs recoiled at the sudden blast of winter. Matlock looked about him and spied what he was looking for several blocks to the northwest. A clean, white steeple rose above the roofline. He started walking in that direction, keeping the steeple in his sight. He realized that his little girls were

73

# Stolen

probably experiencing the same winter weather wherever they were, and he desperately felt the need to pray.

# Stolen

Chapter 6

*6:30 a.m., December 27, 1887*

*Dominguez Adobe, Narvaez*

*New Mexico Territory*

The old man had slept through the night, moving only once when he pissed himself in his sleep. The sun could spread little light and less warmth due to a layer of low clouds that hung over the Llano. The fire in the small hearth had died an hour earlier, and Ramsfeld brought in more wood from the stack next to the lean-to. While he was there, he tossed a bale of dry straw and hay to the horses and a forkful or two for the old man's donkey. When he went back inside, he discovered that Viligry had found coffee and was waiting for the fire to be restarted.

The old man was awake, too. He was cowering in a corner, wrapped in a blanket and shivering from the cold and hangover.

"Has he said anything yet?" Ramsfeld asked.

"Nope, but I can damn near feel him cursin' us in Mexican," Patchelski answered.

Boone Waverly, who was the least talkative of them, said, "Let's see if he'll waggle his tongue for a hair of the dog." And he brought out a bottle of tequila from his pack. "Hey there, hombre. Swallow of tequila?"

The old man's eyes widened, and he reached a wizened hand out from his blanket. "Por favor, Señor. *Estoy enfermo.*"

Boone poured some into a tin coffee cup and reached toward the old man.

Ramsfeld objected. "The old man is suffering, Boone. Please don't make it worse."

"Padre, that old man looks like he's livin' on the stuff. This little touch ain't a-gonna hurry up his whiskey death, but it might help us find them, children."

Viligry added, "He's right, Reverend, anything that might help us, we gotta try."

The old man finally said, "*Por favor, Señor?*"

Boone handed the old man the cup, and he swallowed without missing a drop.

"*Muchimos gracias, Senores.*"

Viligry began with simple questions. "Do you speak English? *Habla ingles?*"

"*Si, un poco.*"

"What is your name?"

"Alexandro Dominguez. *Por favor, uno mas?*"

# Stolen

Boone poured a little less into the cup, and Dominguez drank it quickly. He sighed as it went down, and his shoulders relaxed. *"Bien, esta bien."*

Viligry began again. "Are you alone here?"

*"Si*—yes, I am alone."

Boone handed Dominguez a piece of jerky, but the old man waved it away.

*"Sin dientes, Señor.* Ah—no teeth." The old man was quiet for a moment and then pointed to Viligry's badge. "You are of the law?"

"Yes, we are."

"You are seeking las niñas?" A

ll four men reacted to this. Viligry asked, "Yes, we are. Have you seen them?"

*"Por favor, uno mas Señor."*

Boone again handed Dominguez a cup.

He nodded and said, "Yes, here. Um . . . ayer—yesterday." The alcohol was having the desired effect. Dominguez was becoming more verbal. "You will not find them."

"Where are they?"

"They are many miles away now. Maybe dead already." Boone threw the cup aside and grabbed the old man by his tattered shirt.

# Stolen

"You drunken ol' beaner, where are they goin'?" Patchelski and Viligry pulled Boone Waverly back.

Viligry looked into the old man's eyes. Now, they were keen and alert and somehow aware of the power he had.

Ramsfeld said, "Dominguez, if you want more. . *mas tequila*, you will answer. Where are the men taking the children?"

Dominguez grimaced and clutched at his chest. Viligry saw fear and searching in the old man's eyes. His breathing was ragged and short, and he toppled to his side, vomiting up the tequila he'd drunk. Gabe Viligry spoke softly to the old man.

"Dominguez. *Estas muriendo*. You're dying, man. Where are the men taking the children?"

Dominguez rolled his head from side to side and suddenly stopped and whispered,
"They go to the Don." Dominguez gasped twice and then stopped breathing. Reverend
Ramsfeld reached for his Bible.

# Stolen

*7:15 a.m., December 27, 1887*
*An Abandoned Line Shack*
*Sixty Miles West of Narvaez*
*New Mexico Territory*

"Alarid, you and the Cherokee take the horses to the rocks out of the wind. Tie them well, but do not hobble them. Then you both come back to the shack."

"Si, Jefe. Do jue wan the Indian to check the backtrail again?"

Chavez thought for a moment. "No. He is weary, as we all are, though he won't say it. He is to come back for food and sleep. Romero can go when it's light. I will tell him after he has made a fire. Now, you go."

Both girls were too tired and cold from the long night in the saddle to be hungry. Once the old iron stove was lit, they curled up in front of it and waited for warmth. The old flue was leaky, and soon, there was as much smoke inside as out. Alarid opened the door slightly, and the one window that hadn't seized shut was propped up an inch or two. Before long, the girls were asleep.

Chavez wrapped himself in blankets and sat propped up in a corner, taking an occasional taste from the tequila bottle he kept in his bedroll. He pondered the night

# Stolen

'just passed and watched as the sun moved shadows about as it rose into daylight. He allowed that they would have two more nights before reaching Las Vegas, New Mexico, and the relative safety of Señor Silva's *fortaleza*.

The Indian, Cherokee Bill Guerrero, was the only other one still awake. He sat with his back against the wall, facing the door. He looked briefly at Chavez and then dropped his head to his chest, his hat blocking the light. In a few minutes, everyone was asleep.

At 3:30 p.m., Chavez opened his eyes. He was cold. The sun was still up outside, but inside the line shack, the fire in the stove had gone out. Nobody had bothered to check the fire during the day to see if it needed more wood. It was quiet in the shack. There was some very light snoring coming from Romero, who had returned to the bungalow without seeing anything on the backtrail. If he had, the men would have been roused. He couldn't see the girls from his position, but again, he assumed the general stillness meant they were yet asleep. Quietly, so as not to disturb them, he peeked around the corner of the interior wall and saw the Indian, Cherokee Bill Guerrero, squatting next to the older girl, lightly stroking her hair.

Chavez withdrew his pistol and slowly stood up. Moving slowly, the shack's flooring was old and creaked when weight was moved across it; Chavez stepped up behind Cherokee Bill and held his pistol to the Indian's head. The Indian heard nothing or was so engrossed with Ruth's hair that he ignored everything else. When he was ready, Chavez drew the hammer back on his single-action revolver. The unmistakable click of the trigger mechanism was all the Cherokee needed to hear to stop his fantasizing and relieve Alarid as the lookout. He stood slowly, never looking back at Chavez, and silently left through the back door.

Chavez looked down at both girls and watched them for a few moments. He would let them sleep for another thirty minutes before waking them and getting them prepared to travel. Tonight, they would cross the Canadian River at Minese Gap and ride to the rancho of Nicolai Waslaski. Waslaski was another rancher on Señor Silva's payroll. He had often provided shelter, food, water, and fresh horses to those in Silva's employ who needed to be scarce from the Las Vegas area. The next night would see them to Silva's Rancheria, and he would complete his assignment. Vicente Silva would take over from there, and he would handsomely reward his loyal servant Chavez y Chavez.

# Stolen

The Matlock girls came awake near 4:00 p.m., and both were hungry and thirsty. They were also cold and stayed wrapped in blankets as they ate. They drank melted snow and ate cold beans from a can that Chavez opened for them. He also provided the spoons they used. He had left them unbound, hoping his display of friendliness and trust would make the girls more amenable to their condition. After all, they were in the middle of the Llano Estacado, nothing but flatlands and snow for miles in any direction. There were no landmarks to guide them, and the Llano was even more dangerous at night.

He also made small talk with them, which revealed a more human side to the outlaw and the kidnapper he had become. He sat on the floor with them.

"You know, I once had a niña myself. As a young man, I married my sweetheart from our village. We had two bebes, a boy and a girl. Her name was Leticia, and my son's name was Guillermo."

Susie asked in a quiet voice, almost a whisper. "Where are they now?"

Jose Chavez's face became clouded, and he leaned back, looking away, "My bebes are dead, *muerto*."

# Stolen

Susie's brow wrinkled in sadness, and Ruth thought for a moment. "What happened, Jose? You don't have to talk if you don't want to."

"It is sad, Señorita, to speak of it. They were killed in an Apache raid on our village. My wife was killed, too." Chavez cleared his throat and continued, "That is why I promise you will be safe with me and back with your family soon." Chavez smiled at them both and said, "For now, we must go. We are riding tonight to another rancho where you will be more comfortable. Come now, up on our feet and to the horses."

The night sky was clear, and the weather was bitter cold. Thankfully, there was no wind to speak of as the four riders and their passengers, with a trailing horse that was now loaded with supplies, left the line shack.

They moved slowly in the foothills of the eastern Llano as they made for the Minese gap. After that, it would be an easy gallop over the moonlit Llano across the Canadian River and then on twenty-eight miles to the Waslaski rancho. They would stop twice for forty minutes along the way to rest the horses and stretch. No fire would be allowed. The girls, riding double with Chavez and Alarid, would snuggle their heads in close to the men's jackets and even go so far as to open the coat to slide their

# Stolen

faces inside. They couldn't see the trail, and the men smelled bad, but with their heads protected, both girls felt somehow safe and sheltered. In the back of his mind, Chavez knew the horses would be too worn to make the next leg of their trip. He would have to make adjustments.

# Stolen

Patchelski and Waverly finished burying Alexander Dominguez in the yard behind the adobe.

"S'pose that other grave is one a them bastards?"

"Doubtful. That ol' man couldn't hold a gun, much less shoot it. Prob'ly a relative, wife, or some such. 'Sides, don't believe they would a left him alive afterward."

"Whaddaya figure for that damned donkey? Be useful to someone. Just slow us down even more." "Reckon Gabe'll just cut him loose. He'll wind up better 'n the ol' man treated him."

Gabe and the Reverend came around the corner with horses saddled and bedrolls packed neat. As Viligry mounted, he said, "Thanks, fellas. I know that's hard work in the cold. Patch, why don't you go turn that donkey loose? Let him see if he can't do better in the village."

Patchelski walked to the lean-to and untied the animal, shooing him off in the general direction of Narvaez. The little Jenny complained at being rousted but left the lean-to anyway. Patchelski came back to the group and mounted up. They all headed west, following the same

85

five sets of tracks that had brought them here. Waverly, the most experienced tracker, spoke up after a few minutes.

"Hey, Gabe?"

"Yeah."

"It's the same horses, but one's being trailed now. Ain't carryin' no weight."

The three other men immediately thought of the extra grave.

"You sure?"

"Can't hardly miss it, Gabe. Prints ain't as deep on the one with the split left forefoot. You thinkin' bout that other grave?"

"Yuh."

"Explains why it was so fresh."

"It does."

"So?"

"So, we'll find out when we catch 'em. How far ahead are they?"

"Ten, maybe twelve, hours. No more 'n fourteen. Any idea where they headed?"

"West."

# Stolen

"Hell, I know that. You can see their trail for the next hunnert yards. They don't seem to be worried 'bout bein' followed. Whaddaya make a that?"

"Well, we just buried the last three men who followed 'em. Seems like they got bein' followed pretty much handled."

"Yeah. You worried?"

"Right down to my boots. Let's pick it up a bit, boys." All four riders spurred their horses to an easy lope.

# Stolen

Bass walked into the sheriff's office to refill the coffee cup he'd left behind when he went over to his new business, F&Ts Fodder and Grain. As he sat in the chair opposite Bart Mariany, Eddie Voer walked through the office and headed to his place in back. Eddie was the jailer, and he had a small desk opposite the cells in the back of the sheriff's office. He was also responsible for coffee in the morning, sweeping out the office and the cells, seeing to any prisoner's meals, and any repair work that needed attention around the building. Eddie was a big man, over six feet, and weighed nearly three hundred pounds. He was generally in good humor, but this morning he was not. Bass looked at Mariany,

"What's goin' on with him?"

"Not sure, but I believe he intended to ask Luke Jorgensen's daughter to the soda shop. Maybe she said no."

"Jorgensen . . . Jorgensen, why do I know that name?"

"Ran for town council last month. He lost."

# Stolen

"Oh yes, yes, now I remember. She's the tall one, blonde hair, pretty face, figure to stop a clock?"

"Tha's the one. Well, if she said no to our Eddie, she jus' don' know what she's missin'. Hey, Eddie."

The reply was sullen and barely audible. "Yeah."

"C'mon out here, wanna talk to ya."

Eddie walked back out to the office and sat on the divan against the far wall. Bass turned to him, "Say, how come you're so down in the dumps, Eddie? You don't seem yourself this morning."

Eddie hung his head and fidgeted when he answered. "So, I asked Gretta Jorgensen to the social this weekend at the soda shoppe."

"Ah, and she said no?"

"No. She said yes, seemed real anxious to go with me too."

"Well, that's great, Eddie. So, what's the problem?"

"Two things. Her little brother knows I don't read so well, hardly at all, and he was pokin' fun right in front of her. Second, I just flat-out don't know how to dance a lick. Don't even know how to start. Gretta's a real sweet gal and all . . . hell, she's the only gal in town that's my size!"

Bass listened carefully. Eddie was one of his favorite people in all El Paso. "Eddie. Seems to me you

already got the hard part over with. Usually, just the askin'
is where most fellas fall flat. As to the readin'? Hell, that
ain't nothin' but practice. My Sally has buckets full of
schoolbook learnin.' I'm sure she'd be able to help with
your readi'n. And dancin' ain't no secret, neither. She'll
help ya with that, too. Now remember, she's in a family
way and due to deliver next month, so you'll have to go
easy on her. Okay?"

"Sure, Marshal. That sounds just fine."

Bart refilled his cup. "Earlier, there was a fella
named Matlock came in. He's from up to Hartley above
Amarillo. Frank his little girls were kidnapped on
Christmas, fer Christ's sake. He's come all this way to ask
for your help. It's here in the mornin' wire."

Bass read the brief report and shook his head.
"Damn. Where is he now?"

"Stepped out. He'll be back. One other thing you
should know, the assholes that done it cut their baby's
throat."

Bass stood up in horror, his face twisted in rage and
confusion. "It's okay. The baby's okay. Matlock said the
bastards couldn't see very well, it bein' so dark, an' that
musta saved the child from a worse cuttin'. Anyway, the
baby's okay."

# Stolen

Bass thought quietly to himself and sipped at his coffee. "It says in that report which way the bastards lit out?"

Bart looked at the wire again. "Nope."

"Sally'll prob'ly kill me; it bein' so close to her time and all. I'll have to talk to her."

Just as he spoke, Avery Matlock walked through the door.

"Marshal Bass? I'm Avery Matlock." Bass rose to his feet, extending his hand. "Good morning, Mr. Matlock. Bart has shown me our wire report. I am so terribly sorry for your family, sir."

"Thank you, Marshal. Well, I'm sure you've guessed why I'm here, sir. I must humbly beseech you to help us find our children. This ransom letter was found sometime after the girls were taken. We did not see it immediately. The room was dark, and our baby was crying."

"I can well imagine. Let's go upstairs to my office and talk. Would you like another coffee?"

"Thank you. I would."

Bass signaled for Bart to send Eddie Voer up with a fresh pot, and together, they went outside and climbed the steps to Bass's second-floor office. The morning was chilly

# Stolen

and dim, with a thick layer of low clouds in varying shades of gray. Bass raised the blinds to let as much sunlight in as possible. Next, he set a match to the kindling of the stove that had been made ready that morning when Eddie arrived.

"The room will warm up soon, Mr. Matlock, and coffee is on the way." Both men could see the vapor of their breath as testament to the low temperature in the room.

"Please, Marshal. Call me Avery. I'd like to be as informal as possible. Formalities sometimes get in the way of urgent business, I've found."

"Okay then. And please call me Frank. Almost everyone does."

"Almost everyone?"

"Yes, my wife insists on calling me by my given first name, Frederick."

"That's much preferable to my wife's nickname for me, Avy. Oh. And my youngest daughter, Susan, is in the habit of calling me Ivory." Avery caught himself with tightness in his throat, and he dabbed at his eyes with a handkerchief. "I'm sorry, Frank. It was a long day of travel yesterday, and I haven't been sleeping well."

# Stolen

"No need to apologize, Avery. I understand completely." Matlock regained his composure and put away his handkerchief.

"So, to the subject then, will you help us, Marshal? We really are quite desperate."

"Yes, of course, I'll do all I can, but I need to tell you that my wife is within four weeks of her due date, according to the doc. Now, I know that's just an estimate. It could be sooner or later. But Avery, this is my wife's first baby. She's excited and happy, certainly, but she's also understandably fearful and nervous. Now let me see the letter." Bass took a moment to read. "Says they must have the money by the second of January. Is that possible for you?"

"Yes. We have some savings, and my employer, XIT, will give us the rest."

"Good. Put the ad in the paper then today. The telegraph office is at the railroad terminal. Tomorrow, I want you to go home and wait for instructions. As soon as they arrive, I want you to wire me an exact copy, word for word. Can you do that?"

"Of course. You will be here then, in El Paso?"

# Stolen

"Yes. Until we get the instructions, we're kinda stuck. Say, let me ask you. Do you know the direction the kidnappers took when they left?"

"Why yes, it was west."

"Due west? Not northwest or southwest?"

"No, due west. In fact, I foolishly sent my foreman and two riders out to see if they might find them. They hadn't returned by the time I left yesterday morning."

"Well, it's not impossible that your men will find their way home, but from everything you've said and the information on our wire, I gotta believe these guys we're up against are pretty good. Did your man indicate how many there might be?"

"Yes, he said from the tracks, which were all unshod, that there were possibly five horses. Oh, and another thing. We have or had two large dogs that slept in the barn. They were both killed by arrows. The unshod horses and the arrows led me to suspect Indians, but my foreman said no, not likely. Of course, this was before we found the letter."

"Do you know if your foreman had training in tracking... reading sign?"

"No, I'm sorry, I don't. I remember him saying that once in his youth, he was a deputy sheriff in Kansas, but

# Stolen

that's all the background I know on him. He always seemed an honest man. He was hired by the Company."

"I'm sorry, you may have mentioned it earlier, but what is the Company?"

"XIT Ranch."

# Stolen

*5:45 p.m. December 27, 1887*
*An Abandon Line Shack*
*60 Miles West of Narvaez*
*New Mexico Territory*

Gabe Viligry's posse had stopped on a rise overlooking the land surrounding an old line shack. The tracks they had been following led directly to the structure. Gabe was watching the place through his Zeiss binoculars, which he bought from the manufacturer in Germany via mail order. The light was fading, and as the sun dropped, shadows began to obscure his vision.

"No smoke, no horses. Don't see any activity of any kind, but let me ride in a little closer. I'll signal if it's clear."

The men were tired, hungry, and cold. The horses needed a good feed and a quiet night. Boone Waverly spotted tracks leading to a fairly deep arroyo and pointed it out to Ramsfeld and Patchelski.

"Bet's where they hobbled their horses down in that barranca, low, and outta the wind. Probably some graze in there, too, under the snow." Ramsfeld had been watching Gabe, and now he spotted the Sherriff waving to the bunch.

# Stolen

"Gabe says it's all clear. Whyn't you tell him 'bout the arroyo when we get down there."

The three men started moving down the rise. "Yeah, and 'soon as I do, he'll say, 'okay, sounds good, Boone. Why don't you put the horses up for the night seein's how you spotted it an all.'"

"Boone, I swear you'd argue with your shadow. Makes you feel any better, I'll put 'em up myself."

"Now, Reverends, I didn't mean fer you to do it."

Patch spoke up. "Hell, now it's on me? I'm mindin' my own business, enjoyin' a pleasant winter's eve a horseback, and somehow you both shifted the horse tendin' chore to me?"

"He's right, Boone, this is just 'tween us: you an' me. We got to be careful not to involve ol' Patch there, delicate and frail as he is."

"You're right as usual, Reverend. Why ol' Patch prob'ly just wants to get to his knittin' by the fire."

"No, ya don't. I see what you boys is tryin'. You're tryin' to goad me to it, and it ain't gonna work. We get down to Gabe. Let's let him decide."

# Stolen

The others were in agreement with Patch's plan, and as they approached Gabe at the front of the shack, Boone was first to speak.

"Say, Gabe, uh, we all took a vote and elected you to put up the horses' yonder in that arroyo outta the wind."

Gabe looked at each man briefly and said as he remounted. "The arroyo, huh? Okay. Good a spot as any, I guess."

The three men dismounted and slipped off their saddles and gear, grinning at their cleverness.

As Gabe collected the reins to their horses, he said, "Reverend, why don't you walk out and scare up some firewood, see if you can't get somethin' burnin' in the hearth? Patch, I want you to take whatever you can find and collect some snow for cookin'—maybe yonder, to the south. Boone, you take all the gear inside and lay out the bedrolls by the hearth. I'll meet y'all back at the shack. Won't take me but a minute."

And Gabe rode off to the arroyo with the horses. The three men were left standing in the snow looking at each other when Boone said. "Now, how the hell did he do that?"

# Stolen

Patch told Boone of a convenient place for his future questions, and the Reverend threw a snowball at him.

# Stolen

Chapter 7

*8:15 p.m., December 27, 1887*
*Front Room, Main House*
*TwainHeart, Ranch*
*El Paso, Texas*

"Well, of course, you must go, Frederick. My goodness, two little girls, and on Christmas as well. The vermin! And the baby? You must find these awful people and do them justice." Sally sat on the divan, and Bass gazed out the large front window as snow fell in the yard.

"I knew you'd feel this way, Sal, but so close to your birthing date made me stop and think. I remember what Doc Spalding said about this bein' your first, and I do wanna be here."

"I know, sweetheart, but those two children must take precedence. Besides, I hadn't mentioned it before, but there's a very good chance that Maggie and Elsie will be coming down from Torrington in a week or so. So, you see? I won't be alone at all."

"Sure be good to see 'em again, 'specially Elsie. I'm real fond a' her. Strong youngster she is. 'Bet she's grown since the last time I saw her. When was that last spring, right?"

"Yes, dear just count backward nine months. That'll give you an approximate. I remember you two had a wondrous bond when you first met. You were the only one she'd talk to." Bass nodded along as Sally spoke, "So, it's settled then. You'll do whatever is necessary to return those children to their home, and we'll have another wonderful tale for Annie when she's older."

Bass smiled at how lucky he'd been the day he met Sally. Hardly a year ago, and here she sat, so pregnant she needed help to stand up.

"Frederick, Junior."

# Stolen

*The Abandoned Line Shack*

*West of Narvaez*

*New Mexico Territory*

Patchelski was the first one awake. He'd made the mistake of laying out his bedroll too near the hearth. As the sun rose, light pierced through the gaps in the wall around the flue and hit Patch square in the forehead. After relieving himself outside near the door, he came back in and started a fire using the still-glowing coals in the hearth. He fixed coffee, set the pot on a stone near the fire, and then rolled back up in his blankets.

"Patch? That you?"

"'Tis."

"What's it like outside this mornin'?"

"Fuckin cold is what."

"Damn. I hoped I'd been dreamin'."

Boone Waverly crawled out of the tangle that was his bedroll and, like Patch before him, went outside to relieve himself. "God damn, I believe my pee froze 'fore it hit the ground."

# Stolen

The Reverend overheard the conversation and slowly sat up in his blankets. "Coffee? Is there any coffee here?" Ramsfeld's eyes were still closed, but he turned his head in the direction of whoever spoke.

"Just about, Deacon. Startin' to boil just now."

"Thank you. Who are you?"

"It's me, Deacon, Patch Patchelski."

"Oh yes, fine fellow."

"Say, Boone?"

"What?"

"Where's Gabe at this uh . . . day?"

"I do not know. I suppose that he's well, though, as he did not drink but little with us last night."

The night before, the posse-men allowed that since it was so cold, it was hard to sleep, so they decided to share a bottle of 'who shot John' that Boone brought with him from his private supply. They all agreed that the liquor was good and clear, with few impurities and a heady bouquet. Also, it kicked like a mule when it hit bottom and smoothed out as more was taken. Just as the men were becoming resolved to the new day, the door opened, and Gabe Viligry walked in, slapping his gloved hands together and heading for the hearth.

"Mornin' boys, sleep well, did ya?"

# Stolen

There were groans all around, and Reverend Ramsfeld cursed. Gabe smiled as he sipped at his coffee.

"Snowed during the night, but I picked their trail 'bout a half-mile out. Same as we followed yesterday. C'mon boys. We're burnin' daylight . . . saddle up, and let's go."

The Reverend Ramsfeld cursed several more times that morning.

# Stolen

*8:45 a.m., December 28, 1887*
*Nicolai Waslaski's Rancho*
*Sabinoso Canyon, Canadian River*
*New Mexico Territory.*

The four men had been walking the horses since sunrise while letting the girls ride. Three days of hard travel had taken a toll on the animals. They needed at least a full day of rest and plenty of sturdy fodder. Jose Chavez knew this, but he also knew Señor Silva had a timetable to keep. The girls would have to be at his rancheria by tomorrow morning.

When the group arrived at Nicolai Waslaski's small sheep ranch near the Canadian River, both the men and the horses were exhausted. Waslaski had done as he was told. There was shelter, oat hay, and water for the horses, but the small shack he lived in had only one room, and with six people, accommodations were cramped.

As usual, Chavez saw to the girls' comfort first. Waslaski had a fire going, and a large iron pot of mutton stew was hanging from the hearth crane to keep it warm. Chavez saw that the girls' blankets were laid out carefully in front of the fire. Alarid, the Cherokee, Romero, and Waslaski were putting up the horses in the barn.

# Stolen

"There you are. Warm beds for the fine ladies, eh? Soon, you will have food and a long sleep."

As he spoke, Eugenio Alarid walked in carrying his saddle and a large canvas bag filled with hay he'd picked up in the barn. Deliberately, he flopped his saddle at the rear of the room away from the fire and brought the bag up to the girls to use as a pillow. He covered the coarse fabric of the bag with a blanket, smiling and saying to the girls, "*Para tu comodidad, Señioritas.*"

When he was finished, he picked up his wide sombrero, held it over his chest, and backed away, saying, "*Gracias, gracias.*" It was the most conversation he'd made during the whole trip.

A smallish black and white herding dog dashed through the back door and lay on a straw mat by the fire that evidently was his sleeping quarters. Waslaski, a short, round man with a black stubble beard and long, greasy, black hair, filled two bowls and made sure the girls got only the most tender pieces of the mutton. He also provided a large round bread that he indicated he'd made himself. It was fresh and flavored with the wild thyme and sage that grew near the river. The girls ate first and threw small pieces of mutton and bread to the dog, who ate quickly, wagging his tail and begging for more.

# Stolen

Once the girls had eaten, Waslaski delivered the pot and the rest of the loaf to the men who remained in the background, sitting at a table, talking quietly in Spanish, and drinking from a bottle of tequila that their host had given them.

Chavez approached the girls as they settled in their blankets, "You both ate the stew well. Was it to your liking?"

"It was all right. We were hungry enough to eat anything," Ruth answered.

Chavez smiled. "That is good. Sleep now. We begin the last part of our journey this evening. But I am afraid it is a long one. When we get to the rancheria tomorrow, it is like a palace. You will be able to wash and sleep in real beds until it is time for you to go home."

Susan started crying and saying in a very soft voice, "I wanna go home now. Please, can we go home?"

Chavez could only look kindly at the children and say, "Don Vicente is a kind and generous man." With that, Chavez stepped away. He sat down at the table and ate a few bites of the mutton stew and bread. He did not drink the tequila.

# Stolen

Chavez, Alarid, and Romero were at the barn with the horses. The animals had been well-fed by Waslaski (Chavez made a note to commend Nicolai Waslaski to Don Vicente), and now their heads were held up, their tails switched back and forth, and they appeared ready to leave. The men waited for Cherokee Bill Guerrero to return from his backtrail check and chatted amiably among themselves in Spanish.

The girls were still asleep in the shack a short distance away though they both were starting to wake and feel the need to relieve themselves. They went out the front door and circled around to the outhouse on the side. It was small and rank, like most of the commodes they were used to. They both went inside to get out of the fierce wind as it roared through the Canadian River canyons. While inside, they heard the arrival of the Indian and supposed that it was close to being time to leave.

As they walked back to the front door, they were jolted by two loud bangs, one right after the other, that came from the barn and echoed out to the river. They quickly dashed inside, thinking it may have been wrong to go out without permission, and they didn't want to make

108

# Stolen

anyone angry with them. As they were rolling up their blankets, Chavez and Alarid came in.

"Niñas, we are about ready to leave. Mr. Waslaski will bring the horses around to the front door, and we will leave from there. Just so you know, our friends Jose Romero and Cherokee Bob will be remaining here to help Mr. Waslaski with his sheep. They have graciously given us their horses, as they will be needed during the last part of our ride. Now, Señor Alarid will help you with your things, and I will say goodbye to Nicolai Waslaski."

The girls walked back out the front door to find Eugenio Alarid holding five saddled horses. The Indian and Romero were nowhere in sight, and neither was their host, Nicolai Waslaski. They all rode away to the south, partnered as usual, Ruth sitting on the rise of the saddle against the pommel and Chavez sitting far back on the cantle. Susie was in the same position, but as she was smaller, Alarid was much more comfortable. As they rode away, Ruth looked back and saw Mr. Waslaski behind his barn digging a hole.

# Stolen

Bass had just tipped the delivery boy two dollars for riding all the way out to TwainHeart to deliver a telegram. He was standing in the front room reading the message as Sally walked in from the kitchen.

"From Avery Matlock. He's back in Hartley already. Musta' rode the train all night to get there." Bass began reading the telegram.

Sally was trying to sit on the divan but needed Bass's help. "What does he say? Anything about the condition of the baby?"

"Only that all's well, that he has the money and is waiting for instructions. The foreman and two of his men never returned. I don't know if I mentioned that Avery sent his foreman and two riders out to follow the tracks left by the kidnappers. He says at the end here, they never returned. I imagine he's pretty broken up over it."

Sally thought for a moment and said, "In a situation like that, I can understand his motivation. He must've been very desperate. I'm sure he would have gone himself if he wasn't so badly needed by his wife and baby."

# Stolen

"Hm. You're right. Well, it says he has the money and is awaiting instructions. 'He will advise,' he says."

"So, we wait for more news. How do you think you'll handle this, Frederick?"

"Well, as soon as Avery knows what he's supposed to do, I'll join him. I imagine he's being watched, probably by someone he knows. Could be more than one of 'em too."

"Shouldn't you have gone back with him?"

"No, nothin's going to happen 'til he gets the instructions from the kidnappers. He'll be okay 'til then. I'll leave as soon as I hear from him. Likely be tomorrow. When is your sister due?"

"Sunday. They'll probably be getting on the train tomorrow."

Bass didn't want Sally to see he was nervous about her being alone. "Nesta will be here for the next few days, right?"

"Yes, dear. I'll be fine." Sally thought for a moment, "Dear, how long do you think you'll be gone?"

"Four or five days, Sal. A week at the most. I'm just gonna be there for the exchange, the money for his children. Make sure it goes smooth and safe. Then, I'm

# Stolen

gonna kill as many of 'em as I can." Bass smiled at Sally, even though she knew he was telling the truth.

She smiled back, "That's my Marshal. Do be careful, though."

"Deputy Marshal, actually."

# Stolen

*5:30 p.m., December 28, 1887*

*Nicolai Waslaski's Rancho*

*Sabinoso Canyon, Canadian River*

*New Mexico Territory*


The posse-men plodded within one hundred yards of a shepherd's adobe. They viewed it and the surrounding terrain from atop a rise near the river. Gabe put his field glasses away.

"Smoke showin'. Sheep to the left, down in that little coulee. Animals in the corral, probably in the barn too."

"Think they're there, Gabe?"

Viligry thought some more as he watched the small house. "No, I don't, boys, tell you why. 'Twas me holed up in there, I'd have a lookout sittin' right up here where we are. No, sir, I believe it's just the shepherd and his family down there. Let's pay a call. Bet them outlaws was here for certain."

The four riders wove their way down the slope to keep the horses from slipping in the new snow. When they got to the yard, Gabe sent Boone to check the barn, and the other two tied off the horses and then went to the door with Gabe. Before he could identify himself, there was a loud boom from inside, and the wooden door exploded outward. Patchelski, standing just to the right of the door, was caught in the middle with birdshot and flying splinters. Fortunately, his heavy clothes took most of the shot pattern, but Patchelski was knocked unconscious by the door swinging on its hinges.

"Jesus! Stop your shootin' in there. We're lawmen! God damn, Patch, you okay? Can ya hear me, Patch?"

Patch opened his eyes and began blinking and coughing at the same time. "Oh, Lord. Holy Christ, Gabe! I'm shot!" The wool on his jacket was smoking, and he tried to blow on it as he spoke.

"Shoot that son of a bitch, Gabe. He'll kill us all."

"Calm down, Patch. I think you're okay. Hello inside? You speak English?"

After a moment, they heard, "I speak. Go 'way now. You don't belong here."

A dog barked in the room somewhere.

"We're lawmen, duly-appointed posse chasin' kidnappin' outlaws. I'll shoot you if I have to. Don't want to."

"Then go away now."

Once he saw that Patch was all right, Ramsfeld circled around to the back, where he joined Boone.

# Stolen

"The hell happened, Reverend? 'Scuse my language."

"Whoever's inside just blew the door off when Gabe knocked. Door hit Patch. He's okay."

"Whew, glad a' that. It's just an old man is all I see. Got a clear look at him from here, s'pose Gabe wants me to shoot?"

"No, no. Gabe wants to talk to the guy, find out 'bout them outlaws."

They could hear Gabe still talking to the man. "We just wanna ask you some questions, fella. Ain't gonna shoot. I'm comin' in. Don't you shoot now. My hands are up."

Gabe took a small step into the shattered doorway and peered around the room. He saw an old man huddled behind a tipped-over table, holding onto his dog.

"See? Got no gun. Now. I have three deputies with me surrounding the house." Gabe showed his badge. "All we wanna do is talk to you."

The old man lowered his shotgun and stood up. "All right, for only talking. You may come in."

"It's ok, boys. Come on in."

All three men walked into the adobe, holding badges plainly in view. The old man saw how Patch's jacket was damaged and made a guilty-looking expression. "I'm sorry to hurt you. I not know who you are. I will pay you for your coat to fix."

"Well, that's just fine, mister, but who's gonna pay to have my heart restarted? Mighta been kilt, old-timer."

"I'm sorry, sit, sit, have drink. It will warm you." The old man passed around a bottle of clear liquid.

"What is this? You make it yourself?" Boone asked.

"It is Polish Vodka, drink." They all swallowed the liquor down.

"Say, this here's might fine. How do you make it?" Boone asked.

The old man smiled, "Potatoes."

Boone stared at the man for a few moments. "Say what?"

"From potatoes." The old man gestured as though he was digging.

"Damn me. Potatoes. Who'd a thought?"

Gabe Viligry finally brought the conversation to the men with the little girls. The others sat by the fire, and the Reverend began petting the dog.

"First, tell me your name, please."

"Nicolai Waslaski. I am shepherd."

# Stolen

"Okay, Nicolai, we've been followin' a group of outlaws who kidnapped two girls from their home near Amarillo, Texas. Their tracks have led to your house. Were they here?"

"Yes, but I not know about kidnap. They pay me for food and shelter and for their horses. I have not to do with them." Waslaski had a very concerned look, and he spoke very quickly as if he was worried he'd be arrested.

"Okay, how many men were there?"

"Four mens and two childs. The, ah the *dziewczynki* . . . ah were not hurt and were treated good."
Waslaski was stumbling for his English, and Viligry was becoming more suspicious by the minute.

"When did they leave?"

"Yesterday…in *wieczor*, ah—ah eventime."

"Evening time?"

"Yes, yes. Then."

"What happened while they were here, Mr. Waslinski?"

The old man was sweating visibly now, and he looked up when Gabe asked the question.

"They…they. How is it—shot some." The man's shoulders slumped, and he began to mumble in Polish.

"They shot some? You mean they killed someone?"

# Stolen

"Yes, yes. I am not here, but they say to dig hole. I do it for the money. I do it for the money." Waslaski was obviously shaken by what had happened, and it explained why the posse was greeted with a shotgun.

"Who did they kill?"

"Two of them. One is Indian. The other is Mex, I think."

"We tracked five horses to your home. Was it three men that left with the girls?"

"No." Waslaski held up two fingers. Gabe nodded. And turned to the three men.

"I think we were right. For whatever reason, that fresh grave at Dominguez's place was one of the kidnappers. He was killed for some reason, I s'pose, and they took his horse with them. Then here, according to what I think Waslaski's saying, two more were killed. He says he buried them. Says he wasn't here when it happened but that it was an Indian and a Mexican that he buried."

Boone spoke up. "Indian lines up with the three men we found, scalped and shot full of arrows. An' he's dead, this ol' bird says? Too bad, I was lookin' forward to killin' that one myself."

# Stolen

Gabe smiled and said, "Yeah, so the odds are improving. Hell, maybe by the time we find 'em, they'll have all shot themselves, save us the trouble."

"So what do we do now, Gabe?" Ramsfeld asked.

"Well, he says they left yesterday evening. I bet they 'been travelin' at night all along. Horses are 'bout done in, and we all need some rest. We'll pick it up again in the mornin'. Patch, why don't you see to the horses? We'll settle in here."

Everyone nodded their agreement.

"Say, old man, got any more a' that Polish Vodka?" Boone asked.

# Stolen

"Time to get movin' boys. Gonna be a long day, I'm afraid. We're gonna have ta' walk the horses 'bout as much as we ride 'em. That's how broke down they are."

Gabe was the first one up, he generally was, and he'd already been out to check on the horses. They were all worn, not by the weather, but by the constant travel on poor fodder. All four animals needed a good feed and a full day off.

"You know, I wonder if that's why them two men were killed? For their horses, maybe?" Patch added, "If that really is the reason, we're trackin' some pretty cold-blooded outlaws. We better rethink how we're gonna handle 'em when we run 'em down."

Boone added, "Animals, animals is what they are. Animals, boys. Cut a baby's throat, murder and scalp, strangers, shoot your own men for their horses? All I plan to do is kill as many as I can."

"They're still the Lord's work, boys. Let's not forget that. Wayward and ruthless, that's true, but still the Lord's work."

# Stolen

Waslaski provided simple breakfasts of bread, eggs, and pork belly. The men brought their own coffee. By seven-thirty, they were back on the trail, and after two hours, they came to a stop.

"Still the same five horses, Gabe. The cracked wall on the right forefoot is still leading." Boone was doing the tracking. His eyes picked up some things the others might miss.

"Two are laden, and three are bein' dragged behind."

Gabe Viligry explained, "Backups. They killed two men for backup horses, is what they did. Jesus, what kinda people are these?" Gabe talked softly to himself, but the other three were thinking the same thing.

By midday, the posse had covered fifteen miles. They were slowed by the need to rest and walk the horses. It had been a hard trail for the animals, sparse grazing and ice and snow for thirst. The horses did get a suitable watering at the Canadian River before striking out to the west.

"Gabe, we're about a day's ride behind these guys, right?" Patchelski spoke up.

"'Ats how I figure it."

# Stolen

"Well, don't it seem strange they don't seem to care 'bout being tracked? I mean, after them, three poor scalped bastards. And now they up an killed the Indian. He was the one that covered their back trail early on, and they killed him. What's all that mean, Gabe? Must mean somethin'."

"You're right, Patch. Know what I think? Could be wrong, but I think it means they're close to home. And they ain't worried cause they know they got us outnumbered."

Everyone became quiet. All that could be heard was the creak of saddle leather as each man became conscious of an ambush.

After a minute or so, Gabe said, "Boys, we're gonna get off this trail now. We're gonna parallel the bastards 'til we see what's what. We'll follow from up yonder in the hills to the north. We know where they're headed. Hell, they're headed west. Only thing out that way I know of is Las Vegas, which might just be the most wide-open town in the territory. We'll climb up into them hills and ridgelines and keep our pace along up there. Once it gets dark tonight, we'll see if anyone comes lookin'. Anyway, we'll get off this track. Let's camp up in the trees yonder. Bank the fire high and leave around midnight."

# Stolen

Chapter 8

*8:55 a.m., December 29, 1887*
*Matlock House*
*Hartley, Texas*

The telegram read:

> *Congratulations, Matlock. You are getting closer to*
> *retrieving your daughters. Tomorrow at 4:00 p.m.,*
> *you are to meet my representative in the lobby of*
> *the Farview Hotel in Amarillo. Have the money in*
> *cash. You are being watched day and night, even on*
> *your trip to El Paso. Don't stumble now that you*
> *are so close.*

Avery explained his plan to go to Amarillo to Alice,
who had become braver and more capable in the four days
since the break-in and kidnap at their home. She was even
more hopeful when he explained that he'd gotten the
money from George Findlay. She was more confident still,
when he told her that Frank Bass would be there to help
out.

"I have to go to the bank in Hartley and ask the
manager to send a wire to Marshal Bass. I'm being

watched, and a trip to the telegraph office might cause difficulties if the kidnappers find out. This will appear as though I'm making arrangements to pick up the cash in Amarillo."

Avery asked one of the wranglers to saddle a horse for him. He was particularly obvious in his remarks about where he was going. He wasn't sure if one of the wranglers at the house was an informant, but he didn't want to take a chance either.

The First Texas Republic Bank was at the corner of Seventh Street and Dodge, about a twenty-minute ride from the Matlock house. Avery tied the horse outside at the hitch rail and walked in. He turned right toward a series of small glass-walled offices lined up along the rear of the building and noticed the manager, Jerry Feckle, was busy with another customer. Avery sat in one of the comfortable chairs outside the manager's office and waited as patiently as he could.

After about ten minutes, he stood up and began pacing. He would occasionally stop and throw quizzical glances at Feckle, sending as clear a signal as he could that his time was being wasted. Finally, both men in the office rose and shook hands, and the customer took his leave. Matlock removed his hat and closed the door behind him.

# Stolen

"Avery. How can I help you today?"

"I want you to send this telegram to the gentleman indicated in El Paso. Please don't ask any questions. Just do this once I'm mounted and gone from the street. It is of vital consequence to my family, Jerry."

Feckle understood the urgency. Almost everyone in town had heard of the calamity that had fallen on the Matlocks at Christmas. Feckle nodded, "You can count on me, Avery." And with that, Matlock was out of the office, on his horse and away.

Thirty minutes later, a Western Union delivery boy handed the message to Frank Bass. It took only moments to compose his response, and once he handed the folded note to the delivery runner, Bass told Bart Mariany that he would be out of the office for a few days.

"I'll ask Paulo to stop by just to check on things. If something should come up, he's perfectly capable of handling 'bout anything. Otherwise, this is where you can reach me tomorrow, and I'll try to keep you informed of my movements."

Bass handed the note to Mariany and left through the back door. He saddled Emma in the small barn behind the office, headed past the Chamizal, and continued on to TwainHeart.

# Stolen

# Stolen

*Noon, December 29, 1887*
*Main House*
*TwainHeart Ranch*
*El Paso, Texas*

They stood in the foyer talking about Bass's ideas. "My plan is to be in the hotel before Avery arrives so I can see the man who takes the money and hopefully follow him, undetected a course, to the head conspirator. Once I see the girls are safe, I'll kill everyone involved in this monstrous scheme and return the children and the money to Avery back at the hotel. Sounds simple, right?"

"Indeed, dear. But where is the part where you don't get killed in the offing?"

"Well. That's a bit sketchy right now, but I plan to work on it on the train."

She hugged Bass as if it were her last chance, and in the back of her mind, every time he left, she knew it might be. Bass kissed her long and deeply. It was a scene they played out each time Bass left for parts and persons unknown.

"Nesta will be over shortly, and I think Marianna will ride over too. Theo will pick her up on his way home from the feed store."

# Stolen

"How is the new venture progressing?"

"I think pretty fair. 'Only been open a couple months, but we're picking up new customers every day. Folks are all pretty sick a' Sherm Radabaugh, and by the time we're through with him, he won't be able to sell water to a thirsty man."

Bass threw the strap of his valise over his shoulder and grabbed his rifle. "I'll check in when I get there. I love you, Sal."

Sally kissed him again, and he walked out the door.

# Stolen

*10:15 a.m., December 29, 1887*

*Vicente Silva's Rancheria*

*Outside Las Vegas*

*New Mexico Territory*

Chavez and Alarid had been walking the horses for the last six miles. One of the animals had stopped after fifty miles and was no longer able to stand. Alarid shot the horse, and the party continued on its way. Susie had never seen an animal shot before, and it upset her to the point of tears.

After the next rest stop, Chavez decided that each girl should ride her own horse to relieve the burdens on his own and Alarid's mount. He reasoned that the animals were too tired to run and the girls too scared. They had been lucky for the past two nights in that the moon was full to waning gibbous, and the sky was clear. This night was overcast, and only a faint light could be seen in the southwestern sky. Chavez had been carrying a torch for most of this leg of the trip, replacing it as needed from one of the four other saddles. Each man had been equipped with a torch and fuel oil for the trip. The sun had been up since just after six, but the light was gray and muddled.

They spotted the low roofline of the hacienda and then the barns and corrals behind. There was some sparse

# Stolen

activity around the barn, but the rancheria still looked to be asleep. As they approached, a tall, slender man in a dark suit appeared on the veranda, and he began waving to the group as they rode single file through the gate and up the drive.

Chavez was first to dismount as he approached the man. They smiled and embraced one another and then talked for several minutes. Alarid had helped the girls off their mounts and, after bowing to the older man, led the four horses to the barn behind the house. Chavez called to the girls, "Señoritas, please come greet your host, Señor. May I present Señoritas Ruth and Susan Matlock? Ladies, this is Don Vicente Silva."

Silva was older, with silver hair and a mustache that extended an inch or so on each side of his mouth. He wore a black suit and vest and a white shirt with a stiff collar and a string tie. His skin was ashen, and his teeth were yellow. Ruth thought he looked sick, but he smiled.

*"Buenas Dias. Chavez te mostrara tu habitacion."* His smiled faded then, and he turned back to the door and went inside.

Chavez handed each their blanket roll and said, "Come with me, please. I will take you to your room."

# Stolen

They walked around the side of the house, and the girls were able to get an appreciation of how large the place was. The house had two wings in the rear with a fountain inside in the middle. The floor was all colored tile, and many vines grew on the walls of the house. There were two large barns and several corrals for each. There was also a long, low building with windows and a chimney between the two barns.

They were led into the barn on the left, and Chavez opened a small hatch that led into a room that Ruth thought must have been an addition to the barn. There was no light, and the air smelled musty, like the attic at home when mama needed extra dishes.

"Señoritas if you please." Chavez was no longer smiling. The look on his face was more of regret than anything else.

"But there is no light or heat," Ruth said.

"It's too scary." Susie was in tears, sobbing.

"Please, Niñas, I will hand you the lantern and blankets. There is a small stove and chairs to sit on and a bed for sleeping. I will bring your food and water. There are books to read, too. Please go inside."

# Stolen

Ruth started but stopped and said, "Mr. Chavez, how can you do this to us? We thought you were our friend?"

Chavez was visibly upset as well. He turned away. "It is the will of Don Vicente. Please, no more talk. Go inside your fine new room."

Both did as they were told and when they got inside, Chavez handed in a lantern and then some blankets.

"I will bring wood for the stove, *muchachas*, and food and water from the house."

He was thinking of his own children as he closed and latched the door. Susan began crying, and Ruth hugged her until she stopped.

# Stolen

*7:50 a.m., December 29, 1887*
*El Paso & South Western Terminal*
*Amarillo, Texas.*

Bass stepped off the Pullman Sleeper and onto the platform of the E. P. & SW passenger station a few minutes before eight. The morning was crisp and clear, perfect for a bracing walk to the Fairview hotel. He'd slept only sporadically in his compartment. The noise of the tracks was bothersome, but the occasional sudden jarring of misaligned rails kept him awake. Bass knew the hotel and went directly to the café, where he ordered coffee, ham and eggs, fried potatoes, and more coffee. He decided to wait on getting a room and opted to walk about Amarillo to get a sense of where things were. Bass was somewhat familiar with Amarillo as he had purchased several cows and two bulls from the livestock auction not far from the train station. He kept track of the auctions as he was interested in purchasing a Shire horse broodmare for his stallion Willy.

Bass checked his Elgin timepiece and noticed the morning had closed in on eleven, so he turned toward the hotel and sat down in the lobby, his back to a corner near the fire, reading the Amarillo Twice Weekly Herald and smoking a cigar. He couldn't tell you what was in the paper. His eyes were everywhere but the paper. He had no idea who he was looking for, what sort of man it might be. He assumed it would only be a messenger, that the leader of this kind of outfit would insulate himself from actual contact. Still, he scrutinized the men that came and went from the hotel one by one.

At 11:45, Avery Matlock walked through the front door carrying a black leather bag and looking slightly anxious. As per their agreement, Avery paid no attention to Bass and sat at a table for two near a front window. He ordered a whiskey, and Bass saw his hand trembling as he lifted the glass.

At exactly noon, a well-dressed young Mexican in a light brown suit with a straw Panama hat, *out of place in winter*, Bass thought, appeared at the doorway and walked immediately to Avery's table and sat down. Bass could not hear their conversation, but in short order, Avery handed the bag to the man, who promptly stood and left. Bass rose to his feet—slowly, in case the room was being watched— and walked to Avery, still watching the man through the front window. Avery passed Bass and said under his breath that there was a message waiting for him at the front desk. Bass continued through the front door, his eyes still focused

# Stolen

on the brown suit and Panama as Avery caught up with him.

"They want more, dear God. They want more money."

Bass turned his eyes to Avery, who looked achingly desperate and lost. Instinctively, Bass bolted after Panama hat, who had just gotten into a buggy across the street. Bass pulled the smaller man out of the two-seat buggy by the lapels of his brown suit and threw him to the ground. On the ground, the man reached into his vest for a small pistol. Bass kicked the man's hand away, cracking his wrist at an unnatural angle and leaving a small gash on the man's face with his spur. Bass held the barrel of his Colt directly in front of the man's nose and pulled the hammer to the fully-cocked position.

"We're gonna have a serious talk, you and me, *comprende*?" The man was visibly shaken and could not take his eyes away from the barrel of Bass's gun.

"*Si, Si Señor, para*—I ah—ah . . . have nothing. *Por favor*, I'm not knowing."

"Uh-huh, we'll see about that." Bass threw the satchel to Avery and lifted the man from the street, who then clung to a wheel-spoke for support.

# Stolen

People had started to gather as the street scene unfolded, and it became necessary for Bass to identify himself and ask that they all move on. As they dispersed, Bass and Avery walked the dazed man back across the street to an alley alongside the hotel. Once all three were in the alley, Avery stood watch while Bass and the man stayed in the shadows. Bass began questioning the young man.

"What's your name, buster. *Tu nombre, tu nombre?*"

"Señor please I beg, please Señor they will kill me . . . *muerto*, Señor, please!"

"*Tu nombre, te quedes*, your name!"

"Tomasino, Señor de Rivera, Tomasino de Rivera." De Rivera looked dejected and reconciled to his position. They will kill me now."

"All right, Tomasino, what were you supposed to do with the money?"

"I cannot say, please do not make me. I am…they kill me, Señor.

"Tomasino, they're gonna kill you no matter what, amigo. They ain't gonna believe you kept quiet no matter what you tell 'em." Bass drew his pistol again and applied it as he had before.

# Stolen

"You talk to me, tell me the truth, and I'll see you get protection . . . protection, so you can testify. But if you keep up this 'they will kill me stuff,' hombre, I'm in the here and now. You'll be *muerto* in thirty seconds . . . *treinta segundas, comprende?*"

Tomasino nodded quickly, still staring at the barrel of the Colt.

"Good, we're making progress here. Now, I only have two . . . that is *dos*, questions, amigo. If I believe you, *proteccion*. If I think you're lying, *mintiendo, Tomasino es muerta. Lo entiendes?*"

Tomasino's shoulders sagged, and his chin dropped to his chest. The beads of sweat that had formed on his forehead and upper lip began evaporating as his new situation took hold.

"*¿Qué preguntas?* Ah . . . what questions, Señor?"

"Good. Who approached you with this job?"
Tomasino took a deep breath,

"Pasquale."

"Full names, Tomasino. Full names and addresses, *por favor.*"

"Pasquale Sumarez. He lives near me in Agua Negra Chiquita. He is a friend in the gang." Bass's face turned darker at the mention of an organized gang.

"What gang is that, Tomasino?"

"Señor, *por favor*. I am not even to say the name."

Bass raised the pistol once again.

"What gang, Tomasino?"

Tomasino was getting used to the gun now. He swallowed hard. "The White Caps."

Bass lowered his Colt and nodded his head at Tomasino. He understood the young Mexican's fear. "Okay, Tomasino, one last question. What were you supposed to do with the bag?"

Again, Tomasino drew a long breath. "I was to give it to a man on the train at two o' clock."

"Do you know the man?"

"No."

"Does he know you?"

"No."

"How was he to know you had the bag? Many people have bags at the train depot."

"The hat, Señor. He would see the hat."

Now Bass understood the plan. The people actually exposed to apprehension knew only enough to complete their task. The Gang was insulated. Bass took Tomasino by the arm to the front of the alley.

# Stolen

"Avery? See if you can find some kind of local law enforcement and bring 'em by, will you?"

"Right away, Marshal."

"What we're gonna do here, Tomasino, is turn you over to the police to be held in what's called protective custody. You won't be charged with a crime so long as you agree to testify at trial if one should come up. Otherwise, you'll be safe with the police."

"Señor, there are many of the police paid by the White Caps. Even here in Amarillo. No Señor, I am a dead man."

Bass thought about it and realized that the young man was probably right about crooked lawmen on the take.

"Ok, Tomasino, here's what you do. Here's twenty dollars American. Get on the next train that will take you to El Paso. When you get there, go to the town sheriff, man named Bart Mariany. I'll send a telegram to him to expect you. Now, if you decide not to go, you decide instead to run, you're right. They will find you and kill you. If you go to Bart Mariany, you'll be safe. I'll leave it to you to decide."

Tomasino wasn't expecting to be released, much less with thirty Yankee dollars. Then he thought some more and knew what the big man was saying was true. If he ran, he could never come back, never see his family, his mama again.

"I will go to El Paso, Señor, *muchas gracias*."

"You stay low till you leave. Stay in the shadows, out of sight. Bueno suerte Tomasino." The young Mexican took the money and walked down to the end of the alley, staying as close to the shadows as he could. Bass figured he'd sell the suit and buy some old work clothes at a second-hand shop. Maybe he'd get on the train, maybe not. Bass knew Tomasino was right. If he ran, they'd find him.

"Avery, never mind the copper. It's 1:15. Let's get to the train station."

Avery, carrying the bag, and Bass, trying his best not to stand out, difficult for a man his size, arrived at the station at 1:45 p.m. The chalkboard said the train due at 2:00 was from Lubbock and bound for Albuquerque. It was running fifteen minutes late.

"It's the only train due at two o'clock. The next isn't till four, and it's heading south." Bass thought, *Maybe Tomasino will get on that one.*

"Ok, so what's our plan, Marshal?"

"First, let me see that letter."

Avery took the letter from his breast coat pocket and handed it to Bass. The hand that wrote this one was

# Stolen

different from the first. It was smooth and neatly spaced.
'Easier to read too.

> *Mr. Matlock,*
>
> *That went so well, and I'm enjoying the company of your daughters so much that I believe I'll raise the price. Another ten thousand dollars, please. I will, of course, extend the waiting period past the second of January to allow you more time to raise funds. Let's say to the fifth of the month. Can't be too generous now, can we? I know you're thinking, What if he raises the price again and then yet again? Well, fear not. As well-behaved as Ruth and Susie are, I will be tired of them by the fifth, and you'll get them back.*
> *Adios, amigo.*

Bass was steaming as he finished the note.

"God damned, son of a bitch. I'm gonna shoot that asshole so dead it'll hairlip his parents. Sorry, Avery, I know you're God-fearin', but sometimes a good cursin' is the only way to get it out.

Now. You're going to have to take Tomasino's place. I just don't fit the bill. Once the train arrives, people

# Stolen

will be getting on and off, so you just stroll the platform wearing the hat and carrying the bag. I'll be nearby, and when the man makes his move to you, I'll nab him, just like with little Tomasino. My guess is each of these . . . *couriers* are unknown to the other. It's the way conspirators insulate the ringleaders. We'll play their game with them, and eventually, we'll find who's got your girls. So, put on the hat and try to look innocent, and if you can manage it, a little dumb, too."

# Stolen

Chapter 9

*2:00 p.m., December 29, 1887*
*EP & SW Passenger Station*
*Amarillo, Texas*

Bass picked up a newspaper and sat on a wooden bench along the loading platform near the door to the ticket counter. Avery Matlock stood in the middle of the arrivals ramp, wearing the straw Panama hat and holding the bag containing twenty-five thousand dollars. The train was listed as fifteen minutes late, so Avery paced the platform back and forth several times as he waited to hear the steam whistle. He heard the bell first, clanging as the train entered the yard, and a split second later, the ear-piercing sound of the steam whistle when the engine negotiated the first switch to its siding.

It took the train three minutes or so to come to a stop at the platform. Regulations required the engineer to roll to the platform at dead-slow speed. Once the brake locked and the checking mechanisms thrown, the engineer released the bladder of the air brakes, and the train began settling into rest.

# Stolen

Bass kept his eye peeled for another man dressed similarly to the way Tomasino had dressed, but the cars were empty by 2:20 p.m., and Bass was still looking for the second man. As he turned to check on Avery, he noticed that Avery was talking with a woman: young, Mexican, and attractive. She smiled and tried reaching for the valise in Avery's hand. Bass approached and heard the conversation between the two.

"Gringo, give me the bag. Did they not tell you I was to pick it up from you? *Maldito Dios!* Give me the bag, or I'll miss my train! You are not the right man, gringo. How if I speak to Chavez y Chavez? *Bastarda.*"

Avery did not speak at all; he kept the bag at arm's length. There were several travelers nearby, but no one seemed to notice.

Bass decided to interrupt.

"What's going on here between you two?"

"Oh, Señor, there is no thing here for your worry. We are friends, *si*, amigos, eh gringo?"

Avery spoke to Bass. "She seems to think that this belongs to her, and she threatened to tell someone named Chavez y Chavez if I didn't hand it over right now."

Bass recognized the name, a longtime outlaw and killer who was last heard to be in Nogales. Bass grabbed the woman's arm at the wrist and dragged her to a corner of the passenger platform, where he spun her around, face to face. A few straggling passengers still on the platform retrieving luggage began to take note of the large fellow manhandling the girl, so Bass flashed his badge.

"Move on, move on. Nothing to see here."

As the gawkers passed, he turned back to the girl. "What's your name—*como te llamas hermana? Habla maldita sea? Pronto, pronto.*"

The girl was frightened by the large man with a gun, but she would never show it. "*Los hombres blanco son cerdos.*" She spit in Bass's direction.

Bass stopped a moment and took a breath. He decided to try a less aggressive, more sympathetic approach.

"Look, whatever your name is, do you know why you were sent to pick up this satchel?"

The girl was still fearful and continued to put up her best bravado.

"Yes. I am to take it on the train to Agua Negra Chiquita, where a caballero will give me one hundred Yankee dollars for it, and then I will be rich, hombre, and you *vete a la chingadal.*" At that, the girl insulted Bass further by wiping her chin at him and sneering. Bass did not have fluent Mexican, but he understood *chingadal* well enough from the jails around Juarez.

"Now listen to me, you foul little *puta*, there is no way Chavez y Chavez is letting you walk away with money. And I'll tell you why. You know too much, *muchacha*. Hell, you already told me you work for Jose Chavez. No tellin' what you'll say once we put the screws to ya."

The girl listened now. She had not meant to let the name Chavez y Chavez slip, but she was scared and did not know what else to do. Chavez had taken her aside and laid with her when he gave her the assignment. She was his favorite, he had said. Then he told her the bag transfer would be easy, that this Tomasino was a stupid boy, not smart like her. But now she was caught, and she knew what jails were like for young women. She began to relax her shoulders and ease her fighting stance as she listened, and Bass noticed it.

"So. Let's try again. What is your name?"

"Maria. Maria Dolores Quintasemos."

"Very good. Now Maria, have you ever met a man named Tomasino?"

"I have ah, no, not met. He was to give me the bag."

"Okay, anything else?"

# Stolen

"I was to bring him on the train, to get his money, and make sure he wore his hat." Bass looked away and nodded.

"Maria, you are in great danger right now. Do you know what's in this bag?"

"Yes. Money."

"Do you know what it's for?"

"No, Señor." Maria was wavering now and curious about the bag.

"Maria, the money in that bag is to pay a ransom, *comprende* 'ransom'?"

She nodded, and Bass continued, "Ransom for this man's two little girls. Did you know that?"

As soon as Maria understood the crime, her eyes opened wide, she caught her breath and brought her hands to her mouth. Tears began to well, and she tried to wipe them on her sleeve. Bass handed her his kerchief and backed away slightly.

"*Por favor, hombre*, I did not know." She turned to Avery Matlock, who had been standing close and listening. "Señor, please, I am so sorry for your niñas. I did not know. I did not know."

She cried then, and Bass allowed her some time. He also looked over his shoulder at the train and saw two men in a window watching the scene as it played out on the platform. The three of them were standing in shadow, but he could not be certain how much the two men saw or would recognize again.

"All right. Maria, there are men on the train who were sent to kill you and Tomasino, probably on the train tonight. Do you know where the train is headed?"

"I was told Agua Negra Chiquita. I was told to get off and give the bag to a man who will pay me."

Bass thought for a moment. He looked at Avery and saw a confused, tired, and all-but-hopeless man standing in a strange city, clutching the lives of his children to his chest. He saw in Maria's flushed, wet cheeks sorrow and desperation.

"Ok. Here's what we're gonna do. . . ."

Twenty minutes later, at 3:10 p.m., the west bound's steam whistle sounded, signaling to all that it was about to leave. Avery and Maria took adjoining seats in the first of two passenger cars and were—as inconspicuously as possible—scanning the rest of the passengers for likely assassins. The cars behind were a second-passenger day coach, a dining car, and two Pullman Sleepers.

As the steam engine's drive wheels began to grab, the train moved slowly forward, achieving eight miles per hour, the speed limit for this yard, until the last car cleared the platform. Bass stood near the final steps of the platform pretending to read a newspaper, and as soon as the final Pullman passed, he jumped to the center of the tracks and chased after it, grabbing the handrail of the car's last steps before the train was switched to the main line.

At top speed, the engineer could make the trip to the next water stop in just under five hours. This put them in Agua Negra Chiquita at 9:00 p.m., assuming there were no mechanical issues or unplanned stops. The train would then continue to Albuquerque, arriving at 1:15 a.m.

Bass stood on the small landing and waited for the conductor to open the door as part of his routine ticket check. The train had picked up speed on the flats of the Llano and was traveling at thirty-five miles per hour, fast enough to make standing outside in the winter cold uncomfortable. Bass sat, huddled in a corner for nearly thirty minutes before he saw a shadow in the glass panel of the doorway. Finally, the conductor unlocked the door and opened it only part way to see that all was well. It was wide enough for Bass to stand to his full intimidating height and force himself past the smaller man in the black uniform and cap.

# Stolen

"See here, mister. You'll need a ticket and a good explanation if you want to stay on my train. Busting through the door like that, it's—it's more than rude, I can say."

"I know, sir, I know. I apologize, but it's colder than a whore's heart out there." Bass was blowing on his hands to warm them. He cursed himself for not bringing his new Christmas gloves along.

"My name is Frank Bass. I'm a US Deputy Marshal on official business." Bass produced his ID card and showed his badge.

"Sorta official business, son?"

"There are two people in the first car in grave danger from, I believe, two men on the train. I don't know their names, but I think I spotted them on the train while back in the station. Can you be discreet about this kinda thing?"

"Why, 'course. T'aint the first time, you know. Say, back in '79 I was on the New Orleans Special and . . . ."

"Okay, okay, I believe you. What's your name?"

"Clancy Mulacky."

"Okay, Clancy, how many folks are in these sleepers?"

# Stolen

"Right now, none. Everybody's up to the dining car for drinks and dinner. Later, there be two of 'em occupied."

"Okay. I don't think anything will happen until after dark. Do you leave the lamps lit in the coaches all night?"

"Not if there's nobody out there. I generally shuts 'em down and draw the shades. There's always some folks want to nap or such on a long haul like this."

"Gotcha. Is this last compartment here in use?"

"Nope. Just the first two. One couple's headed all the way to Yuma!"

"Long way. Since it ain't bein used, I'll take this last one here. I believe if mischief's afoot, the villains'll want access to that little porch thing."

"Vestibule."

"Right, Vestibule. They'll have to come right past me here. I'll leave the door open a crack to spot 'em."

"Want me to report anything suspicious?"

"Nah. 'Preciate it, though, if you'd just go about your business normal. Do what you'd usually do. Okay?"

"Will do, Marshal."

"It's Deputy Marshal, actually."

"Say what?"

# Stolen

"Nothin'. Thanks for your help, Clancy."

Bass opened the door to the sleeping compartment and was impressed at its size. One large window with two upholstered benches facing each other against the front and back walls. From experience, he knew the berths pulled down from above the benches, but the compartment he had on his trip back from Wyoming the previous year was smaller. Different railroads, different accommodations, he assumed.

There were two current newspapers on the rack under the window, along with a couple of books. One was a primer on speaking Spanish, and the other was a novel titled *A Study In Scarlet* by someone named Arthur Conan Doyle. The jacket said it was a mystery featuring a new detective, Sherlock Holmes.

"All these funny names . . . must be a fine detective. Not from 'round here a' course."

Up in the first coach, Avery and Maria were getting acquainted. It was much noisier sitting at a window, but a small coal-burning stove warmed the car, and the train was always faster and generally more comfortable than traveling by stagecoach.

"How did you get mixed up with a gang like this, Maria? You seem far too bright to fall for their schemes."

# Stolen

Maria hung her head, looking into the seatback ahead. "I'm from a very *pueblo pobre*...a broke village?"

"A poor village, I understand."

"*Si, si,* and my brother, Miguel, would often get into trouble with stealing. The Rurales would catch him for stealing fruit or eggs and would beat him before sending him home. When he got older, he stole cattle and horses, usually from the Indios, and the Rurales would keep what he stole and beat him more. One day, he tired of the beatings and took Papa's gun. He killed a Rurale, one that had beat him hard, and they put him in jail. One day, he had a visitor, I do not know his name, but he was the gang's...yes? *Comprende?* He got Miguel out of jail and promised him wealth. Soon Miguel was sending money and presents to us. When he came home, there was fiesta with dancing and tequila.

One day, Miguel did not come home, and *mi madre*, please, my mama asked me to go see him, to find out where he was. That is when I met Señor Chavez y Chavez. He took me to a party in a grand Palacio with handsome men and beautiful ladies. He took me to a room where he gave me tequila . . . and had me. I was drunk on tequila and fell asleep right after. I woke up in the Palacio, and a very nice lady explained that Miguel was away on important business

# Stolen

and asked if I wanted to make some money. I was still sleepy, but I said yes, and she took me to another room with two men. They gave me more tequila, and I fell asleep. When I woke, I was sore in my . . . my places, but I had one hundred dollars American in my bag. When Jose Chavez said I was his favorite and asked me to do this for another one hundred dollars, I said yes."

Matlock had been listening intently, careful not to appear shocked or condescending in any way. After a few seconds, she looked Avery Matlock in the eye and said, "I'm so sorry about your niñas, Señor. I'm so sorry to have been in it."

"Maria, how old are you?"

"Almost sixteen, Señor."

Avery nodded. "We'll get you out of this. The Marshall will see to it. He is a good man.

Maria's eyes began filling again, and she settled a little further down in her seat. After some time, she said, "Thank you, Señor." And she closed her eyes to sleep. In a short while, her head was nestled against him, and he'd put his arm around her shoulder.

Sitting in the back row of the second passenger coach, two men waited for darkness. Occasionally, one would go

# Stolen

forward to the gangway connection between cars. There he would have a smoke and sneak a look through the glass panel on the door of the forward coach. He watched the heads of two people moving in unison with the rest of the passengers to the rhythmic swaying of the car as it rolled on steel wheels and springs. Satisfied that all was as it should be, he returned to his seat.

"*Ellas estan dormidas. Que hora?*"

"*Ocho, ocho y media.*"

By 8:10 p.m., the sun had long given up the Sandia Mountains, and the western Llano Estacado was swallowed in darkness. The moon was waxing gibbous and provided some illumination from its position in the eastern sky. The two Mexican killers found the time to be right. Most of the lamps had been snuffed, and the shades had been drawn. One of the men, a tall, thin fellow with greasy-looking hair and a handlebar mustache, walked through the gangway connection and into the first coach, moving very slowly, trying not to disturb the sleeping passengers. He carried a revolving pistol in his belt and a long-handled knife strapped to his boot. He spoke in hushed tones as he leaned over to talk to Avery and the girl.

"*Desculpame, por favor*…er, excuse me, please. You are the ones I am to pay, *si*? Is that the bag?"

# Stolen

Avery spoke up. "Yes, it is, and it will remain with me until I see my fee." Maria was completely still, moving only her eyes.

"Oh, but of course, Señor, we are fine, just fine. It's just that I was expecting only the girl . . . but no matter. Please come with me to a safe place where we will not disturb anyone with our business."

"We can talk right here, amigo. We won't disturb anyone." Avery's stern manner was not appreciated, and the exaggerated smile that the man wore began to slide from his face.

"Oh, but Señor, my *compañero* has the money. It is best if we go to him." The Mexican moved his right hand slowly to rest on the butt of his pistol.

"Very well, it may be best after all." Avery and Maria both stood and moved to the aisle with the gunman following.

"Where is this *compañero* of yours?"

"He waits in the last car where it is quiet, and people are sleeping in the little rooms. No one will hear our business."

As they entered the final car, they could see the second man through the glass of the rear door. He smoked a small cigar as he stood on the vestibule. Avery realized then that was where they would make their play. He hoped Bass, wherever he was, had been watching.

"See right through that door on the small veranda, please."

As they went through the door, all pretenses were dropped. Maria and Avery were pushed to the railing, and the two Mexicans had them under their guns. The second man was shorter than the first and heavy. He wore a black vest with crossed bandoliers and held a nickel-plated revolver. Avery thought he seemed the more-likely assassin. The noise from the undercarriage and the wind made it difficult to hear as, once again, the tall fellow spoke, "Now, Señor, we will have the bag, *por favor*." The large grin reappeared.

Bass had seen the first man walk past his cabin. He'd left the door to his cabin very slightly ajar and had pinched out the lamp. With the cabin blacked out, he could not be seen watching the narrow passageway outside. Though he could not hear any of the conversation outside, the lamps along the inside passageway and the two signal lamps outside on the vestibule wall cast enough light for Bass to see what was going on. The noise produced by the undercarriage increased as he opened the vestibule door.

# Stolen

Bass held his gun barrel at the heavy man's ear and stepped to the man's right side. As he moved, he pulled the Colt's hammer to full-cocked. "Consider your next move carefully, *tu jodes*."

The Mexican froze and began slowly turning toward Bass. As he did, he tried to bring his pistol to bear, but the close quarters made him fumble his piece. Bass pulled the trigger on the Colt, the bullet taking the man in his right temple, killing him, and lodging in the woodwork by the door. The concussion, smoke, and noise created enough confusion for Avery to swing his satchel at the tall Mexican, knocking him backward into the blood-splattered wall. Maria instinctively crouched down low to make herself as small as she could. Once Bass had the tall one covered and on the floor, Avery reached slowly for Maria's hand.

"Come, child, you're not hurt. All is well. Let's go inside and get warm."

The two stepped inside while Bass remained outside with the Mexican.

"What's your name, *proscrito*?" Bass smiled as he spoke. He removed the .32 caliber Remington-Smoot model two pistol he kept in his vest.

# Stolen

"I will tell you nothing, gringo. *No te molestes, comprende, hombre?*" The Mexican grinned, his brown and broken teeth visible in the lamp light.

"Oh yeah, buster, I *comprende* real well." And Bass shot the man in his right knee. The .32 Remington-Smoot made a sharp pop, barely audible above the noise of the train, and the Mexican screamed in pain as he grabbed his leg and tumbled to the floor.

"*Bastardo! Cabron. Ah, Dios Mio.*"

"Hurts, don't it?"

"Agh, *vete a la mierda.*" The Mexican was sweating profusely and salivating.

Bass feared he might work himself into shock, so he wasted no time with his questioning. "Now. Let's try it again." Bass held the muzzle of the small pistol above the Mexican's left knee.
"What is your name?"

"Agh, Diego, ah. *Mierda.*"

"Last name too, Diego."

"Rolandes de Checheria."

"Good. Wasn't hard, was it? Don't you pass out on me, Diego? Y'hear? Take this belt and wrap it around your leg. Pull it tight. It'll stop the bleeding."

"*Vete al infierno, gringo.*"

# Stolen

"Uh-huh. Now, who were you supposed to give the money to, Diego?"

The Mexican just shook his head. "If I tell you that, hombre, he will kill me if I tell."

"Say. You know, that's the second time tonight someone's said that to me. I'm gonna tell you the same thing I told the other guy." Bass got down close to Diego's face and scowled as he looked into the wounded man's eyes. "I'm gonna kill ya . . . if ya don't tell me. And Diego, I'm right here with a pistol at your head. You really wanna take that chance that I won't do it?"

Diego Rolandes was frightened now. He had a white lawman on top of him, ready to shoot, weighed against the probability that El Chalequero would find him someday.

"Shall I ask again, Diego? Or should I just shoot you now?" Bass cocked the Remington-Smoot pistol making sure Diego could see.

And he began talking.

"I am to give the money to people waiting for the train at Agua Negra Chiquita. When the train stopped for the water, we were to get off and hand over the money to the vaqueros waiting there. Then Pedro and me, this was his name, Pedro, we ride the train to Albuquerque."

# Stolen

"Excellent, Diego. You just might live through this night."

Diego Rolandes managed a weak smile.

"One more thing, Diego, who runs this gang, and where is he?"

Diego hung his head again. His teeth, what few there were, chattered both from the cold and the loss of blood. "Hombre, I only know the name of his Segundo. I don't know where he is now, but I think he has a rancho in the Sangre de Cristo Mountains, Señor."

"Okay. What's his name?"

"Jose Chavez y Chavez."

Bass remembered that the girl had threatened Matlock with that name, so he figured it was safe to believe Rolandes. Bass could see that Diego was wearing down, so he pulled him to the other side of the vestibule and turned to the dead man, Pedro, still slumped against the back wall. Bass unhooked the gate in the railing and wrestled Pedro's dead weight to the edge. The train's movement rolled the man forward and over through the open gate. Bass watched as he tumbled alongside the tracks and slipped over the side of the elevated roadbed.

Clancy Mulacky walked back through the final sleeper car, checking on a passenger's report of gunfire nearby. As he approached the last compartment, he noticed a blood trail leading from the vestibule door into the last compartment. When he looked into the compact little room, he saw a wounded Mexican, one he'd noticed when taking tickets, and the Marshal he'd met earlier. The Mexican was passed out on the forward bench, and there was bandaging around his knee. The Marshal was sitting up on the opposite bench, his legs crossed, sipping a glass of whiskey.

"Clancy. Just the fellow I wanted to see. Come in and have a drink."

# Stolen

Chapter 10

*8:45 p.m., December 29, 1887*

*Outside Agua Negra Chiquita*

*Western Llano Estacado*

*New Mexico Territory*

Clancy Mulacky and a porter had moved Diego to the first coach where, as luck would have it, a doctor from Lubbock, on his way to a wedding in Taos, was tending to him. A porter cleaned the blood from the vestibule as Avery and the girl joined Bass in the compartment. Bass and Avery talked of their next move.

"Avery, do you trust me?"

"Of course I do. Certainly."

"Okay, cause from here out, I oughta do this alone, and I'll tell you why. The men comin' to meet the train at the water stop are gonna be a different kinda animal than the ones we've dealt with so far. They're gonna be older, more experienced, and more ruthless, kinda like ol' Pedro, only ten times worse and twenty times more able. They'll be from the backbone of whatever gang we're up against, and frankly, I'd be nervous for you. Hell, I'm fearful for myself. And 'sides there's a few things I'd like you to do for me anyway."

"I understand, Frank. I appreciate your candor. I don't have the experience or expertise to deal with those types of villains. So, what do you want me to do?"

"First, I'd like you to take his train to its stop in Albuquerque and see that Diego up front there is able to get off the train. See that he understands it's his life if he don't get far away. Second, take care of Maria. I think of all the wanna-be outlaws we've come across, she's the most savable. And finally, if it ain't too much trouble, send a wire to Sheriff Bart Mariany in El Paso . . . check if Tomasino ever made contact. And then take the next train back to Amarillo."

"Of course, I'll do as you ask. It'd be my pleasure, Frank. Good luck with whatever comes your way. I know you'll bring my girls home soon."

"I'll certainly do everything I can. I don't know where this thing's gonna take me, but I'll wire you at Hartley when I know something."

# Stolen

*9:10 p.m., December 29, 1887*
*Agua Negra Chiquita*
*Western Llano Estacado*
*New Mexico Territory*

The whistle signaling the approach to the water tank at Agua Negra Chiquita sounded about one-quarter mile down the track. Bass felt the train slow down and finally lurch to a stop as the engineer positioned the tender's reservoir collar beneath the filler spout. It would take at least half the water in the tank to fill the tender's reservoir and a good twenty to thirty minutes to complete the procedure.

Bass stepped out again on the vestibule and checked both sides of the train, looking for riders, but saw none. He was taken by how quiet the setting was compared to the last time he was out there. He set the valise down and began to light a cigar when he heard horses approaching from behind and saw torches being lit. Three men, all Mexican and all armed with long guns and revolvers, reined up, spanning the tracks. They were dressed similarly in wool trousers under chaps, heavy jackets lined in fur, crossed bandoliers over the chest, and wide sombreros. Silver Conchos decorated the saddles and bridles of one of them, and the rowels on his spurs were long and sharp. Bass continued smoking his cigar while he slowly removed the Colt from his holster and held it in his right hand behind his back.

The man with the spurs spoke first. "My name is Guillermo Sotros, Señor. Is the money in that bag on the floor?"

"It is." The three men smiled at one another.

"All the thirty-five thousand Yankee, Señor?"

"No, twenty-five thousand. Mr. Matlock had to go back to get the rest."

"That is well. You are smart not to waste time on our *lacayos*, Señor. Please, throw the bag here. When we have the rest, we will release the children."

Sotros and the others were smiling, trying to put Bass at ease. Bass took two long pulls on his cigar and stepped it out on the plank flooring of the vestibule.

"No, Guillermo, I don't believe I'll do that. I think I'll wait 'til I see the girls first."

"Oh, but Señor, I do not think you have carefully considered. How if we just kill you now and take the money?"

Bass nodded and smiled at all three. "Think you're good enough, Guillermo?"

# Stolen

"Señor, it is our business. It is what we do for many years." Guillermo smiled again, mumbled something to the others in Spanish, and went for his pistol.

Bass saw it coming and raised his Colt, firing in rapid succession, first at Sotros. He went down, taking two slugs squarely in the chest. The force of the double impact toppled him back over the rump of his horse. He was still pulling the trigger on his pistol and firing wildly. One of his bullets struck the horse of the man on his right in its neck. The animal screamed and went down where it stood, kicking violently in pain and fear. The horse's rider went down as well, but he still managed to get off several rounds, all of which struck the siding of the vestibule.

The third man, the one on Sotros' left, saw the carnage and quickly dropped his pistol and extended his arms to his sides, showing his empty palms. Using only his knees, he backed his horse a few yards back down the track, hoping for a chance to run.

Bass walked to the fallen horse and finished it with a bullet to the skull and then turned to the rider, who was struggling to withdraw his right leg, which was wedged under his horse. The man threw his empty pistol at Bass and began to curse as he grabbed for the rifle in its

# Stolen

scabbard. Bass pulled the hammer of his Colt to full-cocked, aimed, and shot the man in the head.

Next, he turned his attention to the third man, who was still trying to coax his mount backward. The torches on the ground continued lighting the scene, and the lamps on the train were still burning. Bass calmly reloaded his pistol.

"Stop where you are, or I'll shoot you too."

The man, who seemed older, did as he was told and nudged his horse forward into the light making sure Bass could see he was still unarmed. The sudden explosion of firearms caused most of the train's passengers to open their windows. They were met with a scene of moving shadows and the sharp, acrid smell of spent powder. Bass called to the man on the horse.

"Slide down from your mount, hombre. Keep your hands where I can see 'em."

Again, the man did as he was told, and Bass used a leather strap to cuff his hands behind him.

"How are you called? What's your name?"

"I am Miguel de Storano, Señor."

"Uh-huh. Well, Miguel, you're gonna tell me where those children are."

# Stolen

As they got closer to the light, he saw that Miguel was indeed older than the other two. He also showed good sense, throwing his hands up and making no sudden moves.

"Ah, I'm sorry to say I cannot do this. I have given my word, Señor." De Storano had a slight grin on his face that made him look a little too cagey.

"So, you're a man of honor, eh, Miguel? Maybe you can tell me how a man of honor, such as yourself, settles his conscience with stealing children?" Bass made no attempt to hide his disgust.

"I did not do the thing, Señor. Others, younger men, sought to take the children as a message to their father. He has closed the range to us, keeping us out of the Llano."

"You mean, he closed the range to keep you from stealing horses and cattle. Ain't that right." Miguel de Storano grinned again as he nodded.

"It is our life, Señor. It is all we know." Bass's ire was up now.

"Well, my my, pobrecito. Thieving is all you know? I'll tell you what you know . . . lazy is all you know, Miguel. Lazy and dishonest is all you know. Stealin' from hard workin' people because you're too damn lazy to work for yourself. By God, if I wasn't such a peaceful man by nature, I'd tar and feather you myself." Bass raised his pistol and held the barrel only inches from Miguel de Storano's forehead.

"Now damn you, Miguel, don't you dare tempt me. I'm gonna ask you again, and if I don't like the answer, your brains are gonna decorate the railroad tracks behind you, *comprende*?"

The Mexican nodded his head all the time, watching Bass's eyes, but he did not seem afraid. Bass assumed this was not the first time de Storano had been held at bay, and he cocked the hammer of his pistol slowly.

"Not good enough, Miguel. Out loud, I wanna hear you agree with me out loud."

"Si Señor, I understand, and I will answer your questions."

Bass released the hammer to safe and took the gun away from the older man's forehead. Trying now to calm himself, he said, "All right. Come with me then, man of honor."

Bass forced de Storano to sit on the rail as he moved the dead men off the tracks. Bass took whatever weapons were still on the bodies and threw them out onto the prairie out of sight. There was no time for burials or readin' over bodies. The dead horse had fallen off the tracks and lay on the slope of the roadbed. Bass tied off the

# Stolen

two remaining horses to the train and went to pull de Storano to his feet. The two men climbed back onto the vestibule.

Bass took de Storano to the compartment and told him to sit down. Storano immediately noticed the bloody floor and bench.

"You have killed many people, hombre?"

"When it was necessary." Bass turned to face the older man. "Ain't made my quota fer today yet, if that's what you're askin'."

"No, Señor, I am not. It is only... I see your badge. You are the policia?"

"Yeah, So?"

"You do not act like one, is all I say."

"Yeah, well, the law has a perplexin' way of protectin' folks like you and your friends. So, I'm gonna tell you this, and you can, by God, take it to the bank. 'Til I find those children and get 'em home, don't expect the law to protect you any. Far as I'm concerned, anyone involved in stealin' those babies oughta be shot. And I'll be happy to pull the trigger. Right now, you're first in line. You got that?"

"Si."

# Stolen

"What?"

"Yes, I understand."

"Good. Now I'm gonna ask you some questions. If you're lyin', I'll know, and I'll kill ya right on the spot. Got that?"

"Yes, I do."

Bass settled himself and began. "Where are the girls bein' held?"

"I do not know for certain, but I believe they are at the rancho of Don Vicente Silva. I do not know exactly where. The rancho, it is *muy grande*—very large."

"Where is this rancho?"

"It is outside of Las Vegas. I have never been there, Señor. I am not high in the rank. That is all I know about it."

"How far away is it from here?"

"Two days ride, one night. To the northwest."

"This Don Vicente, he the boss?"

"Yes. Ah . . . he has many, what is it . . . followers?"

"I get it. All right now, Miguel, I believe you. Here's what's gonna happen. I'm tying you to this bench, and you're ridin' all the way to Albuquerque. The

172

# Stolen

conductor will hand you over to the town sheriff when you get there."

The older Mexican hung his head and nodded. It was what he expected. He also knew he would be marked for death in Albuquerque. Bass leaned out of the door and called for Clancy. A porter in the first compartment heard him, waved back, and said he'd go find him. After a few minutes, Clancy walked into the compartment.

"Yes, sir? Oh, ya kept one, did ya. 'Spect you'll wanna question him. What can I do for ya?"

Bass moved Clancy out of the compartment to the aisle. "Clancy, I know the engineer is waiting for a go-ahead, and I don't wanna hold these folks up any longer. I'm gonna get off the train in a few minutes, and I'm leavin' this fella here tied to the bench in the compartment. Hand him over to the local law when you get to Albuquerque. And Clancy? This fella's been an outlaw all his life; it's all he knows. Don't trust him 'far as you can throw him."

"Well, that's fine, Marshal. 'tain't my first opera, neither. Can I get you anything for your travels? We carry breakdown provisions aboard."

173

# Stolen

"Could use blankets if you can spare 'em. Maybe some food and water."

"Sure, sure. We keep a lot a that stuff in the baggage car. I don't believe we have anything like a tent, but we do have one er two a' them new 'mummy bags,' you know, with the zippers? Don't know how well they'll work in this weather, but gotta be better 'n just bedrolls alone."

"That'd be fine, Clancy. Thank you. I'll ride up to the baggage car in a few minutes, and then you can all be on your way."

Bass went forward to say another goodbye to Avery and Maria and to tell them what he'd learned from Miguel de Storano.

"I figure it'll take two days to get to Las Vegas. Never been there before, an' I don' know who the law is, but from my experience, if a gang runs a town, the sheriff is in it, too."

"But the weather, Frank. The cold. How will you manage?"

"Done it before, 'couple times, with the right gear. 'tain't as bad as ya think, and the conductor has some stuff for me. I'll be all right. You two mind your step, too. Once you get Diego off the train, head on back to Texas. Oh, if you don't mind, send a wire to my wife, let her know I'm okay and what I'm up to."

Bass shook Avery's hand, patted Maria's shoulder, and walked back through the train. He mounted the taller of the two horses—they were both small—took the reins of the other, and walked up to the sliding door of the baggage car. Clancy had already packed two canvas satchels and filled a canteen. Bass lashed the blankets and the sleeping bag to the 'D' rings of the second horse's saddle and hung the leather satchels around the horn. He checked his Elgin 10:15 p.m. and opened his compass for a bearing to the northwest. After a final thank you to Clancy and a tip of his hat, Frank Bass crossed the tracks and headed into the night.

# Stolen

*8:15 p.m., December 29, 1887*

*Don Vicente's Rancho Outside Las Vegas*

*New Mexico Territory*

"Ruthie? I need to, you know. . . ."

"Well, Suze, there's a bucket in the corner. I think that's what it's for."

"That's just awful. I can't do that. Mama would be so angry."

"I know, but Mama's not here now, and it's all we have. I'm sure she would understand."

"All right, but don't you watch."

"I won't. I'm gonna keep readin' this magazine."

Susie used the bucket as best she could. She felt a cold draft as she was fixing her trousers and decided to move the bucket to see where it was coming from. She noticed that one of the slats of the outside wall was cracked off, and she could see daylight coming through.

"Ruthie? Come here. You should see this. I think I broke their wall."

Ruth put down her magazine and walked to where Susie was standing.

"See? This board was already broken, but the one next to it is loose, too. Are we in trouble?"

# Stolen

"No, you goose, let me see." Ruth pushed the loose piece of siding with just enough force to see it was close to opening. With both boards open, there would be enough of a gap for both to squeeze through.

"Shh. We can't tell anyone about this. I think if we try, and we're very quiet, we might be able to escape through here."

"Oooh, fun. Let's do it right now and go home."

"No, Sis, we wait for later tonight when it's dark and quiet and everybody's in bed. Maybe I can steal a horse from the barn, too, so we won't have to walk all the way."

"Okay, What do we do in the meantime?"

"Same as yesterday. We'll read and take naps. And tell story games. And tonight, late, we'll try to get away.

# Stolen

The train stopped at the platform at 2:50 a.m., exactly one hour and thirty-five minutes late. Even at that hour, there was still plenty of activity at the station. Passengers were getting off and on, traveling to points beyond. Avery was exhausted. He felt it best not to sleep on the train as long as Diego was wounded. He wanted to be available in case the boy got worse. He got up once to check on the Mexican in the last car and stepped outside on the vestibule for a smoke. When he returned to his seat, he coaxed one of the porters to make coffee, and it didn't take long for other passengers to call for a cup as well.

Once he and Maria were off the train, they walked to the front of the building, hoping to find a sheriff or some kind of law official,l to help with Diego, who was still in the parlor car. He also wanted an official to relieve Clancy and take charge of the outlaw, Miguel de Storano. He asked one of the passengers he recognized from the train about the local police and was told,

# Stolen

"You'll never find a copper this time of night, but the railroad bulls'll help you out. 'Ats actually part a' their job. Inside, there's an office by the ticket counter. Try them."

Avery and Maria went inside and found the office marked 'EP& SW Police. Safety for the Rail Roading Public.' After knocking, they were admitted to a small office with two desks, one occupied.

"What's the problem?" The uniformed officer did not get up but continued reviewing the paper in front of him.

"My name is Avery Matlock, and I have been traveling with a US Deputy Marshal named Frank Bass. I have a request to make on his behalf." As soon as the man heard Bass's name, he dropped his newspaper and jumped to his feet.

"Frank Bass? Is he here? Where?" The man was short, round, and bald with stains of some kind on his vest, and his collar was open even though it was chilly inside.

"No, he is on official business, but he has left two prisoners on the train, and I would like you to take charge."

"Take charge? Of course. It's my job, you know. Tell me where these two are while I arm myself."

"Of course. And your name is?"

"Al. That is Alfred Shoenstien at your service."

# Stolen

"Uh-huh, Pleasure. The first is a young man named Diego. He has a gunshot wound and will require treatment. Marshal Bass asked specifically that he be released on his own recognizance after he's seen a doctor. The other is locked in the Marshal's compartment on the train. The conductor, a fellow named Clancy, has the key. Marshal Bass thought the man a bad enough outlaw that he left him tied up and locked in. It's the last car out there."

Avery asked Maria to wait in the office while he escorted the officer first to Diego and then to the last car. When the officer and Matlock got to the compartment, they walked in to find Clancy Mulacky dead, tied to the bench where de Storano had been. His throat had been cut.

The officer had a look of confusion as though he was suddenly overwhelmed. "Ah . . . I better call my supervisor. Ah, I mean—ah—that guy's dead."

"Yes, well, please hurry. I believe there's a very bad man on the loose, and he needs to be apprehended quickly."

Avery was shaken himself at the notion that a killer was again at large. His thoughts returned to the girl, and after excusing himself, he went to find Maria. At first, he was afraid she'd taken off too, and he ran back to the terminal, scanning the area around the Police Office.

# Stolen

He was about to give up hope when she walked up behind him and tapped his shoulder.

"Thought I had…what is it…skipped, eh?"

He told her what had happened to Clancy and that de Storano had fled. Also, that Diego would receive medical attention and then be free to go, hopefully far away from the White Caps and New Mexico Territory. Then, he led the girl to the telegraph counter, where he sent a wire to Alice at home with a cryptic update of progress and, of course, his love. Next, he wired Sally Bloom, advising her that Frank was well and in hot pursuit, and finally, as promised, he sent another telegram to Bart Mariany to be on the lookout for Tomasino. Finally, he took Maria next door to the Harvey House Café for something to eat while waiting for the train ride back to Amarillo.

"Señor, I am very sorry that I was a part of your *tragedia*. I swear I knew nothing about the crime. If I did, I would not have done it. You believe me, Señor? Please?"

"Yes, Maria, I believe you. And right now, it's important that we get you out of the territory as fast as possible."

# Stolen

Chapter 11

*12:15 a.m., December 30, 1887*
*New Mexico, Territory*

Bass had ridden about ten miles in the darkness, trusting in the outlaw's horse to put his feet right in the dark. Bass used the glow of his cigar to recheck his compass, and when he felt the terrain begin to dip, he decided to stop for the night. He knew the Pecos River was around somewhere and judging by the scrub oak and mesquite he could make out around him, he figured it to be nearby.

He found a bare patch that seemed dry enough and dismounted. The first thing he did was to light the small oil lamp Clancy had packed to have a look around. He saw several bare scrub oak trees growing in the little swale, along with a few Screwbean mesquite shrubs where he'd stopped. He'd never liked Mesquite. The thorns were stiff, toxic, and long enough to penetrate even heavy clothing.

Tonight, though, he was grateful for them. Now, he saw in them firewood and possible-shelter. He stretched a rope between two of the low-growing oak trees and tethered the horses with enough slack for them to graze on the little amount of Indian and Buffalo grass they could

# Stolen

forage under the snow. Bass then hung a large woolen blanket over one of the lower mesquite branches, creating a kind of wind break. He moved the saddles and gear under it to help keep the bottom of the blanket in place. As he worked, he thought of how much the Crow Woman's buffalo robe would be welcome tonight. But it was home, upstairs, keeping Sally warm at night.

Bass made a small fire, protected from the wind by the stretched blanket, and rolled out the 'mummy' bag between the saddles. He opened a can of cold beans, a package of jerky, and the bottle of Old Crow that Clancy had the forethought to provide. As he ate, he watched the horses in the soft glow of the fire, and by 1:00 a.m., he was asleep.

It wasn't long after, however, that he was awakened by the horses becoming agitated. They stomped, tugged at their tethers, and nickered enough to startle Bass, who immediately grabbed for the Mexican's rifle, a 45-70 Hotchkiss bolt-action carbine. There were fifteen rounds on a sling sewn onto the scabbard, and he chambered one and took four more in his pocket.

Mexican Gray Wolves were no longer common on the Llano, but their predation still occurred around cattle ranches, and Bass knew in winter they'd be more

183

aggressive. He quietly moved from his mesquite cover toward the horses, staying deathly quiet and watching for movement. Without warning, from behind, he heard a terrible high-pitched scream, and as he turned, a human form was on top of him, howling and wailing like a banshee.

The carbine flew loose, and Bass's arms were trapped, fending off the assault by what Bass assumed was an Indian. He suddenly noticed the glint of a steel blade and felt it puncture his middle as the Indian leaned on it. There was no immediate pain, and while the Indian's hands were holding the knife's pommel and trying to push it deeper, Bass was able to withdraw his Colt and fire it, point-blank, into the Indian's face.

Immediately, the dead man crumbled, and Bass pushed him off to the side. It was then he noticed the pain in his gut and the wet, sticky feeling at his belt. The horses were panicked now, and one tore free of his tether at the sound of the gunshot. Bass felt weak and a little chilled as he tried to stand to secure the remaining horse. He managed to tie off the horse's rein directly to a mesquite tree and returned to the body of the man he'd killed and said,

# Stolen

"Who the hell are you, you God damned, middle a' the night son of a—" Bass could not finish his curse. He fell face down in the snow next to the Indian, unconscious.

# Stolen

*3:15 a.m., December 30, 1887*

*Don Vicente's Rancho outside Las Vegas*

*New Mexico, Territory*

Ruth and Susan, both wrapped in blankets, had been listening carefully for two hours. It had been that long since the Mexican men stopped talking, and Ruth now felt it would be safe to move around outside. Susan had been asleep for about two hours after dinner. Ruth had no way of knowing the time, but she knew she could read her circus book in about one hour. She asked the man who brought their dinner the time, and she estimated from then. She also knew the Mexican men drank and played some kind of game in their quarters, which was near enough to them. They stopped talking at about the same time every night. Ruth thought now would be a good time to go. They would not discover they were gone for five hours when the woman brought breakfast, and she knew they could go a long way in five hours.

Ruth moved the bucket that hid the loose boards and slowly, quietly slid the two boards to the side. She was the first one out, and she helped Susan follow after.

"You wait here. I'm gonna look into the barn and see if I can find a horse for us."

# Stolen

"Okay, but not too big. They scare me."

"Don't be a ninny. You'll be fine. Wait here." Ruth walked around the corner to the sliding barn door near the stalls. She slowly slid the heavy door as far as she could, and it looked to be wide enough for a horse to walk through.

The moon was in the west and bright enough to cast shadows, so she stayed near the sides of the stalls. She had no idea how to judge a nice-tempered horse, so she picked the oldest looking, a small mare that stood with her head to the corner. She grabbed a bridle nearest the stall and slipped the headpiece over the horse's ears as she'd been taught. She coaxed the mare to take the bit and led the little horse out of the barn to where Susan waited.

"We don't have time for a saddle. I think it's best if we walk her away from the barn and into those trees. We'll get up on her there and head east."

"Is east where our house is?"

"All the way here, we rode with the sun at our back in the morning. That means we were heading west. To go back, we'll ride toward the sun in the morning and go east, see? Simple."

The two girls walked the mare to the thicket, and each stood on a log to climb on the horse's back. Ruth

# Stolen

looked back at the ranch buildings, and everything seemed quiet. *Even the dogs must be asleep*, she thought. Slowly and carefully, Ruth nudged the mare, and the horse started walking east.

# Stolen

Bass opened his eyes to piercing white light, and without moving, he took a moment to analyze his condition and try to remember how he'd gotten into it. He discovered first that his left eye was working, but his right eye, for some reason, would not open. He was extremely thirsty and had a dull ache in his belly. All that was for starters. The right side of his face was numb, and he couldn't feel certain parts of his body. He could feel his left hand but not his right. His right leg felt fine, but his left leg hurt.

It all came back to him quickly as realizations were made. His location was somewhere near his camp, face down in the snow. That also explained his right eye not opening and the right side of his face feeling numb. Both were pressed into the snow, which at some point had melted and frozen again in the night. He saw the deerskin leggings of a dead Indian, and those memories now flooded home. That explained the ache in his gut. Finally, he recalled that one of the horses had bolted and had stepped on his leg in its panic to escape.

*Now I have it*, he thought. *Shit, I 'been stabbed.*

# Stolen

Bass struggled to his knees, and the pain in his middle became sharper. So bad that for a moment, he thought he might get sick on the spot. He swallowed several times, putting handfuls of snow in his mouth. When he felt strong enough, he slowly got to his feet and looked at the frozen blood that clung to his jacket. He knew he had to deal with the wound right away, so he opened his jacket, vest, and shirt, finally seeing the jagged red puncture inside his torn drawers. He couldn't tell how deep it was but knew his heavy clothing had protected him to some degree. He saw his makeshift windbreak had survived. Everything, including the money, was still in its place, which told him the Indian he was looking at now was alone last night. The horse he'd tied off was still there, and he saw the second one some ways off, calm now and cropping the grass and weeds he'd found under the snow. His fire had gone out. Even the embers were cold. This bothered him because he had no medical kit with him, and he would have to cauterize the hole in his belly, which had started to bleed again. He'd burned a wound closed once before and remembered how unpleasant it was. He'd gashed his leg in falling from a horse and couldn't stop the bleeding.

Moving slowly and bending as little as possible, he gathered enough fuel to start a fire. The hard wood of the mesquite would make the fire plenty hot enough to do the job. He set the blade of his ten-inch Bowie knife in the flames and got out the bottle of Old Crow. After dripping some of the whiskey into and around the wound, he was ready.

"God damn, I hate this."

He took a long pull on the whiskey bottle and quickly laid the glowing knife blade over the wound. He smelled his flesh burn before he felt the pain. His cry was agonized. He began shaking and had to force himself to leave the blade on the puncture until he was sure the alcohol had sealed the skin shut. Then he threw the blade off his stomach and fell to his side, curled to protect himself from the pain that he knew would come. He felt the intense agony climb up his spine and hoped it meant healing. As it faded, he fell asleep again.

# Stolen

*Noon, December 30, 1887*
*New Mexico Territory*

Bass woke for the second time that day feeling surprisingly well. He checked his stomach and was pleased that he saw no fresh blood. There was a raw-looking welt on his gut just above the belt line from the hot blade, and he knew that it would scar. He considered it a small consequence of a potentially fatal wound.

He stood, slowly wincing as the skin stretched, and walked over to look at the dead Indian. As he suspected he was young, late teens or early twenties, it was always hard for Bass to guess ages. His paint was red at the eyes, white on the cheeks, and a black handprint across his mouth. The colors were common to many tribes and usually meant the warrior was ready for a fight or blood. Otherwise, there was nothing telltale about his appearance. His leggings and footwear strongly suggested Apache. He knew there was a Mescalero reservation to the south, but he estimated it would be over a hundred miles away.

A closer inspection revealed his headband and talisman to be Comanche. The boy had no spear or bow that might help verify this, but Bass knew that the western Llano Estacado, in fact, most of western Texas, was

# Stolen

considered Comanche territory or *Comancheria*. Bass had experience with a Comanche Chief named Small Horse the previous summer. Small Horse had led a band of Comanche off the *Comancheria* and into Devil's Canyon near La Luz in the territory, nearly two hundred miles away. He guessed the boy may have been on a vision quest or some other rite of passage, and Bass unknowingly interrupted him, somehow violating a sacred setting. Members of his tribe would eventually come looking for him. Bass hoped it would be soon or at least before the scavengers came. In as much as the boy had tried to kill him and had caused him great bodily distress, Bass was not inclined to be too concerned about the kid's remains.

It took almost an hour to make the horse ready for travel. Bass had to favor his wound to keep it from opening, and he also tried to walk out to the second horse who had grazed to within one hundred feet of the other. He was able to grab the reins at one point, but as soon as the animal approached the mesquite stand, he bolted, and Bass had to let him go. Bass took the remaining horse to a large rock where he was able to mount more easily and without stretching the cauterized skin. He had wrapped a second shirt around his middle as bandaging, and once underway, he ate more jerky and drank from his canteen. He was able to make better time without the drag of the second horse trailing behind, and he checked his compass at regular intervals to make sure he held his course. After two hours of riding, Bass would rest the horse and himself. The time made up by not trailing the other horse, Bass assumed, was lost in multiple rest breaks.

Shortly after noon, the bright sunlight gave way to deep gray clouds that rolled over the high prairie and brought a light drizzle that turned to sleet as the temperature fell. Bass began to smell snow in the air but dismissed that notion as it had become too cold. The rain and wind had picked up, and the droplets froze as they fell. Bass began looking for shelter ahead and, after a few minutes, spotted a copse of madrone and scrub oak maybe a quarter-mile ahead on the right. Bass urged the horse on, but the most he could get out of the beast was a high lope. As he approached, he began to see other trees and low vegetation stretched along what must be a waterway of some kind. He had never spent time in this area either as a Ranger or with the Marshals service, but he recollected that the Canadian River was somewhere in the far western Llano Estacado. Maybe this was it. As he got closer, he saw large rock outcroppings and steep banks to the water below. There was no access to the stream anywhere near him, but

# Stolen

he saw a small limestone overhang large enough for a man and horse to wait out the weather. Once he made it to the overhang, he noticed that the river had smoothed the stone wall underneath into a concave shape that provided further protection from the gusting winds of the winter squall.

The moisture on the horse was steaming as Bass unsaddled the little gelding. Careful not to stretch his wound, he threw a blanket over the horse, hoping he'd cool down slowly, and tied him off close into the overhang. He then began the search for dry firewood. There was little of it handy. He searched through the madrone and Oak thicket, picking up deadfalls as he found them. He had no ax or saw blade, so his search was limited to usable sizes. Realizing he was doing his wound no good, Bass had to settle for what he could carry and would have to make several trips. All the while, the skies continued to drop, freezing rain and drizzle on the area, and gusts of chilling wind.

Eventually, exhausted from his search, Bass used his matches and was able to get an encouraging amount of smoke to waft out over the rocks. He provided a steady bellows, blowing into the base of the kindling, and soon, the bright yellow and orange licks of flame appeared. The fire danced slowly at first, but with more fuel, it began warming and then drying the small shelter. He considered hiding the valise in the rocks somewhere away from his camp but thought better of it. He was too tired to move anyway. Bass wrapped another blanket around himself and pulled the bottle of Old Crow out of its pouch. He took two good pulls before turning over, where he lay for several hours of rest. His sleep was fretful.

# Stolen

*7:30 a.m. December 30, 1887*

*Don Vicente's Rancho outside Las Vegas*

*New Mexico, Territory*

"Segundo! Segundo! Come quick, *por favor*. De little niñas are gone, Señor. Gone! What shall I do?"

Jose Chavez y Chavez was alongside a corral watching the vaqueros breaking mustangs when he heard Nardo's voice. Nardo had been put in charge of feeding the girls and tending to their needs. Chavez's eyes widened at the news, and all he could think of was how he would tell Don Vicente.

Nardo was small and thin, almost frail-looking. His serape was heavy wool, uncolored, and a bit too big. He was a naturally nervous little man and terrified of the vaqueros about the ranch and especially of the Segundo, Chavez.

"Nardo, first you must go and saddle my mare, the yellow one. Then you should save me the trouble and go quietly to the trees and shoot yourself *en la cabeza*!"

Nardo held his sombrero and pinched the brim as he scampered to the barn. Chavez decided he did not want to involve others. Since it was likely that he would find the girls quickly, the fewer that knew of this, the better. He walked over to the small shed attached to the barn where the children had been held and examined the area.

He found the loose planking immediately. There was snow blown up to two feet against the wall, so the bottom of the wooden slats would not be visible from the outside. Now that the girls had gone through the opening and left a trail in the snow, it was easy to spot. Nardo had been reprieved. The footprints in the snow led around the corner to the sliding barn door. It occurred to him now that the little demons might have taken a horse. He walked into the barn and discovered an empty stall. One that should not have been empty. It was stall *cinco*, number five, near the barn door. The horse assigned to that stall was Kahlo, named for the famous painter. More importantly, the horse belonged to, and was much loved by, La Señora Francesca Silva, the wife of his Don.

He mounted his horse and began searching the yard for Kahlo's hoof prints. Finding the children's prints was easy enough, but they stopped at Kahlo's stall. Finding one unshod print among many others was not a skill he possessed. The yard around the barn was covered with hoof prints, and, as Chavez had never become familiar with La Señora's horse, to know her manner of walking or the flaws in her hooves, he could not find a place to start. He had no

# Stolen

idea where to begin. He sat on the back of his mare and gazed to the east. The weather was sunny and clear, so visibility was good. After a moment, a slight smile appeared on his face, and he spurred his horse forward.

# Stolen

Chapter 12

*10:30 a.m., December 30, 1887*
*A Narrow Coulee*
*Western Llano Estacado*
*New Mexico, Territory*

Ruth and Susan had been riding the horse for seven hours, though Ruth had no way to tell the exact time. She knew that horses walked between five and seven miles in an hour, so she estimated they had traveled about thirty-five miles away from the barn. Both she and her sister were sleepy, hungry, and thirsty, so they decided to rest in a small ravine that was crowded with scrub oak trees for cover. There were patches of snow around, but the sun was bright and warm. Ruth knew they could not have a fire, and even if they could, she had no way to start one. She decided to let the mare graze to keep her as strong as possible. They had no hobbles or tether line anyway, so it seemed the most logical thing to do; besides, the horse was older and did not wander. They were warm enough in their heavy clothes and blankets, so they quenched their thirst by eating snow and sat leaning against a tree, dozing.

# Stolen

"You know, Suz, they probably saw we were missing maybe two hours ago, and right now, they're following our tracks."

"Ruthie, I don't wanna go back. What if they catch us?"

"They won't hurt us if they do find us 'cause they know Daddy will pay." Ruth thought for a moment.

"You know what we oughta do? We should tie a broken branch to the tail of the horse to wipe out our tracks. Then, when we leave here, we should head north or south, a direction they won't think of. Yeah, that sounds good, huh."

"If you say so. I'm gettin' awfully hungry."

After resting for a few minutes and quenching their thirst with snow, they began collecting thin, lightweight branches that fan out in a wide enough pattern to drag behind and cover the horse's hoof prints. Using their bootlaces, they attached their branches to the docile horse's tail and let them hang just to the point that they would drag out the tracks they left in the high desert sand.

"Well, she doesn't seem to mind the branches hangin' there. 'Course, if she goes to switch her tail, she'll

# Stolen

be disappointed, but there aren't any flies in the winter anyway."

"I hope we can find something to eat soon. My tummy doesn't feel so good."

"Don't worry, Suz. We're bound to come up on a ranch or village somewhere out here." Ruth didn't really believe it, but she wanted to keep her sister's spirits up.

They climbed up on the mare's back using a rock they'd been sitting on and pointed the mare's nose to the south. Ruth knew to keep the sun to her right side as they traveled. She checked the branches every few minutes, and though she had to avoid walking through the snow, they seemed to be doing a good job. The sun was warm, and her plan was working.

# Stolen

*7:00 p.m., December 30, 1887*
*Llano Estacado East of Las Vegas*
*New Mexico Territory*

Chavez had been on the eastward path for nearly two hours when he realized he was not equipped for a prolonged search of the countryside. He had his bedroll and rifle, a nearly full water bag, but no food or extra blankets. He contemplated going back for them but decided it would give the girls too much advantage, and he cursed himself for discounting the children's capabilities.

Once he was well away from the rancho, he had begun making wide circles around his path every mile or so. On one of the circles, he got lucky. He managed to stumble across the hoof marks of a single horse that even he could tell were reasonably fresh. Chavez did a close inspection and made a special note that the right rear hoof turned in at an unusual angle, probably due to some long-ago injury. This would make tracking easier, so he quickened his pace. Finally, in a narrow coulee among scrub oak, he found their campsite and where the horse was tied. As the sunlight was beginning to fade, he decided to stop there for the night as well. Now that he knew what to look for, it should be easy to overtake them in the morning.

# Stolen

*11:50 p.m., December 30, 1887*
*Along the Pecos River*
*Western Llano Estacado*

Bass woke up in a heavy sweat, his body racked with fever. The fire had gone out again with a shift in the wind that brought the bitter cold into his shelter. He was lost at first. He had no idea where he was. There was no light from the moon; it was hidden in the clouds. The rain had stopped, but the wind was relentless, gusting from different directions all at once.

He was delirious in his fever, and his recurring visions were of Sally, alone with a babe in her arms, striding through snow and frigid surroundings, pale and blue with cold. He would cry out to her and, in his tormented state, try to join her, but he could not move. And then darkness, blessed sleep when his unconscious mind was idle. Dreams came but were not so vivid. Dreams of the old Crow Woman who healed him years ago and gave him his spirit visions and the buffalo robe.

He saw his first wife, Moon, and his boy grown to manhood, handsome and sturdy and straight. His beautiful Moon in Winter, with her raven black hair loose in the

# Stolen

breeze and the large doe-like brown eyes that he could almost get lost in. And then Sally, fair and lovely but willful too and strong with her arms stretched out to him, ready to soothe and heal him. Finally, sleep peaceful and deep.

# Stolen

Chavez woke shivering in his blanket as the sun poured across the Llano and slowly began warming his back. The fire that had allowed him to sleep in some comfort had dwindled to ash, and he debated starting another or just getting back on the trail. He chose the latter and, wrapped now in his heavy woolen blanket, he saddled and mounted his yellow gelding and rode to the east looking for the tracks of La Señora's horse.

After fifteen minutes of searching, he returned to the camp and examined the girl's footprints more closely. He found where the horse had stood as she was boarded by the two girls and the first few paces after that, but then the trail disappeared. He sat, thinking atop the yellow horse, until it occurred to him that the two niñas had used a branch to wipe their tracks behind them. Maybe they dragged a long branch or tied something to the horse's tail, some branches or a blanket. Chavez smiled again.

"*Estan astucia.*"

Now that he knew what to look for, he found it. A smooth surface where all about it was rough and natural: it pointed to the south. Again, Chavez smiled and spurred his horse in the same direction—this time, at a faster gait.

# Stolen

*7:15 a.m., December 31, 1887*

*Narrow Canyon*

*High Desert, New Mexico Territory*

The two girls woke up almost as tired as when they fell asleep. Ruth had decided to chance a small fire last night, so she used hair from the horse's tail, small pieces of blanket ticking, and dead leaves and twigs from the low shrub growth around them as a starter. They both had a hard time finding larger pieces to burn, but Susie found a few small pieces of madrone deadfall and scrub oak bark.

Ruth remembered watching one of the ranch hands start a fire to burn brush using nails scraped against a piece of jasper. She used her belt buckle to strike a small piece of quartz she'd found, and before long, they had a small but very hot fire going. Ruth knew to bank the fire high so it would not be visible in the dark, and at night the smoke could not be seen anyway.

During the day, Susie complained almost constantly about being hungry, and all Ruth could do was try to comfort her. Eventually, in the afternoon she grew frustrated however, and snapped at her sister. For the rest of the day, they barely spoke. They stopped early at a grassy spot where Ruth thought the horse might be able to graze.

# Stolen

She knew that without the horse, they probably would not survive. Every direction she looked she saw only emptiness. Susie began to complain about not feeling well, and Ruth was too tired to try to help her. Susie began to cry and turned away in her blankets. Ruth was beginning to feel desperate now, too, and she knew if they didn't find something to eat soon, their strength would fail. She wished she had planned better before the escape. This was on her mind until she fell asleep.

# Stolen

*6:15 a.m., December 31, 1887*

*Along The Pecos River*

*Western Llano Estacado*

*New Mexico, Territory*

The sun woke him. The light first, then the warmth. He opened his eyes to a quiet day, clean, fresh, and blue. He was sitting up and could see and hear the river below swollen with runoff, muddy and turbulent. He was still soaked in sweat, but he wasn't cold. The fever must have passed. His blankets were wet, as was the one covering the horse who still stood nearby. The valise was where he'd left it, under the saddle he'd huddled behind. The fire had washed away, but no matter; he felt well enough to build another and sit by it until he was dry.

Standing proved more difficult than he'd thought, and he became dizzy very quickly. He staggered some and held onto the horse for support. He was weaker than he knew. The pain in his gut was sharp again, and he opened his clothes to check for bleeding. The burned skin was black and swollen, and there were tinges of dark blood on the inside of his shirt. He remembered the old Crow Woman gave him willow leaves to chew to ease pain and fever. There were no willows here.

# Stolen

Sally had miraculously cured the infection using bread mold and honey, but, of course, there was no bread or honey nearby. He decided then that he had no choice. His will and his, physical strength and determination would have to prevail. He remembered now that two young girls and their family were depending on him. Sally and his unborn baby were depending on him, too. There was no choice to make. No one or the other to choose. Only his will to push him through.

He decided to move on while he could. The blankets would dry as he rode. The pain in his middle was his only nemesis. It was sharp and bright, not the dull ache it was yesterday. He poured some of the whiskey over the burn, biting down on the sleeve of his jacket until the pain passed. He cut some long strips from the dry end of one of the blankets and wrapped it tightly around his middle, hoping it would keep him from accidentally stretching the burned edges of his skin. Bass tied the valise to a 'D' ring on the saddle and slowly climbed aboard the little horse. As he rode back out through the madrone thicket, he knew he had certainly been tested in the night. He was alive and still on the trail. He took some pride in that.

Bass pointed the little horse to the northwest, away from the Pecos River and more in the direction of Las

# Stolen

Vegas. He had no plan yet as to what he'd do when he got there. He was almost certain that any law in Las Vegas would be corrupt, unreliable at least. The only advantage he had was the money. Until the man Silva got the money, he was sure the girls would be safe. Of course, there was nothing to prevent Silva from shooting the currier and taking the money. He decided he'd better come up with a plan. And quick.

Bass checked his Elgin every time he checked the compass. By three o' clock, he'd come, by his estimation, only ten or twelve miles. His wound was slowing him down more than he expected. On top of everything else, he had a river ahead that he'd have to cross. He had no idea what river it was. It might still be the Pecos. Rivers tend to wind around, he knew. It might be a stream he'd never heard of. He knew it wasn't the Canadian because he was too far west. He decided to stop for the third time that day to rest and then look for a likely spot to cross. He thought if he found an easy ford, he could stop for the day on the other side. He noticed a sheltered spot among some large rocks on a bluff overlooking the river and tied the horse off at a low shrub. He took the whiskey and the money with him and sat in the sun, his back against a warm boulder. After a couple of swallows, he opened a can of pears,

# Stolen

spearing the fruit with his knife, and finally drinking the remaining syrup. He felt completely relaxed and experienced surprisingly little pain.

The horse woke him several hours later while trying to reach a patch of Indian grass that was just beyond the span of his reins. Bass cursed himself for sleeping as he had, losing the last few hours of sunlight and now having to face a winter evening with no firewood. He removed the small lantern again, shaking it to determine the amount of fuel remaining and finally setting a match to the wick. As he moved about, the pain in his gut became more intense, and he was forced to work at a much slower pace.

Once he had collected enough small pieces of tinder, he laid a fire at the base of the rocks and used a match to get a blaze. Once he was warmed and rested, he removed the saddle from the horse and stretched a tether, allowing the animal to crop on the few green spots beneath the snow. With one blanket on the horse, two blankets around him, and a fourth pitched over him using the carbine again as a tent pole, Bass began to feel comfortable again and nodded off at nearly ten.

The fever returned that night, worse than the previous evening. His dreams tonight were of the actions he saw with General Crook and his White Mountain Apache

212

# Stolen

Scouts. Of the battle at Apache Pass and of the old Crow Woman who saved his life and kept him hidden. He saw again her small, pitiable body, hanging from a pinion tree, naked and pierced with the knives and arrows of a group of drunken Apache warriors. He screamed it seemed, for quite a long time as he avenged her death, mutilating the dead Apache bodies as she would have done. His eyes, then, would open to the dark, blind, and fearful, only to close again to relive the horror of that day.

# Stolen

*9:15 a.m., January 1, 1887*

*Shallow Canyon Lands*

*High Desert*

*New Mexico, Territory*

Ruth and Susan had been riding through a series of narrow valleys for about two hours. Ruth had no notion as to how far they'd come, but the sun was bright and on her left, meaning they were still heading south. She believed they were on a high plateau because she could see a great expanse of flat desert land at a considerably lower elevation in the distance. She saw nothing in that remote scene that gave her hope, only a winding greenbelt below and to the east, which she took for a river, though she didn't know which.

The horse was noticeably weaker, being now three days without a decent feed, and though she knew they could last several more days on water alone, her despair was getting the better of her. She kept up pretenses as best she could. It would do no good for Suz to break down or panic now.

By 3:00 p.m., they had descended from the plateau to the lower desert, and Ruth was guiding the horse toward the greenbelt she'd seen from above. Her logic was simple.

# Stolen

People, by nature, seek out water sources to establish farms, ranches, villages, and towns. They had come possibly twenty miles during the day. It was difficult to tell because the path she chose to descend the escarpment was a winding one. Also, at several times during the day, they had stopped to rest the horse, and once or twice, they walked the mare as she remembered Mr. Chavez had done after she and her sister were abducted.

Now, on the low desert, she noticed there were fewer patches of snow scattered about. What was still showing was hidden from the sun in deep ravines and under thick mesquite shrubs. This had been their only source of water, but with a river nearby in the greenbelt, there should be water and graze plants aplenty.

The sun was closing in on the mountains to the west. Evening, therefore, was only two hours off at most. Ruth decided to camp once they entered the trees at a place close to the river. As they approached the trees, they both noticed the scent of wood smoke.

This was good news indeed. Smoke meant fire, and a fire meant people. And people, hopefully, good Christian people, would be their salvation.

# Stolen

*9:15 a.m., January 1, 1888*
*Near the Pecos River*
*Western Llano Estacado*
*New Mexico Territory*

Clouds covered the morning sun, and when he woke, it was past nine. His blankets and clothing were damp again, and the chill in the air caused him to shiver uncontrollably. His wound felt better, thankfully, and though he felt tired from his fitful sleep, he also felt ready to be back on the trail.

He made a small fire using the deadfall from trees along the river and dried his blankets as quickly as possible. He melted snow and made coffee, and treated himself to one of the small tins of corned beef provided by Clancy. He remembered the river crossing that lay ahead and scanned the banks from his position in the rocks.

Using his field glasses, he spotted a broad, flat span of the river with a sand bank showing in the middle and sand at either shore. Access would be easier if he didn't have to scale a steep ledge to get to the river. He took a short swallow of whiskey against the cold and was crossing the river by noon. Only after riding several miles and counting the days until the deadline did he reckon today's date and wished himself a Happy New Year.

# Stolen

Chapter 13

*4:15 p.m., January 1, 1888.*
*Western Llano Estacado*
*New Mexico Territory*

Bass was growing tired earlier in the day, though his
stomach wound had become nothing more than a dull ache.
He recognized the urgency of his timetable for delivery on
the third of January and assumed each day would be better
than the last. He desperately felt the need for sleep, so he
decided to camp at the bottom of a shallow coulee. There
was no snow and plenty of green grass shoots for the horse
to crop, and the coulee protected him from the light winds
that were almost constant.

A fire was made, the horse settled, and a short
swallow of the Old Crow set Bass up to do some serious
planning. He figured he was still at least a full day's hard
ride to Las Vegas. And once there, it shouldn't be too hard
to find this Don Silva. That's where it got tricky. He had
already decided to keep the local law authority in the dark.
A town as wild and open as Las Vegas would mean local
law on the take. Once he knew where Silva's place was,
he'd have to make contact with the man on his own terms.

# Stolen

Doubtless, Silva would have protection around him. A small army, at least. Finding a way to catch Silva alone would be the trick. If it weren't for the pain of his stomach wound, he believed he'd be equal to three or four hired guns. But the wound sapped his strength, so he doubted more than two.

He propped up his makeshift pup tent and leaned back on the saddle, the valise tucked under a fender. He opened a small tin of sardines in oil and ate them with dry biscuits and cheese. Clancy had given him three days' supplies, but since he was eating irregularly, they would likely last the whole trip. Clancy had seen to almost everything Bass would need, and he was grateful. The only thing missing was some kind of medical kit. It was still light out when Bass closed his eyes.

"Mister!? Hey, Mister, are you okay?"

Bass was taken completely by surprise at the sound of a youngster's voice out here in the uninhabited desert. He was still half asleep when he started talking.

"What? Yeah, I'm okay. Who'er you? What can I do for ya? You lost?"

"Sorta. We saw your smoke. We're sure hungry."

Bass started to regain his wits. "Well, come on, get down then. I got some chow." Bass watched as the two girls slid down from the horse's back. He thought *they looked to be the right age of the missing children, who else could they possibly be? But who would expect such a thing as this outta the blue in the middle of nowhere? Maybe another dream? 'S gotta be it.*

"You two got names? Mine's Frank. I'm a US Deputy Marshal." Bass was opening cans of cooked chicken and smoked beef. The two girls were hungry enough that they ate with their fingers, scooping the can's contents into their mouths. Both were so intent on eating they barely heard his question.

"I'm out here looking for two girls your age that were taken from their home up to Hartley in Texas. Their names are Ruth and Susan Matlock. Could that possibly be you two?"

Ruth nodded her head quickly as she chewed. Susan tried to speak, but it came out all jammed up with chicken. Her eyes were wide and moving furtively around as if she was watching out for something.

"Damn. Well, I am snookered. I come all these days expecting you two to be helpless prisoners, and look at ya. Here, all I got to drink is water but help yourselves." Bass handed Ruth a bota, and they both guzzled several long swallows.

# Stolen

When Ruth finally could speak, she began telling of the escape they managed and their days on the trail, trying to avoid being tracked.

"And then I made a fire with my belt buckle, and we got warmer, but we didn't have any food, and Susie was sore hungry, and complaining, but all I could do was hug her. So, we tied some brush to the horse's tail. She's prob'ly hungry, too, and that wiped away our tracks, so I don't think anyone's following. And that twisty path comin' down over the ridge was a long way, but we could smell your smoke . . . oh, and thanks for the tins. And sorry for wakin' ya."

"Well. By God. And all this time, we were worried for ya. Sounds like you had the situation well in hand."

Susan spoke next. Her eyes were wide as she told her story. "Yes, sir and I had to go, and the bucket was in the corner, and I found the loose boards, and we went out really late on this horse, and now here we are. Do you know Mommy and Daddy? Thank you, Mister."

Bass smiled, "Yes, little one, I know your Pa, and I know they both have been terribly worried to get you back. I'll bet this will be the best present they could ever get, havin' you both back with 'em. Now. What do ya think we should do next?"

# Stolen

"Go home. Can we go home now?" Susan asked.

"Of course, but home is still a long way away, honey. We gotta figure how best to get you there fast."

Ruth was trying her best to be grown-up, but she was anxious too.

"I know we rode with those men for four days and three nights. They must have taken us pretty far, huh?"

Bass nodded and said, "Well, yeah, but not so far you can't get back in a day or two on the train. I think our next move is to get to the train station in Agua Negra Chiquita. I can send a message from there to your Ma and Pa that you're all right and comin' home. Let me build up that fire a bit. 'You sure you weren't followed?

"Pretty sure. Didn't ever see anyone."

"That's a clever trick to tie switches to your horse's tail. Indians do that when they don't want you to know how many of 'em there are."

"Do you know real Indians? Scalpin' ones?"

"I do."

"I don't like them. They hurt White people and children. I don't like them at all."

"Your name's Susan, right?"

"Uh-huh."

# Stolen

"Well, you know Susan, the Indians ain't so very different from us at all. I know they look different and speak a different language, but they're really pretty much like we are. They love their children and their families. They take care of their horses and animals. They hunt and fish and farm like we do. They even have their own kinda school for their kids. And us Whites have been pretty bad and hurtful to them, too. I know 'cause I've seen it."

"Oh my, they have to go to school, too?"

"Oh yes. They have to learn picture writing and the stories of their families. They learn how to cure sicknesses by using plants. Say, I knew an old Indian woman once who healed me of a broken leg, and she used different plants to fix me. Indians know more'n we do in a lotta ways."

"Gee. They get to write with pictures?"

"Yup. They're mostly very fine folks."

Susan was sitting cross-legged near the fire, her blankets still wrapped around her. "So, how far is this Agua town?"

"We'll be there tomorrow, maybe thirty miles or so. You two can get into my little tent here. I'll sit up by the fire and keep watch. You're gonna be fine, just fine. Now get some sleep."

# Stolen

Bass got up and stoked the fire, wrapping himself in another blanket. He took a long swallow of Old Crow for inner warmth and perched himself with his back against a warm rock by the fire. He heard Ruth say they weren't followed, but he checked the loads in his Colt and the .32 Remington-Smoot anyway. The Hotchkiss Carbine was presently employed as a tent pole, but he remembered it being ready to go if need be.

The hole in his stomach had remained a nuisance through the day, but he was confident the infection had passed. Still, he wondered what Sally would say to the new scar. He'd come by more than a few in the last year, two bullet holes last summer alone, and he'd been lucky just to have survived a couple of them.

The young Indian with the knife still stayed with him mostly because it came as such a shock, out of nowhere in the middle of the night. But also because it was the first time he'd ever been stabbed with any real effect. He'd been cut once or twice in the Cavalry and had even fallen on an arrow during a drunken fight at the Sutlers at Fort Apache. The puncture actually hurt more than being cut. *Anyway, it's the burn that's gonna scar*, he thought, *not the hole.*

# Stolen

"Lay off that poison, Boone. I need all you boys alert and sober for what's likely comin'."

"Jeeze, Gabe, it's cold out here. We can't have no fires showin', so startin' one inside's all I'm doin'."

Gabe gave Boone a grin followed by a 'means business' scowl. "Just keep that hooch corked till this is over."

Viligry took the field glasses from his saddlebags and looked out over the desert to the west. In the hazy distance, he could make out a large ranch, and as he scanned further, he saw several clusters of black cattle huddled about the corrals and even more grazing in the meadows outside the fences. He could see two barns and several corrals, and off to the left was a long, low building with windows and smoke drifting up from two chimneys. Privately, he thought to himself, *Christ if they have men enough to fill that bunkhouse, we're in way over our heads.*

"Boys, we're gonna stay up here for a while, least 'til we know more 'bout what's goin' on with Mr. Matlock

224

# Stolen

and the ransom. For all we know he's already paid it and taken his children home. Say, what day is it?"

"It's Sunday, Gabe. I can always tell," Ramsfeld answered.

"Ha. I believe ya, Al, but the date, what's the date?"

Boone started counting on his fingers, thinking out loud. "Thirty days has September . . . so, that's thirty-one for December . . . damn Gabe, it's the first. January first. Happy new year, boys. This calls for a drink. Whaddaya say, Gabe?"

"Go ahead, Boone. Just one, though." Gabe began thinking. "The first, huh? That means we been on the trail for six days. And up here watchin' that spread for two of 'em. Boys, listen up. Since we got no idea what's what with the kidnappin' and ransom and all, I think it's time we took some action."

The other men all agreed. Sitting around, not knowing what was happening, was eating at all of them.

"Hand me that jug, Mike. Okay, first, we're gonna do a little reconnaissance on that hacienda down there. Late tonight, one of us, yet to be determined, is gonna go down for a closer look. Now we got a pretty good notion that if they have the girls, that's where they'll be. Damn, that's good stuff. Hand it back, Reverend. If they're there, we'll

225

create a plan of action. But if they're not, I'm thinkin' we go into town, quiet-like, and see what we can find out there. At least from the town, we can send a wire to Mr. Matlock. My guess is he'll be glad to know we're still on the job. So, whaddaya say?"

"I'm with you, Gabe," Patchelski was first to agree, but the other two followed along. After a long swallow.

# Stolen

"You sure you're up to this, Boone?" Gabe Viligry called for volunteers to reconnoiter the buildings a half-mile away to try to find where the children were being held.

"Hell, I'll be all right, Gabe. That big house has been dark all night, and there ain't no smoke comin' out at all. Long as I don't wake the vaqueros in the bunkhouse, I should be fine."

"All right, but remember this is just a look-see trip. Don't try to be a hero if you find the girls. Come back up here, and we'll work out a plan. Got it?"

"Don't worry 'bout me, Gabe. You're the boss. I'll go in an hour or so."

"Remember, I got no jurisdiction out here, so if you get caught, I can't help you. Your badge won't do no good. I don't believe we're even supposed to be here, officially."

Boone went back to the other men and drank some of his homemade. Then, he tidied up his saddle and stopped at Reverend Ramsfeld's tent.

# Stolen

"Deacon, I'm headin' out in a bit to sniff around down yonder. Y'all watch out for Gabe now. Don't let him do nothin' foolish, er get himself hurt."

Patchelski added, "You just watch your own top-knot. He'll be just fine. I'm more worried 'bout you, old as you are. Hell, bet ya can't see neither."

"Well, enough to thump you, youngster." Then Boone called, "Reverend? Say a prayer for this fool. He's gonna need it when I get back."

"Be careful, Boone. And quiet. I know that'll task you some."

Waverly smiled and mounted his horse. "Well, see you, boys, later. And leave my hooch alone!" Boone rode down the slope and disappeared in the dark.

The moon was waning gibbous, but the cloud cover filtered the light to show only faint outlines and shapes. Boone didn't want to take a chance that an unseen stallion might pick up his scent and feel like an interloper was at hand. Any commotion was to be avoided, so he tied off his horse downwind of the barn, about a quarter-mile out. There was a small arroyo that ran alongside the barn and then behind the bunkhouse. He decided to check the main house first.

# Stolen

There was no sign of life at all in the house. No lamps were lit, no hearth fires or stoves burning. If the children were in there, they might be alone in some kind of lockup. He went around to a rear door that was out of sight of the rest of the yard. The covered veranda wrapped around the corner from the front of the house and ended at the entrance where Boone stood. He tried the latch, and it gave way, so he opened the door and stepped inside. The first thing he noticed was how cold it was. *If the girls are locked in here, they better have a bunch a blankets.* He also noticed the smell of onions and garlic, so he assumed he was standing in the kitchen. The darkness was even deeper as the window shades were partially drawn. He had to move slowly so his eyes could adjust with each step he took.

He had walked through two large rooms which were facing the front of the house. When he came to a corner that he assumed might have been a hallway, the darkness was complete. He felt along the wall, moving his hand for guidance. Once or twice, he felt the corners of pictures and moved more slowly past. He tried three doors along the hall, and all were open, dark and cold. If the children were in the house, he finally determined, they were well hidden, near froze, and able to see in the dark. He made his way back to the rear door and carefully closed it behind him, making sure to set the latch as he'd found it. The moon had moved, and the clouds were shifting from west to east. Boone could smell snow in the air. He had a bit more light now, and he made his way back to the arroyo and crept along the side of it until he was behind the bunkhouse. Two vaqueros were smoking outside, chatting about something as one relieved himself at the edge of the arroyo. It was hard for Boone to understand. They'd obviously been into the tequila bottle. He knew some of the Mexican dialects from his time in the Cavalry, but it was rusty at best.

*"Ellas escaparon a traves de una pared, amigo. Ahora los esta persiguiendo."*

Both men laughed, and the other said, *"El Segundo se lo merecia."*

They both laughed again and walked back inside the bunkhouse.

Boone heard this and started repeating the words to himself, trying to gather a meaning.

"They '*escaparon*' . . . they escaped!? 'Traves' through the what . . . the 'pared' . . . the fence? The gate? The . . . shit, the wall? God damn . . . the girls escaped through a wall?"

# Stolen

Quietly but with more speed, he made it back to his horse and headed back to the high ground where the others were waiting. He slid off his horse before the animal had stopped moving. Ramsfeld held the animal as Patch and Gabe came up for his report.

"Excuse me for a minute, boys, but the wind's up, and it's cold enough to freeze the devil's dick out there." He walked to his saddlebags and took a long pull on his jug.

"Feel better, Boone?" Gabe was being stern with the older man, but he was grateful to see him back in one piece.

"So. What did you find out?"

"There's nothin' in the house. I went there first. It's cold and dark as a tomb in there. But on my way back, I snuck along a little stream bed. I heard two cowboys, sounded drunk, saying something like 'the girls escaped through a wall, and it served a second right.'"

"What?" Gabe was confused. "Don't make sense, Boone. Them cowboys was drunk like you said."

"Yeah, yeah, they was, but they was laughin' about it like it was important," Ramsfeld spoke up.

"Do you remember the exact words, Boon?"

"I remember '*ellas escaparon*' and '*pared*,' and the '*Segundo se lo mercy.*'"

"*Merecia?*"

"That's it, yeah. You speak Mexican, Preacher?"

"Yes, I do. What you heard translates to the girls escaped through a wall, and the Second had it coming."

Gabe stepped back, startled by the revelation. "They escaped, Reverend?"

"*Escaparon*. Sounds like it."

"What about this 'had it coming' stuff?"

"Oftentimes, Gabe, in Mexican parlance, the second in command is called the Segundo. 'The second in command had it coming,' is what I hear."

Patchelski spoke next, "Well shit, Gabe. What do we do now? You think them two little girls is out on the desert alone? Hell, they won't last a night."

"I know that, Patch. Lemme think."

After a moment, Gabe turned to Boon. "That's all? They didn't say anything about when they escaped?"

"Nope. It was just them two phrases."

Gabe considered for a few more moments and said, "I'll have to report this to the girl's parents, of course. Telegraph down in Las Vegas town. Don't know how they'll take it. Might be happy they're free or afraid for

# Stolen

their survival. Hard to say. In any case, we have no idea as to the whereabouts of the children. They could be hiding nearby, or they could be miles away. But we do know who's responsible for taking them, and he has a ranch about a mile away. My guess is we'll find him, whatever his name is, in Las Vegas. Town should be just a little bit to the south. I figure until we know better, it's the most likely place to start looking again. I know you boys have been through a lot, and I got no right to ask you to stick it out. Hell, 'don't have any legal authority as it is. 'Left that behind at the Hartley city limits. If you wanna go home, I'll understand, boys, and I'll not hold against ya. Thank you for your service. I'm gonna go into town, send that telegram."

He looked into their faces, and all three were looking right back at him.

Boone was the first to speak up. "Quit now? Are you crazy? Just startin to get interestin', Gabe."

The other two heartily agreed, and they all passed Boone's jug around. Again.

# Stolen

Chapter 14

*10:00 a.m., January 2, 1888*
*Along the Pecos River*
*New Mexico Territory*

Bass and the two girls had started out after a cold breakfast of canned fruit and coffee. Bass was feeling better than he had in the last few days, even after getting fairly little sleep. He had woken Ruth around five to keep watch so he could 'catch forty winks,' as he described it. For two hours, she sat, tending the fire and cradling the Colt pistol he'd left with her. "Don't try to shoot anybody. Just wake me up if you see or hear anything."

It started snowing an hour after they left, and now it was coming down thick enough to impair their vision. There was only a light wind blowing, and Bass toyed with the idea of moving closer to the river where it might be a bit easier to see. He decided against it, believing if they were being followed, poor visibility would work more for them than against. The blowing snow would cover their tracks, and the natural move would be to follow the river. Outlaws would assume that, too, and know where to find them.

# Stolen

"Best to keep headin' south, girls. Quicker, too."

The snow slowed to flurries at noon, and Bass began looking for a sheltered spot to stop and rest. He was nearly out of canned food and only had a pouch or two of jerky left. About a quarter-mile ahead on the right was a small knoll with a cluster of large rocks and boulders on the top. Bass pointed to it and headed the small group in that direction. He tethered the horses on a short line so they could crop the sturdy green prairie grass and swallow snow as they needed.

He and the girls sat among the rocks, where they were sheltered both from view and the light wind that still blew. When Bass stood to retrieve the Old Crow from his saddlebags, he was struck in the left arm by a bullet that passed through and lodged in his bedroll that was tied to the cantle D-rings behind the saddle. He heard the report of the rifle a split second after being hit, lost his footing, and fell to the ground, bleeding into his jacket and cursing at the pain.

"Argh, God damned, son of a bitch. Agh!"

He knew the bullet had gone through as he heard it hit the bedroll. Once again, his heavy clothing had absorbed some of the impact. He raised himself on his elbows long enough to tell the girls to "stay down" while

# Stolen

he scrambled as best he could to the other side of his horse to remove the Hotchkiss Carbine.

His left arm was in serious pain and difficult to move; he thought it might be broken. Bass settled the barrel over the saddle of his horse. If this was Emma, she'd know enough to stay put, but the gelding he inherited from the dead Mexican was probably going to bolt with the first shot.

Fighting the pain, Bass laid his left arm alongside the rifle and took hold of the fore stock. He took one of the large .45-70 cartridges still in his pocket and bolted it down into the receiver. Looking down the barrel sights, he watched the desert floor for movement.

"There he is, on horseback, coming this way. Girls stay down. I'm expectin' this horse to startle when I shoot, so don't be scared."

Bass was sweating now and feeling light-headed. He knew he was losing blood and in danger of blacking out, but he fought to maintain his senses, at least until he had done for the villain that ambushed him.

Bass looked through the rear dovetail, laid the front bead sight on the mark, and squeezed the trigger. The powerful cartridge caused the gun to leap backward, and without his left arm for support, the carbine bucked up over

# Stolen

Bass's shoulder. The horse, surprisingly, stayed fairly still, and Bass supposed this was not the first time the animal had braced a long gun for aiming. He picked up the weapon and, as quickly as he could, loaded another round into the chamber.

He slammed the bolt home as he blinked away the fog that was settling over him and could just see that his opponent was down, with his dead horse on top of him. Bass had decided it best, in his condition, to go for the horse, the larger target. The man was trapped under his horse about ninety to a hundred yards out, pushing frantically at the dead beast, trying to free his left leg. Bass had no desire to live looking over his shoulder for this man, so he leveled the barrel once again and placed the front sight on the distant target. He pulled the trigger just as he passed out.

# Stolen

Jose Chavez y Chavez limped nearly a mile to a scrub oak thicket beside the Pecos River. He was feverish and light-headed from loss of blood, and his steps were wobbly and labored. The pain in his side had diminished, but he knew the bullet was still in him, just below the surface.

It had hit the hard ground first and bounced up into his side just above his belt. He would cut it out, he decided, after he'd rested. He kneeled first at the stump of a crooked, leafless tree and eased himself to a sitting position. As he did, a sharp pain rose up his back and made him cry out.

"You sound like a child, hombre. It is nothing, a scratch, a small thing. You have had worse, heh heh, and often."

Still, he winced and grunted as he fumbled for his pocketknife. Somewhere in the back of his mind, he knew he should clean the blade, but the small bottle of tequila he carried was with his saddle on his dead yellow horse. "Ay, cha."

238

# Stolen

After a few minutes, he decided it was time. He picked up a stick to bite down on. From experience, he knew he would need one. He was sweating heavily, and his vision was hazy, but he knew if he didn't get the slug out, he would likely die of the poison from it. He remembered someone saying it was better to leave the bullet in sometimes. He did not believe it was so. "Is it not better to suck out the poison after the bite? Of course, it is."

Chavez tested the blade's sharpness with his thumb and was pleased. Next, he opened his shirt, feeling the cold immediately and thinking that perhaps the cold would clean the blade. It hurt to twist his body but once in position, he held firm and brought the knife to bear.

With a small cut on either side of the bullet hole, he could not tell if the pain was from the new cuts or the existing hole in his skin. He began pinching the folds of skin in an effort to locate the bullet, and when he found it, he needed to rest. The pain was wearing on him. After a few minutes, he started again. He pinched the area and inserted the blade, feeling for metal-on-metal contact. Once he found it, he would have to slide the blade in even further to gently pry up and lift the slug out.

Again, he rested. He was very near to blacking out and needed a few moments to calm himself, take a few breaths, and wait for his nerves to quiet. Finally, it could wait no longer. He put the stick between his teeth, and with his eyes closed, he pushed the blade into the wound to the bottom of the bullet and pried it up and out. He screamed the pain into his teeth and spat out the stick.

"*Santo maldio Dios!* Mmm. I owe that one, the hombre who shot me and killed my yellow horse, but maybe by now, he is dead. Heh heh. Serves him right."

Then Chavez passed out.

240

# Stolen

*3:40 p.m., January 2, 1888*
*Along the Pecos River*
*New Mexico Territory*

"Marshal? Mister . . . Mr. Marshal? Can you hear me?"

"Hm. Oh, yes . . . yes, I can hear you."

"Well . . . your eyes are still closed. Tell me what I can do to help you."

"Water, please. Water . . . in the bota."

Ruth ran to the horse and returned with the water bag. "Marshal, sir, you've been asleep for over an hour. I bound up your gunshot with some of Susie's shirttail. It was too big for her anyway. And I think the bleeding has stopped. I didn't want to check 'til you were awake."

Susan added, "Yes, and I've been watching the man you shot. I'm afraid he's not dead, but I think he's hurtin' really bad. When he finally got free of his horse, he lay real still for a long time, but then he got up and started walking funny over toward those far trees." Susan was pointing, but Bass was lying on the ground with his eyes still closed, thinking.

# Stolen

"Stabbed in the stomach and now shot up in my shoulder. God damn, what's to be next? Wait'll Sally hears 'bout this. My, my."

"What do we do now, Marshal?" Ruth was beginning to sound worried, and Bass tried to reassure her.

"Now, don't fret, girls, I'll be fine in a little bit. Ruth, you did a first-rate job on my bandage. Say, I feel better already." Bass winced and growled a bit at the pain as he tried to stand. "I think it might be time that we left this camp, whaddaya think, ladies?"

Both girls agreed, and Ruth helped Bass to stand up. Once standing, Bass tried moving his left arm and decided maybe it wasn't broken after all. *Nevertheless, I'm gonna treat it like it is.* Bass withdrew his belt and made a viable sling out of it. Ruth helped get the belt over his head and around the elbow of the bad shoulder.

Getting up on the horse proved problematic without the use of his left arm and hand. He decided to mount from the right while standing on a rock. Right foot in the stirrup and right hand on the saddle horn, he was able to pull himself up to a pretty good seat. He asked Ruth to hand him his Old Crow and took a couple of long gulps against the pain in his shoulder and gut. Ruth helped him wrap his heavy wool blanket about himself and then got Susan up on their pony. The three of them walked off the prairie and into Agua Negra Chiquita just before midnight.

# Stolen

*4:30 p.m., January 2, 1888*

*Along the Pecos River*

*New Mexico Territory*

Chavez woke to the sound of horses plodding up the trail he lay on. The jingle and creak of wagon fittings and wooden wheels lit the fires of hope in the old outlaw, so he put on his hat and a smile as the teamster, driving a two-horse freight wagon, pulled up beside him. Chavez checked the road for others, but this was the only wagon in view.

"'S" matter wit you there, beaner. Too mucho tequila?" The driver was fat and slovenly dressed. Torn britches, a ragged shirt collar, and a threadbare wool coat. His round face was red from cheap whiskey and time spent in the weather, and he squinted through crossed eyes that made it difficult for Chavez to know which one of them to talk to.

"No, Señor, my horse is falling on me, and I have hurt my side here." Chavez turned to show the man his wound. Do you have bandages, Señor?" Chavez smiled as best he could, knowing it would put the gringo at ease.

"I might have, Pepe, and then I might not. You got money to pay? American?"

# Stolen

"Oh si, Señor, plenty of silver in my pocket. I will show you." Chavez drew his pistol and shot the man in the head. He did not fall from the seat but slumped to one side, so Chavez painfully climbed up onto the wagon and painfully pushed the man over the side into the snow. Then he took the reins and headed the wagon into a thick copse of leafless Cottonwood trees and desert scrub. He took his time searching the contents of the wagon, finding mostly farming tools but several boxes of guns and ammunition. "I could be better off finding medicines or whiskey. I already have guns."

There were dry goods and blankets, which he felt would be useful and boxes of canned meat, vegetables, and fruit. He checked under the driver's bench last and was surprised to find a strong box. He also found a medicine kit, but it contained only bandaging and tape. There was also a half-drunk bottle of whiskey tucked in a blanket at the far end of the foot-well near the brake.

He threw the strong box to the ground and gingerly stepped down from the wagon. Then, using his pistol once again, he shot the lock off. Inside, he found a watch, three gold coins, two silver metal necklaces with lockets, and sixty dollars in American paper money, all of which he stuffed into his pockets.

# Stolen

He poured a little of the whiskey on his open wound and covered the rent with bandaging and tape. He took a long swallow of the whiskey but had to fight to keep it down. He did not care for whiskey anyway, and this was very bad whiskey. He unhitched the team, large draft animals, and led them away from the wagon. He stood on a log to help him mount, and now, with some of the harness leather still in place, he rode south along the river, trailing the second horse behind. He considered going back for his saddle, but he decided it would be too difficult to pull from beneath the dead yellow horse, and he could always buy another with the sixty dollars he had just 'found.' He knew he could not go back to Don Vicente without the children, so he would continue trailing them from the spot of his ambush.

It took almost two hours to find the rocky hill where he had exchanged bullets with the gringo. It was dark now, but in the morning, he would see the tracks. He was certain the gringo would take the niñas to the train at Agua Negra Chiquita. He would know in the morning, and he would go, too.

# Stolen

Chapter 15

*8:15 a.m., January 3, 1888*
*Cantina de Rebeldes*
*Agua Negra Chiquita*
*New Mexico Territory*

The pain in Bass's arm woke him when he moved in his sleep. Again, he was soaked through his clothes and felt chilled and achy. He remembered talking with a bartender at the Cantina. They woke up in a room with a lock on the door. Most of the rooms had no lock. They were used by the girls who worked there, and no valuables were ever left behind.

The girls had slept on the bed while he took the floor. Bass had wedged a wooden chair under the latch that would prevent an intruder from pushing the handle all the way down. He raised his head and confirmed two little girls, still asleep, one valise full of money, and a beat-up US Deputy Marshal clutching his blankets with one hand and his pistol with the other.

"Ruth. You awake?"

# Stolen

"Uh-huh. You feelin' okay, Marshal? You were fussin' all night long. Your wound might have taken septic."

"Oh, I'm okay, honey. But once you two are awake, I'm gonna get you some breakfast and see if there's a saw-bones in town." Bass was struggling to move without using his left arm or stretching his middle.

"A saw-bones?"

"Yeah, you know, a doctor."

"I've never heard a doctor called that before."

"It's called slang, like a nickname kinda."

Ruth started smiling. "Oh. Okay. That's a corker. Know anymore of slang?"

"Sure, sure I do, like, uh . . . chew-the-fat."

"Yuck. Who eats fat?"

"It means to talk or have a conversation."

"Okay. I don't get that one."

"Yeah. I know it's a little far-fetched. Hey... there's another one. Far-fetched."

"I already knew that one. It's what my dad says when we fib to him."

"I guess fibin's not so bad. Unless it becomes a real lie, that's when you hafta draw the line."

"Is that one, too? Draw the line?"

248

# Stolen

"Well, not really. That one's pretty accurate. Okay. I'm gonna go downstairs now. Ruth, you come lock this door after me. We'll have a code, so you'll know it's me when I come back. I'll say, 'Alice sent me.' Not too many folks out here know your mama's name."

"Okay. That's a cinch."

Bass walked downstairs to the Cantina and found a bartender already serving cervezas and tequila.

"Excuse me, do you speak English? *Habla Ingles*?"

"Yes, Señor. A little I speak."

"First, I'd like somethin' to eat. *Huevos*—er, eggs and ham or bacon?"

"Yes, of course, Señor. I will be right back."

"Make it two orders . . . no three, make it three *platas*, three orders. Gracias."

The bartender returned in a few minutes, and Bass asked for coffee.

"Yes, black is fine, and tell me, is there a doctor in town?"

The barman went to get Bass a cup and brought the pot from the corner stove. "A doctor, Señor? No, no, but I know a doctor of the horses, Señor. He sometimes heals the people, too. Will that help?"

"Yes, anything will help. Say, what's your name, friend."

"Guillermo, Señor. Guillermo Luis Mendoza. But I am called Memo, Señor."

"Well, that's fine. Yes, thank you, Memo. The horse doctor, where will I find him?"

"He could be anywhere now, but he always comes here for his a—*comida*."

Bass sipped his coffee and waited for his breakfast order. When the plates arrived, he realized he'd have to make three trips upstairs as his left arm would not hold up. He took the first plate up, whispering the password to gain entry, and set it on the bed.

"You two start on that, and I'll bring up another plate. Do you want anything else?"

"Milk." Was Ruth's request, and Susan wanted juice. Any kind would do, but she wanted juice.

"Do either of you drink coffee at all? I can get coffee real easy."

"Coffee? Ew. That's for grown-ups, and I'm a kid, Marshal," Susan answered.

"Yes, yes, I know that. And it's Deputy Marshal, actually."

# Stolen

"I don't care, Marshal, I think you're a real one."
Ruth was watching Bass, following his movements about
the room.

"Okay, now I'm gonna go down for another plate.
Remember the secret password."

"Marshal?" Ruth asked him, "Are there any
biscuits?"

"Those flat things there are like Mexican biscuits,
Ruth. They call 'em tortillas. I'll be right back." Bass shook
his head as he walked back downstairs. "Tell me, Memo, is
there a livery in town? Like to get my horses outta the
street, get 'em a' good feed."

"Si, Señor. Down this street on, around the corner,
is my cousin Mano's barn and corral. He will care for *los
caballos*."

"Many thanks. Oh, do you have any milk or fruit
juice of any kind?"

"Oh, no, Señor. Just tequila, whiskey, and coffee.
And water, Señor, water from the Blue Hole, not just
melted snow. Blue Hole water is special, Señor. It's how
the town got its name. The water is so blue it looks black. It
will make you well."

251

# Stolen

"It will, huh? All right, I'll take three Blue Hole waters, Memo. Thank you." Bass took the second tray, balancing the cups of Blue Water, upstairs and into the room again.

"Girls, this is Blue Hole water. They didn't have juice or milk, but they had this Blue Hole water. Supposed to make you well."

"But I'm already quite well, thank you. So is Ruth," Susan said.

"Well, that's just fine to hear, and I'm glad of it, too, but think how much better you'll be for drinking this Blue Hole water. I'm gonna have some right away."

"Yes. But you're shot. We're not shot."

"That's right, so I'm going to go downstairs now and drink my Blue Hole water. After a while, I'm gonna walk the horses down to the livery. Wanna come?" Both girls certainly did want to come.

"Okay then. Now soon as you're done eatin', I want you to try to go back to sleep. I'll be downstairs, and I don't want either of you leavin' this room for anything, Got it?"

Both girls seemed tired and bored, but they both said, "okay," and Bass headed back downstairs to his breakfast.

# Stolen

"I believe I'll pass on the Blue Hole water, Memo. Coffee for me."

Dr. Randall Fontane was not technically a veterinarian in the sense that he was not licensed or educated in the profession. What Doctor Fontane did have was a working knowledge of equine and bovine medications and some of that transferred pretty well for humans. He also had books, was a fast learner, and usually had on hand what was needed for most any situation. He could set broken bones and also deliver babies of all kinds.

True to his routine, he stopped by the Rebledos Cantina for lunch at a little past 11:00 a.m. and sat at his usual table against the far wall facing a window. The Cantina was quite large and had clear demarcations between the drinking and dining sides of the establishment. The doctor was sitting in the café side. The barman saw him come in and gave Bass a high sign pointing at the doctor's table.

"Excuse me, are you Doctor Fontane?" Fontane was older, mid-fifties, trim but not thin. With short brown hair and round spectacles perched on his nose, he had the look of a teacher or businessman, except that his clothing was frayed and his boots muddy. He spoke through a thick salt and pepper mustache that hadn't been trimmed in some time.

"What do you want?"

Bass could meet surly with surly but felt it wise to be diplomatic with the fellow you want medical help from.

"Doctor, my name is Frank Bass. I'm a Deputy Federal Marshal from El Paso, and I need your help." At the words 'Federal Marshal," Fontana became a good listener.

"Oh? And how can I help you, Marshal?"

"I've been shot through the arm and stabbed in the stomach."

Dr. Fontane nearly spit out his whiskey. "You say you're shot and stabbed?"

"That's right. Several nights ago, I've forgotten how many I was attacked by, I believe, a young Comanche warrior. During the scuffle, he stabbed me in my middle, and I managed to shoot and kill him. Then yesterday, I was shot from ambush by a man I don't know. It's not uncommon in my line of work. Anyway, the bullet hit my arm and went through. No broken bones. I cauterized the stab wound and bound the bullet wound."

"Good Lord, man, sit down, sit down. You say you cauterized the puncture wound? By yourself?"

# Stolen

"Uh-huh."

"By your...self."

"Yup."

"My, my. Well. I imagine you've lost a lot of blood.
I'm concerned for the stomach wound becoming septic.
Pull up your shirt. I'd like to see this."

Bass stood and opened his blood-stained shirt. The
doctor also felt Bass's neck.

"Yes, yes, Marshal. The red streaks and discharge
around the burn are signs of infection. Your glands are
swollen as well, so everything points to sepsis. You've
been pretty sick, haven't you?"

"Mostly at night, sweats, chills. Some fever during
the day. Better lately, though."

"Well, the infection isn't advanced, or you wouldn't
be sitting here. Now show me your arm."

"Hmmm. Clean and well bandaged. What astringent
did you use, sir?"

"Whiskey."

"Internally or externally? Ha ha, my little joke
there. No, the arm looks fine. I'll put in a stitch or two,
fresh astringent, rebandage, and there you are. As to the
stab wound, I'm afraid all I have is Bromine and Iodine.
When combined, both are effective, but I'm afraid the

Bromine hurts like the dickens. I can give you laudanum for the pain. Put your hat on. Off we go, young man, to my office."

"Whoa, hold on there, Doc. The bartender said you're a vet."

"Yes, well, I treat all manner of illness and disease. I attended medical school in Illinois but never got my diploma—the war, you know. I worked in a medical unit in South Carolina, Fifth Cavalry. Assisted Surgeon Dr. Waddy Thompson."

"So, how did you wind up here?"

"After the war, I kicked around some and toyed with the notion of going back to school. But I decided to see the western frontier first. I was on my way to Albuquerque and got off the train here. 'Never got back on. I stayed. These folks don't care about diplomas, you see, only in healing. And yes, many of my patients are animals. Fairly healthy group a folks in Agua Negra, you know?"

"Doc, is this something you can do here? Reason I ask is I have a couple of little girls upstairs, kidnap victims. I'm taking them home to their parents in Texas, and I really don't want to leave them alone."

"Kidnapped, you say? Good Lord. How old are they?"

# Stolen

"Nine and seven, I believe."

"Do you want me to check them over as well?"

"Might be a good idea at that."

"Very well. I'll hop over to my cabinets and get a few things. Be right back. Wait here and finish your lunch."

"I'll do that, Doc. Thanks."

Fontane rose, putting on his bowler, and left six bits on the table. Bass went back to his seat at the bar. "Ok, Memo. I'm ready for lunch. Make it a double."

# Stolen

Chapter 16

*1:15 p.m. January 3, 1888*
*Mano Orelia's Herrero y Librea*
*Agua Negra Chiquita*
*New Mexico Territory*

Jose Chavez was bent over as he rode into the village. He reined his draft horses up at the first barn he saw and waited at the corral gate for someone to come out and help him down. He didn't have the strength to call out. A stable boy dragging a hay bale because he was too small to carry it saw the stooped figure and approached him.

"*Hola Señor. Estas bien?*"

"*Si, si niño. Ayudame a bajar, por favor.*"

The boy helped him get down from the horse, and Chavez steadied himself against the corral. He asked, "*Hay doctor?*"

"*Si. Un medico de animales. Lo necessitatos, Señor?*"

"*Si si, niño.*"

The boy ran off looking for Doctor Fontane. Chavez watched him go and eased himself down to sit on the ground and wait. Mano Orelio emerged from the barn looking for his son and saw the man sitting on the ground by the corral gate.

"Can I help you, Señor? Do you want me to care for your horses? Are you sick?"

"No, I am not sick. I have an injury, and I asked the boy to find a doctor."

"Ah. Can I make you more comfortable, some water, maybe?"

"Yes, *muchacho, gracias.*"

Mano went to draw fresh, well water for a bota and brought it to the injured man.

"*Muchas gracias, mi amigo.*" Chavez drank deeply from the bag, and when he finished, he tried to stand. The effort to straighten himself caused his wound to bleed more profusely. He became dizzy and collapsed.

"*Señor, you are bleeding very much.* Please don't move. I will get a—ah . . . *toalla.* Wait here."

Chavez was sweating badly, and even though he had two blankets wrapped around him, he was shivering so that his teeth chattered.

The boy found Doctor Fantane at his usual spot in the Cantina. "Señor doctor, please to come fast. There is a hurt man at our corral."

# Stolen

"Good Lord, two in one day. Injured men seem to be falling from trees today."

Nevertheless, Fontane followed the boy and knelt to the man's level to speak to him.

"*Hombre.* Can you hear me?"

"*Si.* Who are you?" Chavez spoke his name without opening his eyes. "I am Doctor Randall Fontane. The boy here says you're hurt."

At that point, Chavez toppled over, exposing the blood-soaked blankets that covered his wound. The doctor opened Chavez's shirt and saw the gunshot wound exacerbated by an advanced infection.

"My God, man. This is bad. The infection is very near to being mortal. I need to get you to my office and on the table immediately. Niño, get some men, hombres, to help move this man."

The boy ran into the barn and came out, followed by two hands that appeared to be in their teens.

"*Muchachos, a mi officina por favor.*"

The two men understood immediately and gently lifted Chavez to his feet, helping him to walk down the block to the doctor's office. Once on the examining table, Fontane began asking questions.

"This is a gunshot wound?"

# Stolen

"Yes."

"How old?"

"Eh?"

"When were you shot?"

"Oh. Yesterday. Afternoon, I think."

Fontane was now certain that this was the man that Marshal Bass had been ambushed by. Still, he needed treatment, and Fontane would do his best.

"You know it's infected?"

"Uh."

"I'm going to give you something for the pain so that you can talk to me. Do you understand?"

"Si—yes."

Fontane slowly injected 10 mg of morphine sulfate into Chavez's left hip. Within minutes, Chavez was alert and responsive.

"What is your name, sir?"

"Chavez."

"Mr. Chavez, how did you get shot."

"It was an argument with another about a girl. Can you fix?"

"Yes, I can, but you'll have to be unconscious. Reversing an advanced infection is tricky and painful. You must be asleep."

# Stolen

"Do it, please."

"Can you roll over onto your right side?" Chavez moved slowly, but finally, he was comfortable on his right side. His left side and the wound were accessible.

"Mr. Chavez, there is chloroform on this napkin that I will put over your nose. Please breathe normally."

Several minutes later, Chavez was asleep. Fontane knew he had an obligation to report this to Bass, but he decided to wait until Chavez was recovering from the chloroform and the infection had been cleaned out. He would be lucid then and able to understand who Bass was.

Chavez had been breathing normally for several minutes, so Fontane began. He used a probe and forceps to locate and remove a small piece of the slug. As expected, when the fragment was removed, blood gushed from the injury, and it took Fontane a few minutes to clean and disinfect the wound with bromine and iodine before he could stitch the hole closed. After the astringent and bandaging, Chavez appeared to be resting comfortably, and that's when Fontane decided to find Bass.

He checked the Cantina first and was told that 'they' had gone to the livery to drop off their horses. Fontane walked down the street and found them outside the Mano's barn. Bass saw him coming and said. "Doctor.

# Stolen

Thanks for taking such good care of me today. I feel much better."

"That's fine, Marshal, and who might these two ladies be?"

"I'm Susan Matlock, and I'm going home soon."

"Well, that's just wonderful, Susan, and you are?"

"I'm Ruth Matlock. The Marshal rescued us from kidnappers and is taking us home."

Bass was quick to add, "Actually, they escaped on their own and pretty much rescued me in the desert." Then he said to the girls, "But first, we need to see to the horses, and then we're going to send a wire to their parents."

"Um, Marshal, can I have a word?" They stepped out of earshot. Fontane thought it best the girls not know yet about the man up on his table.

"Marshal, I just treated a Mexican gentleman for a bullet wound in his left side. He said it happened yesterday, so naturally, I thought I'd best let you know."

Bass's expression turned official on hearing this. "Where is he now?"

"My office. Same table you were on two hours ago. He's asleep, chloroform. Should come around within the hour."

# Stolen

"Okay. Go on back and watch him if he wakes up. I need to take the girls back to the Cantina, and I'll come over to make the arrest. Is there a sheriff in town?"

"Yes, but not for the last three days. He had to go to Albuquerque to pick up a prisoner."

"No matter. Means there must be a lockup in town somewhere."

"Oh yes, further down the street from my office."

"Good. I'll be back in ten minutes or so." Dr. Fontane turned and walked back past the Cantina and then into his office. When he opened the door, Chavez was sitting up at the table, buttoning his blood-stained shirt.

"Señor Doctor, you have done very good. I feel much better now. What is your fee?"

"Well, I'm certainly glad to hear you feel better, but I caution that it's likely the morphine that's hiding the pain. You still have an infection that needs treating."

"This cannot be so. I am feeling well. What is your fee, doctor?"

"There is no fee, Mr. Chavez, but you must listen to me. Your infection needs additional treatment."

"You know my name? How is it you know my name?"

"You told me when we brought you here."

# Stolen

"I do not remember this. Who else knows, doctor? Who else have you told?"

Fontane was nervous now, and it sounded so in his voice.

"Well, ah—no one really . . . the men at the corral, they all heard you say your name."

"They do not bother me. I think you told someone. Another man, here with two niñas. He would need the doctor, too."

"No, really . . . no!"

Chavez drew his pistol and shot Ronald Fontane twice in the chest. Then he finished buckling his gun belt, buttoning his jacket and walked out of the door and into the bright, cold daylight. He noticed his side beginning to hurt as he moved, but he decided once he had found the girls and killed the hombre with them, he could rest for a few hours before heading back to Don Vicente.

He turned toward the Cantina, certain to find the girls in a room there. *They will be glad to see Chavez. They know he is always good to them*, he thought as he walked in the street. The sunlight reflected off the snow that remained in scattered patches about the village. The glare hurt his eyes and made him squint. His head began to hurt, and sweat beads broke out on his forehead and neck around his collar. He was feeling queasy as he headed to the Cantina door, and he did not see the tall man standing in the shadows on the boardwalk. He had just started down the street when he heard a voice.

"Chavez, stop! You're under arrest for kidnap and murder. Drop your weapon and keep your hands where I can see them." Bass had Chavez under his gun.

"Hombre, it is you. How is your wound? Does it hurt? Whoo, the pain you put in me, Señor, it was very bad. I think. I think I will pay you back."

"Don't do it, Chavez."

"Yes, now is the time." And with that, Jose Chavez made a slow, awkward attempt for his gun, and Bass shot him cleanly in the center of his chest. Bass walked to the crumpled body and kicked Chavez's gun aside. He could hear the dying man speaking something very softly, almost a whisper, so he bent his knee to listen.

"The niñas are all right?'

"Yes, they are fine."

"Good. Say to them, I had no choice." Chavez closed his eyes and died.

Everyone in the street had heard the earlier gunshot that came from the doctor's office. Bass knew what had happened. He felt no pity for Chavez. He knew everyone had choices no matter what their situation. Even the nine-year-old Ruth knew it.

He stood up, holstered his gun, and turned to walk to Fontane's office. He looked back at the body lying in the street, shook his head, and then looked up at the deep, azure blue of the sky. When he looked at the Cantina, he saw the two girls watching from a window.

# Stolen

Chapter 17

*2:00 p.m., January 3rd, 1888*
*Telegraph Office*
*EP & SW Terminal*
*New Mexico Territory*

"Let's write the telegram together, okay?" Bass had taken the girls to the telegraph office.

"Okay. Send to Mommy and Daddy at home in . . . Ruthie, where do we live?"

"In Hartley, Texas, you goose. And Marshal Bass knows how to get it there. Don't you, Marshal?"

"I do indeed, but what do we say?"

"That we want to come home, of course."

"I think they know that, Susan. How about we start with something like, 'We're both fine, and we love you. Marshal Bass will bring us home. We have a long story to tell.' Somethin' like that. It has to be a short message cause telegram paper is so small." Ruth said, "Yeah. That sounds good to me."

"Me too, but also say, 'We want to open our presents.'"

# Stolen

"Okay then. You two sit on the bench here, and I'll send it. Then we'll go to the store and get some candy to celebrate. How's that sound?"

"Oh, boy! They have candy here?"

"Of course they do. You're being a goose again."

The girls sat on the wooden bench next to the telegrapher's window while Bass read the train schedule and sent the wire.

*Avery,*

*Girls with me. They are fine. Not mistreated. 'Still have the money. Meet at 6:00 p.m. train tomorrow, Amarillo. Happy New Year. –Bass*

Bass gave the clerk eight dollars for the fastest possible delivery.

"So. Let's head down to that general store and see what's what at the candy counter. Okay?"

"Yeah, let's."

Ruth took Bass's hand, and Susan talked almost the entire two blocks about her Christmas presents and her friends at church and how she didn't like Mr. Holcomb, her teacher, because he smelled like moth-balls. Ruth was quiet for the walk, listening to her sister and looking around at the people in the town. But when they got to the store,

# Stolen

Susan ran inside while Bass and Ruth stood on the boardwalk and talked.

"I'm sorry, Mr. Chavez is dead. He was the nicest of all the men that took us, but he shouldn't have tried to shoot you, Marshal. I'm sorry he was an outlaw, too, but it was his own fault. He didn't have to be one."

"You know it's funny you sayin' that, Ruth. Before he died, he asked if you two were all right. I told him you were, and he seemed glad. Then he said he was 'sorry, and that he had no choice."

Ruth thought for a moment. "But that's not so. Everybody has choices, Marshal, even kids."

Bass chuckled and said, "Ruth, you are wise beyond your years. You know what that means?"

"Not really."

"Means you're pretty grown-up for your age." Ruth smiled at that.

Just then, Susan dashed up. "C'mon, Ruthie. They have chocolate bars."

And the two ran inside while Bass followed, smiling slightly, thinking about Sally and the kind of father he might be. The girls spent nearly an hour in the general store, admiring some Mexican and Indian turquoise jewelry, white linen clothing, and hats. Susan ran up to Bass at one point.

"They got a rattler in a chicken wire cage, Marshal. Come 'n see."

So, he did. Bass bought a new shirt to replace the torn, blood-stained garment he'd been wearing for days. He knew a hot bath would straighten him right up, but he didn't want to leave the girls unattended. Forty minutes and six dollars worth of candy and a new shirt later, it was time to get ready to leave on the 4:00 p.m. eastbound. Bass needed to stop at the livery to sell the Mexican's horses and saddle. They wouldn't be needing them anymore. He planned to hang onto the Hotchkiss Carbine, so he kept the saddle sheath to carry it in.

At the livery, the girls roamed the barn looking at the horses and mules that Mano kept there. Susan saw a miniature donkey in the corral and thought it was cute. Ruth stuck by Bass's side the whole time he dealt with Mano.

Orelio allowed twenty-five dollars each for the horses and fifteen for the saddle, blanket, and bridle. Bass took the sixty-five dollars and bought three-compartment tickets to Amarillo for forty-eight dollars and change. He figured between the candy, hotel and the tickets, sixty-five dollars covered his expenses.

Before boarding the train, Bass sent a telegram to Sally.

*Sally Love,*

*Girls are safe and well - so am I - Taking them to Amarillo tomorrow-*

*Home after. – Love, FFB*

Once they were on the train, Bass remembered why he was safe and well. He remembered that Doctor Fontane didn't charge him a fee. And for the next hour or so, he thought about the good doctor and then about the man who killed him. It wasn't the first time he had difficulty fittin' two kinds a people into the same world. *But that's kinda why I have a job,* he thought.

The girls had a great time watching the scenery go by until it got dark, and then eating on the train was a real treat. The food wasn't very good, but they did have cold milk and, of course, whiskey with ice for Marshal Bass. By eight o' clock, the porter had turned one of the compartment walls into a bed, and Bass read them a story from a Good Housekeeping Magazine until they fell asleep. He continued reading from the American Rifleman

# Stolen

Magazine until he got bored with it and decided to visit the dining car again. He was beginning to feel that his bandages might need changing, but there was nothing he could do about it until tomorrow in Amarillo. Bass allowed that maybe he was getting too anxious about his bandages, in fact, and that he needed something to relax him. To that end, he purchased a pint of Colonel Taylor's Kentucky Rye whiskey. Tonight, he would rely on Colonel Taylor's power of sedation.

The next day was spent doing one of the new jigsaw picture puzzles provided by the railroad. The girls put together one with a barnyard scene of children playing with ducks and chickens. When they grew tired of that, they played the seven little words game, or they used colored pencils to draw. Ruth read a long article out loud to Bass about folding proper ribbon knots, boot laces, and the importance of bone china table settings. The train was an exciting diversion for the girls, who both seemed resilient to the trial they'd been through. At 5:30 p.m., there was a notable slowing of speed as the train approached the outskirts of the city of Amarillo, and at exactly 6:oo p.m., the train rolled to a stop at the platform.

Bass spotted Avery, Alice, and Maria holding baby Eddie and waving frantically at each window, hoping to see the faces of their children. As soon as the girls noticed, they both began to cry, and they raced to the end of the car to be the first on the landing platform. Observing all this, the sheer joy in the reunion gave Bass an unaccustomed warm satisfaction.

Bass followed the girls down the stepstool to the platform but stayed in the background until the hugs and tears subsided. When he could break himself away, Avery approached Bass shaking his hand vigorously, thanking him several times over for his heroic effort. Bass tried to correct that it was the children who'd found him after their incredibly brave escape, but it made no difference.

"You're being far too modest, Marshal. I was with you on that train. I saw you in action. I received a telegram from Gabe Viligry just before yours saying they were in Las Vegas and still looking for the girls. If it weren't for you and men like Gabe Viligry and his posse, good, decent people would live in the desperation of lawlessness."

Bass thanked Avery for the sentiment but again indicated that his children were the real heroes. "You say that a posse is in Las Vegas?"

"That's what their message said. There was no return indicated. Just the Las Vegas Telegraph. Should I try to reach them? Let them know all's well?"

# Stolen

"No, better not. Town like that might be giving them away to the wrong people. Let me consider it for a bit, and I'll take care of it. 'Wasn't aware there were others involved. You just take care of your family."

Finally, Bass was able to return the valise containing the twenty-five thousand dollar ransom, relieved to be shed of that responsibility at last. Avery beamed and again thanked Bass for his honesty and diligence and said he was sure the XIT Ranch would be very grateful. It was then that Avery remembered the telegrams that had come for him that he thought Bass would want to see. Bass put the messages into his jacket pocket, said a long farewell to the girls, hugged Alice and Maria, who seemed very happy with her new family, and shook Avery's hand once again. Then, he excused himself to let the family continue to love each other until it was time to board the train for their short trip to Hartley.

Bass ducked into the saloon next to the Harvey House and took a seat near a window with a lamp already lit. He ordered an Old Overholt Rye, lit the cigar he'd bought at the counter, and opened one of the messages. It was from Sally and date-stamped yesterday.

*My Love,*

# Stolen

*'Happy and relieved that you are well and successful. I am the size of Rhode Island still, but Dr. Spalding says I'm fine. Maggie and Elsie will be here in five days. I've missed you so.*
*Love,*
*Sally*

Bass was ready to leave even though his train was still an hour away. He longed for Sally's comfort and the selfless love that he was lucky enough to hold. He was also ready for some time at home to see his baby born, to love his family, and to heal. He carefully folded the telegram and slid it into his shirt pocket. The next wire was from Bart Mariany, time-stamped yesterday, to advise that Tomasino had arrived and Bart had already helped him to change his name and find work. His wire ended, '*Sally said to send this to Avery. He'd be seeing you first.*

Bass took a last swallow of his whiskey and walked back out to the street and down to the passenger boarding platform. Avery Matlock was still there talking with the conductor. Bass called to him, and Avery waved as Bass trotted down the platform.

"Avery, you mentioned a man, Gabe Viligry."

"He's the sheriff of Hartley. Fine, young man. Elected just last November. He took several men in a posse to track the kidnappers the day after the girls were taken. Why?"

"Have you been in any kind of communication with him?"

"Well, no. I mean, I have no way to reach him, except he was somewhere in Las Vegas a couple days ago. I don't know where he is."

"The center of this whole thing is in Las Vegas. He's probably an eager, young lawman, Avery. He may be anxious to prove to his town they made the right choice electin' him, so he's gonna keep trackin' those outlaws right into a nest of rattlesnakes and scorpions."

"Hm, yes, I suppose so. Bring those villains to face the Bar of Justice. I see what you mean."

"And he's on shaky ground to start. Las Vegas is well out of his jurisdiction. Any arrest he might make will be thrown out. The other thing is this town is the most corrupt, criminal stronghold in the territory. Tombstone had nothin' on this place, and Virgil Earp and his brothers were the Federal Officers there. When the Cowboys gang left Tombstone, they went to Las Vegas. And here's somethin' else. Fella I know, Dave Mather, notorious gunman, he took the Marshals job in Las Vegas two years ago. We called him Mysterious Dave Mather 'cause he played everything so close to the vest. And he was good, real good with a gun. Hear-tell, they ran him outta town, and he ain't been seen since. There's plenty outlaws that see Las Vegas as their safe haven, too. All ruthless. All bad."

"But what of the local law there? You don't feel Gabe Viligry is up to assisting the authorities in Las Vegas?"

"No, frankly, I don't. Likely, a town like that won't have any lawmen, or if it does, they'll be on the take and just as corrupt. Take an army of Federal Officers to put a dent in their operation."

Bass thought for a moment. The distraction of people boarding and porters handling baggage slowed him. Avery now had that same concerned look he had on the train when dealing with the Mexican renegades.

He asked, "Do you suppose there's any way we can warn him off? Tell him the girls are safe, and he should return home?"

Bass thought for a moment. "I don't see how, not knowin' where he might be. I'll think on it some more, Avery. Now, you go on home and celebrate."

"Thank you, Marshal. Again, thank you for everything." Avery walked back to his family just as the girls began their story of escape. A few minutes later, the

278

# Stolen

whistle sounded, and the conductor called out, "All aboard."

Bass watched as the train slowly pulled away.

# Stolen

Chapter 18

*6:10 p.m., January 4, 1888*
*Cuddlebees Old Texas Saloon*
*Across from the EP & S. W.*
*Amarillo, Texas*

Bass sat again with his second whiskey and a fresh cigar, pondering his next move. The gangsters that hatched the kidnap plot had almost succeeded. If it hadn't been for the grit and cleverness of the two girls, it may very well have. And his thoughts were not just of the kidnapping. Las Vegas had been a hotbed for violence and corruption for some time. The evil that showed at the surface was deeply ingrained, almost a way of life. Local farmers, ranchers, and citizens were victimized to the point where most decent folks had left. Every bank robber, cattle thief, gun for hire, and assassin at one time or other had drifted through Las Vegas, and some had stayed.

Bass remembered when the railroad line between Albuquerque and Las Vegas was completed it was supposed to bring an influx of businesses and working folks to the area. Now, the train was robbed at least once or twice a year whenever money for a payroll or livestock was on board. Bass was not self-righteous enough to believe that he had to rid the world of the criminal element. Nor was he so egotistical to believe that his were the only skills that could be effective. He was sure, however, that Gabe Viligry and his posse were gonna need help.

It was 6:30 p.m. when the southbound arrived. Bass stubbed out his cigar, swallowed the last of his whiskey, and went to the bar to pay up. The bartender was a jovial-looking sort, young, wide grin, handlebar mustache, and dark hair parted in the middle and waxed down on his forehead.

"Say, uh, what's your name?

"Lucius, sir, a course I tell all the ladies I'm 'Luscious.'"

Bass grinned. He enjoyed saloons and thought all bartenders should be friendly. Congenial is what Sally would say.

"What'll it be?"

"Lucius, I'm 'bout to head home, so I'll pay up. What'd I owe you?"

"Okay, that's two whiskeys and a cigar. Be a dollar fifty. How'd you like that cigar?"

"It was fine. I'm no expert, though." Bass handed Lucius two dollars and said to keep the change.

# Stolen

"Thank you, sir. Anything else I can do for you?"

"Yeah, a matter of fact, you can sell me that pint of Old Overholt there. I gotta long trip home."

Lucius handed the bottle to Bass.

"' At's a dollar, sir."

Bass handed him another dollar. "Tell me Lucius, you ever been to Las Vegas out to New Mexico Territory?"

Lucius stopped wiping down the bar and looked at Bass. "Yes, sir. I was born there."

"Really. Tell me what you think of the place."

"Well, I ain't there anymore. That says somethin', I guess."

"Yes, it does. Why'd you leave?"

"Oh, mister, that town's much too fast for me. Too much everything and not enough of anything, if you follow. I had a couple of pals growin' up there. They stayed. 'Joined up with Las Gorras Blancas, the ah, White Caps. Fella named Vicente Silva. They call him Don Vicente like he's some kinda royalty. He runs everything in that town now. Didn't used ta'. 'Town used to be okay. Now it's all hookers and gambling halls—Lotsa' opium dens. I hear outlaws pay Silva to hide out there. Anyway, my friends were both killed rustlin' cows. Killed the rancher while doin' it. 'At was my Pa." The young man paused and looked away for a moment. "I got no Ma, so I sold out and left. I tell ya, if you have to go there, mister, my advice is don't."

Bass watched the grin reappear on the young man's face. He thanked him for the whiskey and walked out the door and into the street. He looked around at the people and buildings of Amarillo, all looking prosperous and new. Then he crossed the street to the telegraph office and sent a wire to Sally. It was a simple message:

*On my way.*

*– Love FFB*

He hopped onto the train just as it stated moving and settled into a bench by himself. He thought about the last week, everything that had happened. The two little girls, Avery and Alice, and now Maria. He thought about Chavez and the Mexicans he'd killed, about the young Comanche that jumped him. And all the time in the background was Sally and the baby, Theo, Marianna, Paulo, and Nesta. Good people.

He pulled the cork on the bottle of rye, took a long swallow, and thought about Lucius and what he'd said, and then he thought about the young sheriff, Viligry, up against much more than he could handle. There was a man certainly in need of help. Bass had always felt compassion

# Stolen

for the underdog most especially when the underdog was an honest lawman. He took his pistol from the holster, spun the cylinder several times, and thought *Hell. Somebody's gotta do it.*

# Stolen

Chapter 19

*10:15 a.m., January 5, 1888*

*TwainHeart Ranch*

*El Paso, Texas*

Bass got off the train at 5:30 a.m. and saw Theo Treece in a buckboard waiting for him.

"So, you couldn't a waited for a later train, get you here at a reasonable hour, huh?" 'Wind was chilly that morning just before dawn. Bass turned his collar up as he stepped off the platform onto the street.

"Thanks, Theo. I know you ain't used to ranch hours yet, but this is just the start of a typical day for us. Beat the sun risin' to start the day. How's Marianna? Bet she's better used to this hour than you."

"You're right there, Frank. She had coffee and a biscuit ready for me 'fore I left." Theo paused as he pulled his team to the left. "You look a little used, my friend. You feelin' all right, are ya?"

"Feel just fine now that I'm home. Need a hot bath and few hours sleep is all."

"Heard you found the girls. Out on the Llano. Feel good 'bout that don't you?"

# Stolen

"They found me is what happened. Them kids are a tough number, 'specially the older one, Ruth. I was asleep in my camp, and they woke me. Told a story of escape 'make anyone shiver."

"Well, you look pale, and Sally'll see it for sure. Did you get hurt out there?"

"Yeah, some. 'Saw a Doc, and he fixed me up. Sally ain't gonna like it, but what's done is done. Somethin' else she ain't gonna like. I gotta go back."

"What!? No, you're right. Sally'll skin you good. We've been checkin in on her almost every day this last week, and all she says is, 'he must be hurt, or he'd send a wire.' She's fine otherwise. 'Just worried over you.

"What you gotta go back for?"

"There's a young sheriff and some posse-men out in Las Vegas, tryin' to force justice on a town that won't have it. 'Kill 'em for tryin.' I need to bring 'em back."

"'Sat so? You know, I've never been to Las Vegas. I think I might tag along with you, see what's up."

"Thanks, Theo. You're a good man. Too good to waste on a place like that. You've come a long way, pard— but not quite far enough for a place like Las Vegas."

# Stolen

Then he walked back out to Theo and his ride home. The two men talked about several things: their joint venture in the feed business and the Longhorn herd that Theo wanted to start, but the conversation kept turning to Bass goin' back and how Sally would deal with it. Bass asked Theo to drop him at the gate. He wanted to walk up the drive and see the sun come up behind the house. He heard the cattle stirring in the pasture to the north and saw smoke coming from the kitchen stove and the hearth in the front room.

There were small patches of snow on either side of the path to the steps of the veranda. The air was cold and smelled of wood smoke. At the top of the stairs, he turned to watch the Rio a few hundred yards distant, steam rising off the slow-moving stream as the sun warmed the earth. Home. He'd returned here many times after more manhunts than he could recall. But it never felt more like home than it did now.

Sally threw open the doors and rushed to him in her robe and house shoes. She kissed him hard and held him as close as her body would allow. He hugged her shoulders and buried his face in her long auburn hair, kissing her neck and loving the smell of her.

# Stolen

"My God, Frederick. You look like hell, my love. Come in and let me see to you." Sally's face was near to crying as if she'd seen a suffering child. She took Bass by the hand and led him inside.

"The tub is all ready. I still have water on the stove for when this cools."

She started to undress him, kissing his body as each item of clothing came off. It was as intimate as they could be so close to her expected delivery date. When she removed his shirt, she noticed the bandaged arm and said, "What's this then? I should be used to this by now. What happened?" and when he turned around to explain, she saw the bandage over his middle and the bruised and blackened skin around it. Tears welled in her eyes, and her voice quavered.

"My word, Frederick, what have they done to you?"

"It looks a lot worse than it is, Sal. Really. I saw a real fine doctor, and he cured the infection . . ."

"The infection!? What from?"

"Well, I was camped near the Pecos, and late one night, the horses were actin' spooky. When I went to check, I was jumped by this fella, and he ah—he just—well, he stabbed me is what he did, Sal. But I'm fine now, just fine, and he's dead."

# Stolen

"Dear God. Stabbed? Frederick. Stabbed in the stomach?" Sally's face reflected the pain she felt whenever he was wounded. Bass always regretted having to admit he'd been hurt and then seeing the anguish in her eyes.

"Well, yes, but the blade didn't go in very far 'cause a' my heavy clothes, see. But I had to cauterize it with my blade 'cause it bled some. That's why it's dark. It turned septic on me, but the Doc cured it, and I'm just fine."

"And your arm, dear?"

"Shot from behind as I was taking the girls to the train. Doc stitched it up good as new. No infection."

"Well, that's some good news, if being shot could ever be good news."

"Really, Sal, I'm fine now. Knew I would be 'cause I was comin' home to you." He smiled at her then, and she tried to smile back but wound up blowing her nose instead.

Sally carefully removed the bandaging and Bass eased himself into the tub to let warm water soak away the previous six days. Sally seated herself in a chair she pulled in from the front room and sponged Bass's neck and shoulders.

The stitches in his arm and stomach were getting wet, and he'd heard that shouldn't happen, but after everything the wounds had been through, he doubted a little hot water could do worse. And Sally would apply some astringent and rebandage him anyway.

"Who was this doctor then I'm so indebted to?" Sally asked.

"Name was Randal Fontane. He was medic in the war and was workin' as a general healer for man and beast in that small town."

"Was?"

Bass didn't answer right away. "Yes. He was killed by the man who shot me in the arm. Don't know why. I imagine the Doc treated him for the bullet wound I delivered when he ambushed me. 'Good man done in by a bad one. Happens too often. Anyway, I killed the man for it." Bass closed his eyes and settled back against the tub. He knew he'd have to break the news about going to Las Vegas soon. The trip couldn't wait. But for now, he just wanted to be with Sally.

The rest of the day was spent in the barn and around the yard. Sally was strictly limited in activity, and Bass was just as happy doing small chores and caring for the animals. He spent an hour or more with Emma, currying her, cleaning her stall, and checking her shoes. It had been some time since Emma had seen the farrier, and she was

# Stolen

probably due. Bass remembered the time when he would do it himself, but smithing is hot, dirty, and time-consuming work, and his schedule no longer allowed it.

Sally spent time first in the baby's room and then in the barn with Glory. The little chestnut mare was just as sweet-tempered as she could be and certainly disproved the old warnings about 'red mares.' Bass thought the horse could sense Sally's condition and behaved especially quiet when Sally was in her stall. Sally never tired of Glory's company and missed the time they spent together on the plains.

Supper was at six. Bass treated himself to a cigar on the front porch (normally Sally was fine with cigar smoke, but recently she couldn't stand the smell), accompanied as usual by a tall, iced whiskey. They ate sitting next to each other rather than at opposite ends of the table. That way, they were both able to view the Rio through the large front windows. Sally had roasted a goose that Paulo had brought by the previous day. They all knew in advance of Bass's return, and Theo had drawn the short straw for the early pickup at the depot.

After dinner, they sat at the fire on either side of the hearth, Bass with his brandy and Sally her sherry. Bass had

# Stolen

been agonizing over the coming conversation all day, but it had to be said, and now was the time . . .

"Sally, I need—"

"I know, you have to go back. I knew as soon as I heard from Bart about the young sheriff from Hartley. Please don't worry about me, but please don't be long either. Bringing justice to those villains is far more important than my selfish wishes, though I would it weren't so." Sally's eyes were clear, and her voice was strong. "When must you leave?"

"Tomorrow . . . early. The train'll stop at Hot Springs for water, and I can send a wire from there to let you know if the trains are on time. I plan to ride the train first to Albuquerque and then on to Las Vegas. I figure five hours for the first leg and four or so for the second. With water stops, delays, and whatnot, I should be there after dark tomorrow evening. 'Course, I'll let you know."

"Have you ever met this young man? What's his name? The sheriff?"

"Viligry? No, I haven't, but Avery Matlock thinks well of him. He's young but has some military training, so that's in his favor. To hear Avery talk, he sounds like a pretty level-headed guy."

"Who'll be taking you into the depot?"

# Stolen

"Paulo. He's taking me in at four, and the train leaves at 5:10 a.m. 'Same one that brought me here from Amarillo."

"Well, my love, you'd better get to bed then. I plan to knit some before I come up."

"You're right. And thank you for understandin', Sal. You know how much I love you, and it's painful to have to leave again. I promise this'll be the last one of these for some time to come."

"I hope so, for your sake, as much as mine and the baby's. But I also know your heart, Frederick. I know it's impossible for you to turn away from people who need your help. In the end, that's a big reason why I love you so. Good night, my love."

Bass hugged Sally as strongly as he dared and kissed her cheek and neck before heading upstairs.

Bass stripped down to his drawers and opened the closet to make ready his Walker Colts and the 1886 Winchester he routinely carried. He threw his saddle bags on the bed and, on one side, packed in a clean shirt, trousers, and drawers. On the other side, he packed some ammunition for the four weapons he carried and left room for a bottle of Old Overholt. He did not pack his shaving kit, mostly to make the personal statement that his trip

# Stolen

would be short. He wanted to hug Sally one more time, so he opened the bedroom door to go downstairs. From the top landing, he could hear her quietly sobbing as she sat on the divan, staring out the window into the dark. He walked back into the bedroom, cursing the nature he'd been born with and vowing to change his life as soon as he returned.

# Stolen

Chapter 20

*5:00 a.m., January 6, 1888*
*EP & SW Passenger Depot*
*EL Paso, Texas.*

Paulo Armendez pulled his team up at the loading platform just as the conductor was picking up the stepping stools for the passenger coach. Bass saw the brakeman at the rear of the last car swinging his lantern and knew he had to rush. The train was leaving early. Bass only had time to grab his rifle, pistols, and saddlebags and say thanks to Paulo for the ride in. Then he ran to catch the train. As it was, he had to throw his gear aboard and then leap for the grab rail on the landing between cars. Once inside, he settled himself in the dining car and ordered coffee. He had no idea why the coffee on the train was so much better than he could make at home, but it was.

Half an hour into the trip, the conductor walked through collecting tickets or punching those of passengers headed beyond the next stop. Bass bought a ticket to Albuquerque for eighteen dollars and asked the conductor about a connection to Las Vegas. The man was older, his skin was a dusty white color, and he looked generally frail.

# Stolen

When Bass asked about Las Vegas, the older man lifted his head and eyed Bass suspiciously. Bass opened his jacket, revealing his badge, and the conductor relaxed and said, "It's another four hours past your stop on a Local; there ain't no Express. 'Usually runs on time, but not always. 'Might have to cool your heels in Burque for a spell. Harvey House and Silver Bridle Saloon are right outside the station."

Bass assumed they'd stop at Las Cruces, but the train only picked up mail there and went on to the stop at Fort Selden. Bass was very familiar with Selden. It was here during last summer that he and Theo located a gold shipment hidden by his father, a Major in the Ninth Cavalry. It was the culmination of a long chase of renegade soldiers and one particularly evil Captain that Bass had the pleasure of dispatching personally.

The train was rolling again after a twenty-minute stop, and Bass decided not to get off. He'd had enough of Fort Selden to last quite a while. His plan was to stretch his legs at Hot Springs and send a wire to Sally just because he promised he would. It had taken over two hours to reach Fort Selden. Bass estimated another two to Hot Springs, maybe longer; there were scheduled stops at Salem and

# Stolen

Caballo for water and mail. Additional passengers, too, probably.

Bass bought two biscuits and a newspaper from a porter and settled into a window seat to read. He finished his coffee and biscuits quickly; he was hungrier than he thought, and he began reading the Las Cruces Tiempo, noting it was dated the previous week. He'd just gotten into the farm report on page two when his eyes started closing, and his head began falling forward.

He woke when the train stopped at Salem but nodded off quickly when the train started moving. The stop at Caballo was longer and several passengers climbed aboard, one an attractive young woman with a baby. Bass smiled as he watched her play with the infant and could just barely hear the soft coos and gurgles from the baby. He checked his Elgin watch and wound it a bit. He had forgotten to this morning. He estimated they'd arrive in Hot Springs near eleven and Albuquerque five hours later. He was awake now and decided to go back to the bar for more coffee. The conductor was passing through checking tickets, so Bass tried to strike up a conversation.

"Names Bass, Frank Bass. Deputy US Marshal in El Paso. And you are . . . ?"

"Kinda busy right now, Marshal. Lemme finish my rounds, and I'll buy you a drink."

Bass had always been proud of the fact that he'd never turned down free liquor, so he smiled and nodded as the man went about his business. Thirty minutes later, the conductor came back and sat next to Bass at the bar. He made a signal to the barman, and soon, two whiskeys appeared in front of them.

"Homer Fielding, pleased to meetcha." The old man said as he extended his hand.

"Like I said, Frank Bass, US Deputy Marshal."

"Nice to meet you, Frank. You headed to Las Vegas on, ah . . . business?"

"Yes, I am, Homer. Young sheriff and his posse are there, and I believe they might need some help."

"Few honest lawmen ain't gonna make a difference in that Gomorrah, son. Best collect your sheriff and whoever else he's got and high tail it home. Let that cesspool swallow itself and sink into the sand."

"' Can't. 'Promised a man I'd punish the villains who stole his children."

"Oh. That kidnappin' up north? Heard about it. You find them children and give them fellas what for, Marshal."

# Stolen

"Girls are ok, safe, and back with their family. But I'm gonna see 'bout the head man that ordered the thing. Say, how long you been with the railroad?"

"Thirty years, man and boy. 'Started layin' track when I was a young man in the late 50s. 'Stayed with it through the war and seen the Company grow like jeepers. Engineered at one time, and now I'm punchin' tickets. Let you in on a secret. I'm blind as a bat, heh heh. I can't see the writin' on the tickets no more, just pretend to. Punch a couple holes; hell, I can't see what I'm doin'. Figure folks'll get off when they're s'posed to. I can't see to count the money no more, but most folks are honest, and them that ain't; I figure they need to ride bad enough to cheat, welcome to it. Won't hurt the Company none. Don't tell no one now, 'spoil the fun."

Bass laughed right along with the old man and hoped he had the same kind of attitude when he got older.

"Oh, Homer, almost forgot, I know a conductor works on the train between Amarillo and Albuquerque. Name's Clancy, ah . . . last name of . . . ah—"

"Mulacky?" The old man lost his smile and swallowed his whiskey.

"Right, yeah. You know him?"

# Stolen

"Good friend of mine, Frank. He's dead. Some Mexican outlaw cut his throat. They found him when the train got to 'Burque. Mexican was gone."

Bass closed his eyes, picturing Clancy's face as he handed out the supplies Bass needed in Agua Negra Chiquita.

"My God, Homer. I'm sorry." Both men were quiet for a moment.

"Welp. Better get back to work. Nice meetin' ya, Frank."

Frank nodded as Homer left, still thinking about Clancy Mulacky. "What was that Mexican's name? de Storano, that's it. Miguel de Storano."

The train made its scheduled stop in Hot Springs at 11:15 a.m. Fifteen minutes late. The schedule called for water and coal at this stop, so the passengers would have nearly ninety minutes to stretch, get lunch, 'use the comfort facilities behind the Harvey House or shop. Bass went first to the telegraph window and sent a short wire to Sally as he'd promised.

> *My Love,*
>
> *Hot Springs for lunch – Albuquerque around five. Las Vegas late. Will send when*
>
> *I arrive. Love always – FFB.*

# Stolen

Bass walked down the block to the Signal Lamp Café and sat at the counter. The Signal Lamp was like a hundred other cafés he'd been in. A long wooden counter with cane-back wooden stools, seven or eight tables for four, and tables for two in front of the windows. There were always two windows on either side of the door, and the curtains usually were faded red and white checked. There was a stove and cooks hidden from view, and waitresses in gingham skirts and comfortable-looking shoes.

Her name was Dora, and she was born and raised in Hot Springs. 'Went to school through sixth grade and had neat looking penmanship, or rather penmanship, Bass thought because she kept the stub of a pencil behind her ear or in the pocket of her apron. She said most travelers liked the food because it tasted good and 'stayed put' as she said. This meant it didn't run through your system while traveling for a long stretch after eating if you got her drift.

Bass ordered the Blue Plate, which today was roast pork, apple sauce, and green beans. He washed it all down with a soda drink Dora liked called Coca-Cola. The Signal Lamp Café had recently received its first shipment of the drink in bottles from back east, and Dora sold it whenever she could. Bass liked it, but he had to drink it without ice,

# Stolen

which he preferred because he felt it enhanced the 'bubble water.' It was sweet, but not too sweet like some others he tried, and 'seemed to perk him up quite a bit after eating.

He still had some time, so he stopped at Gladstone's Saloon and Card Parlor next door. Again, he sat at the bar about halfway down the length of it. The room was narrow and not very deep. Bass only counted four card tables and assumed that Mr. Gladstone made his living primarily by selling liquor. Bass ordered rye from the bartender, again without ice, and tried making conversation with the short, middle-aged bartender. His name was Ira and that's about all Bass could get the man to commit to on short notice, so Bass bought a cheroot from a box on a shelf behind the bar and smoked as he sipped his rye. At 12:15 p.m., he swallowed what was left of his rye, stubbed out the cigar, and headed back down the block to the train. At 12:35 p.m., he felt the train lurch forward as the whistle sounded. He looked at his Elgin and estimated another four or four and a half hours to Burque.

# Stolen

Chapter 21

*4:05 p.m., January 6, 1888*
*E. P. & SW Terminal*
*Albuquerque, New Mexico Territory*

The train was early, according to Bass's estimate, by at least a half hour. He collected his gear from the baggage handler's cart and went into the depot to check the schedule. He left his pistols, rifles, and satchel behind the ticket counter in the porter's room. Content with their safety there, Bass went back to the front of the depot to find a schedule board. He found the chalkboard with the schedule and checked out today's departures. There was a train leaving at 6:00 p.m. that included Las Vegas in its list of stops, but there were four cities and towns ahead of it on the schedule.

There were stops in Lamy, Glorieta, San Jose, and Serafina, all for mail, water, or coal. This would put him in Las Vegas well after 10 p.m. He wanted to arrive after dark but not so late that the town was closed down. He knew the only people out and about at that hour would be drunks, hookers and drunken hookers. Sure, there'd be a few Sharpies shillin' liquored up rubes, but Bass wanted to get a feel for the whole population of the town. The church goin' Bible readin, backbone of the town. They were there. No matter how wide open a town is or how loose law enforcement might be, there'd still be folks who called it home. Bass wanted a feel for how strongly those people felt and 'could they be counted on in a pinch.

He shook his head, accepting that his arrival time would be what it would be. He needed to take the train at six and get to Las Vegas whenever it got there. The population he was looking for might be more visible in the daylight hours anyway.

As he stood in the busy depot, Bass decided he'd seen enough train travel to last him for a while. It was necessary for this case because so much ground had to be covered in so little time. But he still preferred the tried and true method of manhunts on horseback. He also decided that if he was bein' honest with himself, the notion of days away from Sally and the baby was not a happy one. He still enjoyed his work, except for the parts where he gets stabbed and shot, and 'didn't want to quit it outright, but maybe there was some kinda middle ground he could find.

Paolo'd been helping him a lot with prisoner transfers and court appearances and such. It was safe work, and you were home more often, but Bass knew he'd be

# Stolen

bored down to his boot heels if that was all he did. Still, something needed to be worked out. He made a note to check with District Judge Clarence Hobart and see if maybe he could think of a solution.

Bass walked into the Albuquerque Harvey House inside the Alvarado Hotel and sat at one of the booths they had just installed. He looked around and decided that he liked the idea of the privacy the booth gave, but he thought the backs of the benches were too straight. It was supper time and the café had become pretty busy, so Bass scooted himself over to a table against the side wall and waited there. Before long, a pretty girl in a black and white outfit came to his table.

"How can I help you, sir?"

"What's the house special today?"

"We have several items to choose from, but I recommend the ham and scalloped potatoes. It's the chef's favorite and very reasonably priced."

Bass decided this was not the usual café waitress. She was polite, spoke well, and her appearance was neat and well-groomed. Most of the women servers in cafés and greasy spoons he frequented were just as rowdy and unkempt as their customers.

# Stolen

Bass ate quietly, occasionally looking about the place and admiring the hotel and the people milling about. He finished his ham and potatoes and nursed the iced tea the girl had recommended, *"I'm sorry, alcohol isn't served at the Harvey House."* The tea was sweet and chilled with real ice, not just a handful of snow like most other places. And the price was right: six bits for everything. Bass decided he'd look for more of these places as he traveled.

He left an extra quarter and walked out to the train depot, just next door, and stopped at a news and smoke stand. He bought a newspaper, The Albuquerque Morning Journal, and a cigar, a Romeo and Julieta #1 Corona from Cuba. He planned to smoke the cigar in the depot as he read the paper. He still had an hour before the train's departure for Las Vegas.

He sat in one of the rows of benches organized to face the platform for arriving and departing trains. To his right was the telegraph office, and to his left was the Alvarado Hotel and the Harvey House. He opened the paper and read an article on the death of the former police chief of Albuquerque, one General R.H. Anderson, of pneumonia at his home. Evidently, he had been ill with a cold several days in advance, and took a turn for the worse. He was an older man, of course, but Bass thought what a

# Stolen

sad and mundane end to a life obviously filled with action and command. He thought about it some more, quite a while by Bass's standards, and he came to the conclusion that was a kind of selfish opinion, that a man of action deserved somehow a more glorious ending. He decided it doesn't make much difference how you die, that it's much more important how you lived and how many lives are better off for having touched yours. Bass finally gave up on the subject. It was getting too deep and a little too morbid for him, and besides, Bass wasn't ever gonna die anyway. He knew that.

Bass checked his Elgin and decided he still had time for a whiskey before he boarded the train. He went back to the Alvarado Hotel lobby and, from there, entered the Los Barrilitos Saloon and took a stool at the near end of the bar. A burly-looking bartender in a white apron over a green shirt approached him and only began smiling as he got nearer to Bass.

"Help you, mister?"

"Whiskey, please, rye if you got it."

"We got it all right. Ain't got no ice, though."

"'At's ok. Bring her on."

The barman grunted as he turned, and Bass heard him mutter something about 'drunks and their whiskey' to

# Stolen

the shelves behind him. The man turned back with a bottle and smirked as he poured and said. "'At'll be six bits, fella."

"Hmm. Pretty steep for a short pour."

"What'd you say?"

"Said, lotta money for not much whiskey."

"Why, you saddle bum, who do you think you're talkin' to here?"

"Believe I'm talkin to a sassy barkeep who pours a short whiskey and charges too much for it."

"Why you worth—" the bartender was beginning to climb over the bar, but he wasn't fast enough. Bass pulled one of his Walker Colts and whipped it alongside his head, knocking him backward into a stack of clean glassware. The glassware broke, and heads turned, and as soon as the bartender hit the floor, two mountainous men in derby hats approached Bass with pretty obvious intent to reciprocate.

"Now just a minute here, boys, that fella was comin' at me all steely-eyed and stiff; I had to defend myself." Bass tried defusing the situation, but the men kept advancing. Before any hands were thrown, a smaller, less aggressive, and definitely more female voice was heard from somewhere behind the bar.

# Stolen

"Butch, Herman. It's okay, boys, it's okay. I know this guy. You can go back to the office."

Butch and Herman turned almost in unison and walked away without saying a word.

"Frank! Frank Bass, you ol' coyote, how've you been?"

Bass recognized the voice immediately and called back, "Doxie Slayter, I am surprised."

"What'd you say to Howard to make him want to wallop you across the bar?"

"Howard's a surly nugget, Dox. And he pours short. What's a shot of whiskey cost here?"

"Fifty cents, same as everywhere."

"Well, he's charging six bits a pop. Guess he's keepin' the extra quarter."

"Well, damn. I'll have a talk with him on his way out the door. Surprised nobody ever spoke up about it before."

"Most folks come through here are travelin', Dox. They ain't regulars."

"By God, I've missed you, Bass. You look good." Doxie Slayter was nearly fifteen years older than Bass. She wore a blond wig, heavy makeup, and a shiny red dress with black lace trim that pushed her considerable charms upward and out.

Doxie used to run Slayter's Parisian Salon in El Paso until the city council required her to leave town. 'Seems Doxie also ran a high-priced Cat House in her salon, and some of the upstanding members of El Paso society took issue with that enterprise. Bass had never been a customer, but he liked to drink there, and he liked talking with Doxie, too.

"You're lookin' pretty prosperous yourself, Doxie. Tell me, you really need those two goons?"

"Hell yeah. I got twelve young beauties upstairs who gets nervous 'bout some of our clientele. I don't want any of 'em hurt. Mostly on general principles, you understand, but also it's bad for business. One gets hurt, and four or five leave with her."

"Ah. I see. Albuquerque City Council more lenient than El Paso's, huh?"

"You bet. Three of 'em are weeklies. Need things the wifey won't do for 'em at home. So, you still Marshalin'?"

"Yes, I am."

# Stolen

"You on a manhunt now?"

"Kinda, I got a well-intentioned young sheriff and his posse up in Las Vegas. I'm gonna try to get 'em out quietly. Let sleeping dogs lie kinda thing. If they haven't already busted open the hornet nest."

Doxie's expression became more serious. "Dearie, you be awful careful up there. It's bad, real bad. They have a town sheriff named Belcher, 'don't know if that's his real name, but he's meaner 'an a snake twice as deadly. He has, I think, five deputies, all fast, all ruthless, and not a single conscience among 'em. And then there's Silva. 'Just as evil as he can be. He runs the White Caps up there, and they's just as vicious a group of humans as you'll find anywhere. Get in, get your people, and get out 'fast as you can. I ain't got too many friends left, and you're too good to lose."

"Well, geeze, Dox. Thanks for the up-liftin' talk."

"I'm serious, Frank. You should be, too."

"I'll be careful, Dox. Say, you be careful too. Keep those councilmen happy so you can earn a living."

"Ha, a living. I'm near to retirin' Frank. Say, maybe I'll come back to El Paso all respectable and turned out in proper clothes. Whaddaya think about that?"

# Stolen

"El Paso's gain, Doxie. Though I prob'ly wouldn't recognize ya."

"Ha ha, Bass. I've missed you, boy." Doxie paused and looked Bass in the eye. "You listen to Doxie and be careful, hear?"

"I will, Dox. Thanks."

Doxie Slayter turned and went through a door behind the bar. Bass checked his Elgin and picked up his gear for the walk back to the depot and passenger platform. As he left, he could hear Doxie's voice as she called out, "Howard? Get your fat can in here."

Bass stood on the passenger platform with fifteen or twenty others. His Walkers were slung over his shoulder, his kit was in his left hand, and his Winchester in his right. Among the other passengers waiting, he figured he looked the most likely traveler to Las Vegas. Once the conductor put the stepstool down, people began boarding. Bass waited to the last and settled into a padded bench toward the rear of the car. He hoped he'd be able to sleep. The sun was low in the west and had all but settled behind Mt. Taylor for the evening. A few of the window shades on the coach were drawn, but several were still raised with their windows opened, Bass thought, to rid the car of the cigar smell. At 6:05 p.m., according to his Elgin, the whistle blew, and the

# Stolen

bell rang, announcing the train's departure. Bass picked up his paper, planning to read until his eyes got heavy.

The first stop was for mail only at the San Felipe Pueblo in the north valley. The train hardly slowed at all. The next stop was Santo Domingo, where the train stopped at the passenger terminal, and several people came aboard. No one got off, Bass noticed, so there was no baggage fumbling to deal with. Bass was still wide awake after Santo Domingo, reading the paper, had not had the effect he'd hoped for. It might have been the occasional bumps that shook the car and rattled the windows that kept him awake. Or maybe the rapid side-to-side jarring of the car as it traveled over the uneven roadbeds. One thing was certain, he thought, *the damn springs in the undercarriage don't work worth spit.*

The scenery had changed after San Filipe. They were no longer following the Rio but were traveling now through the desert south of the Sangre de Cristo Mountains, headed to the split in the mainline in the desert, about six miles southwest of La Cienega. It had become too dark to make out anything of interest. Bass was going by the track map posted on the side of the car at either end near the door.

# Stolen

He began thinking how much smaller the frontier had become thanks to the railroads. You could now travel a distance in one day what it would usually take three or four to cover on horseback. On top of that, the passenger traveled in relative comfort, protected from the weather and the other natural bothers inherent in touring in the open air. And it wasn't just passenger travel he considered. The railroads had made moving freight and mail much more rapid. Goods usually only available in eastern cities were now commonplace in borderland towns and cities. Shopkeepers could place orders via telegraph to manufacturers back east and expect to have their delivery within a fortnight. And when considering modern advances and conveniences, the telegraph was another example too often taken for granted. Personal and commercial messages could be transmitted across the country in a matter of hours. There was even talk of completing telegraph service to Europe. Bass wasn't exactly sure how that would work, but smarter folks than him would come up with a way.

Bass had thought himself into a greater appreciation for train travel. He stood up and walked to the rear of the car to look at the track map once again. He saw that a while past Santo Domingo, the tracks split; one headed northeast toward Santa Fe and the other to the south through small

# Stolen

desert towns like Waldo and passed the Devil's Throne at Los Cerrillos. Then, after a while, the track turned north back toward the mountains, winding about through the Glorieta pass and eventually descending back to the desert floor. The track turned northward again at Serafina and went through Telcolte at the eastern base of the Sangre de Cristos, and finally, three and a half hours after leaving Albuquerque, they would arrive in Las Vegas. Looking at the map, Bass suddenly recognized the immense achievement that the railroad was. He walked back to his seat and took a couple of long swallows of rye from his bottle. Then he leaned back, pulled his hat down over his eyes, and let the rocking rhythm of the train lull him to sleep.

Bass checked his Elgin and noted 9:45 p.m. when the wheels stopped. It was late, but not too late.

# Stolen

Chapter 22

*10:00 p.m., January 6, 1888*
*Outside the Passenger terminal*
*Las Vegas, New Mexico Territory*

Bass stood at the entrance to EP & SW terminal facing the town of Las Vegas. It was late enough that most towns would have the oil lamps snuffed by now, but they showed bright tonight in businesses and buildings around what appeared to be some distance away, the town Plaza. A light rail trolley was available to carry travelers to the Plaza. According to the map of the town, the trolley ran down Douglas and turned at Twelfth Street, and then again at National across the Galinas River, and then circled the Plaza for the return trip. Bass had no luggage to speak of, and the weather was chilly but clear, so he decided that rather than wait for a ride, he'd enjoy stretching his legs and walking. He saw a large building on the Plaza Square, and as he crossed a footbridge over the Galinas River, a sign heralding the Plaza Hotel of Las Vegas shone brightly.

He thought he might stand out strolling through town with a gun belt over his shoulder and a rifle in his hand, but the people he passed, and there were more than a

# Stolen

few, paid little mind. He turned west again on National Avenue and walked to the main entrance of The Plaza Hotel Ciudad Las Vegas. The Plaza and the area around the hotel was very active, with people milling about. Everywhere were signs and handbills advertising the Monte Suma Hot Springs, which Bass had never heard of but was probably responsible for some visitors being out tonight. Music and loud chatter, along with sporadic laughter and shouting, spilled from several saloons on the opposite sides of the park. Bass was too tired to pay much attention, so he just shook his head and went inside to check-in.

He entered through double doors to a lobby decorated in white and gold wallpaper. Dark red carpet and polished brass metalwork were all around. It reminded him of the hotel in Cheyenne where he'd first gotten to know Sally. 'Pretty fancy place. Elegant. And seeing that kind of quality in a town that was known to be corrupt bothered Bass. *Who paid for all this, all this finery?* The answer came to him; of course, crime did. It had to be. The town had no industry no capital businesses. It wasn't a cattle town or agricultural area. Some folks came here for the Hot Springs he supposed, but he knew that couldn't provide funding for the riches on display. It had to be criminal activity that supported this kind of generous living. The

317

area outside the park seemed shuttered, and he couldn't say for certain, but strictly by its reputation, Bass believed that the whole town, in some way or another, owed its existence to the criminal element.

Bass approached the front desk and noted that the clerk was sorting mail into mail slots at the far end of the counter. He tapped the bell and set his gun belt on the counter next to the registration log. It made a noticeable thud and the clerk looked over with a sneer.

"Just a minute fella. Busy here, all right?" He said.

Bass had just finished a grueling day of travel and only wanted a bed, but he bit his tongue and waited for the man to finish. He was a younger man in a dark jacket and gray, pinstriped pants. He limped when he walked, favoring his right leg. His short, dark hair was parted in the middle. He was clean-shaven and smelled of lilac water.

"What is it you want, sir?"

"Well, I'm standin here in your hotel, at the registration desk, buster. I'd like a room for the night, maybe tomorrow night, too." The clerk didn't seem intimidated by the tall man, dressed in black and bristling with weaponry. He just nodded.

# Stolen

"I figured that, mister. Most single men who come here also want a little companionship as well. So, what is it you want?"

Bass looked around the lobby again and said, "Doubt I could afford the rates, Sonny. Just a room'll do."

The clerk scoffed and turned to pick a key off the board behind him. "Eighteen, top of the stairs all the way down on the right. Got a view of the hotel privies. Sign the book."

Bass signed in as Frederick F. Bass and dropped the pencil in front of the clerk.

"'At's eight dollars a night in advance; if you want two nights, it's seventeen fifty."

"Pretty steep. Small town hotel. Why is it seventeen-fifty 'stead of sixteen?"

The clerk looked at the log and answered. "Town ain't that small, Frederick. And two nights draws an extended stay fee. Anything else?"

"Nope, can't afford anything else." Bass paid with a twenty-dollar bill and put the change in his pocket.

"Most a' your guests here for the Hot Springs?"

# Stolen

"Don't know, don't ask. A few folks go up there, I guess. 'Water stinks, and it's always too hot. You done yet?"

"Has anyone ever complimented you on your charming manners?" Bass smiled.

"Good night, mister."

"Didn't think so." Bass took his key, picked up his pistol belt, and climbed the stairs. Room eighteen was right where the clerk said it would be, down the hall on the right.

Inside, Bass lit the lamp on the bedside table and set his rifle and pistols on a chair on the opposite wall from the bed. He checked his Elgin, 10:45 p.m., and then hung his heavy coat and suit jacket in the chiffarobe against the wall opposite the bed. An armchair and side table stood next to it. The mattress felt comfortable enough, and the two pillows on the bed were down-stuffed instead of wadded-up cotton. Bass stripped down to his drawers and drank a short whiskey he poured into one of the glasses that sat on the side table next to the chair. He sat on the bed, snuffed the lamp, and lay back on the pillow.

He lay thinking in the near-dark room about his plan for finding Viligry, a man he'd never met and had no idea of his appearance. The town was small but not so small that a man might easily be found. And Bass knew he

# Stolen

couldn't ask around for a Texas sheriff. Surly Viligry would have sense enough to keep his badge hidden. A prolonged stay in Las Vegas, New Mexico Territory, searching for a man who probably was taking pains to keep from being found, was not on Bass's list of favorite things to do. The room was warming up, and the bed and the pillows were comfortable. Bass was asleep twenty minutes after he snuffed the lamp.

# Stolen

*6:45 a.m., January 7, 1888*
*Plaza Hotel Ciudad Las Vegas*
*New Mexico Territory.*

Bass woke to the unmistakable sounds of a Smithy's hammer on metal. He rolled out of bed, put on his heavy woolen trousers over the cotton long drawers he usually wore in winter, and slid on his boots. He closed his sheepskin-lined jacket over his long-sleeve undershirt and, thus attired, paid a visit to one of the hotel privies behind the building. As he emerged through one of the exits, the clangs of hammer and anvil became more defined, and he quickly spotted the reason. Well, to the rear of the hotel was a livery barn and corral. The Smith's shed was across the corral from the barn.

It occurred to Bass that if several men on horseback were to visit a town as part of an investigation, they might well look to board their animals rather than leave them exposed to the elements. '*Good a' place to start as any*, thought Bass as he returned to his room. After using the basin in his room to clean his teeth, face, and hands, he finished dressing, closed and locked his Walkers and the Winchester in the chifforobe, and went downstairs to find breakfast.

# Stolen

The Plaza Hotel had a smallish dining room off the lobby, and as soon as Bass entered, the familiar aromas of fresh biscuits and bacon struck with a vengeance. He became ravenous, remembering he hadn't eaten since Albuquerque yesterday afternoon, and sat down at a table without being directed to it. He chose it because it had a view of the Plaza, and in the gray light of the day, Bass wanted a good look at the town with the worst reputation in the territory. Normally, he would first check in with the local law enforcement office, whoever that might be, but in this case, he wasn't yet ready to reveal his presence. When the time came, if it did, he would pay an official call, but for now, he wanted to remain anonymous.

The waitress stopped by his table first to scold him for not waiting to be seated and then asked his pleasure from the menu on the chalkboard. She was older, short, and heavy, with black hair tied in a tight bun on top of her head. She wore some rouge on her cheeks, but that was all. Pink gingham dress and white apron. She said her name was Maevis.

"You know, they get peevish if you seat yourself here. We get quite a few regulars, and they like their own tables. This one you're sittin at is Harry Roman's table. He's a councilman. If he comes in, you gotta move."

"Say, I'm sorry, mam, I had no idea. Would it suit you better if I moved?"

The woman smiled. "My, you're a polite one. No, you stay here. If Mr. Fatbottom, councilman, comes in, he'll have to wait. 'Usually goes to the bar first anyway. What can I get you, dearie?"

"Ah, coffee, of course, black. Maybe half 'dozen eggs, scrambled. 'Couple slices of ham and a rasher of bacon oughta do it."

"Spuds?"

"Huh?"

"Spuds, taters, you know. You want spuds?"

"Oh. No thanks, Maevis. 'Believe I'll pass on them, but I'd take biscuits and gravy if ya got 'em?

"We do. Be right back." Maevis slid her pencil back behind her ear and left. Bass reread the prices on the chalkboard. Just like the hotel, they were beyond steep.

The café started to fill up, mostly with men dressed well in business clothes, and soon Bass could hardly hear himself think for the chatter going on. He tried focusing on the comings and goings of the people on the Plaza. He noted they all seemed to be in a hurry and keeping to themselves. He was facing the direction he'd come from and could make out the train depot and a flurry of activity

# Stolen

around the entrance. He presumed a train had arrived and people were there to meet passengers.

He noticed more than a few men sleeping on benches in the Plaza in the dead of winter. It was custom among small-town sheriffs in winter to take in drunks and vagrants to the extent that the cots in their jail cells would allow as a humanitarian gesture. Bass counted nine men on benches curled up in the cold. One didn't even have shoes. The railroad provided many wonderful benefits for the country in general, but it also provided a convenient mode of transport for the vagrant and transient populations to move about from city to city and town to town. These people would prey on the citizenry, markets, businesses, and any place where the backdoor was open to petty theft and chicanery. Usually they'd move on when local law enforcement made it too difficult for them to exist in their style. Seeing so many 'down and outers' here told Bass that maybe the local law's attention was focused elsewhere.

The rest of the town wasn't viewable from the café, so Bass finished eating and walked outside. The clouds were low and dark, and chilled gusts were sweeping down the mountains and through town. Bass smelled moisture in the air, which meant either snow or rain, depending on the temperature. The thermometer on the side of the hotel said forty-four degrees, so right now, it was too warm for snow. Being this close to the mountains provided the town with some protection from violent weather, but summer and winter storms were still a threat.

Bass walked back around the building to the livery and the Smithy's shop. It wasn't much more than a lean-to with sides, but the forge and bellows kept the area warm even in gusting wind. The Smith was a young man, powerfully built, as most smiths were, with dark hair under a flat cap worn backward.

"You the owner?"

"Yeah. Whaddaya want? 'Busy."

"I see. I'm interested in renting a saddle horse for a day, maybe two. Can you help me?"
The smith dropped his hammer and set his tongs on the forge.

"S'pose so. 'Got three mares and an older gelding in the barn. Sweet-tempered one's bridle-wise. It's two dollars a day, American."

"Two dollars a day! 'Lotta money bridle wise or not."

"Take it or leave it. Like I said, pal, I'm busy."

"Huh, I'll leave it for now. What's your name?"

# Stolen

"None a' your business, bub. Ain't lookin for any new friends."

"Yeah, me neither. Well, can you tell me if there's any new boarders in your barn? I'm supposed to meet my brother here." The smith started pumping the bellows, and sparks shot from the forge in Bass's direction.

"No new borders. Now beat it. Like I said—"

"You're busy. Yeah, I got that." Bass turned away and headed back to the Plaza. On the way, he decided he'd send telegrams to Sally and Avery, so he headed back to the train depot and the telegraph office.

The wind had become steadier, and Bass noticed the temperature dropping. He still thought checking livery barns for new boarders was a good idea, but he wanted to get a description of Viligry from Avery so he could ask at hotels as well without having to see the guest log. Hotels sometimes were protective of their clientele.

He sent the first message to Sally.

*Arrived late last night. Staying at Plaza Hotel Las Vegas. Alls well. 'Hope same for you. Love FFB*

Next, he sent one to Avery.

*Send Viligry description to Frederick Bass Plaza Hotel Las Vegas.*

327

# Stolen

While he was there it occurred to him to send a request to an old friend, Justice Clarence Hobart. He paid four dollars each for special handling and walked back out. Next, he thought he'd walk around the Plaza and take a look at the various businesses on the side streets. He was looking in particular for smaller hotels, a newspaper office, or a post office, and, of course other livery barns, which he assumed would be located somewhere near the train depot. As he walked, the weather became more threatening, so after examining the shingles and signposts of the first few blocks of National Ave, down to Gonzales Street, he ducked into one of the saloons that fronted the Plaza. He didn't notice the name of the place, only that it was open, had a polished wooden bar down one side, and that it might be friendlier than some of the other service providers in town. As was his custom, he sat at the bar near to the door which was also near to the heat stove. There was nothing behind the bar to indicate the name of the place, so he tried reading the lettering on the front window backward: draC higH smmiS ydduB.

"Huh, Buddy Simms High Card. 'Not very crowded for a Saturday. Early though, I guess." Bass hailed a

# Stolen

bartender who was busy further down chatting up customers with his foot resting on a keg.

"Howdy, friend. What'll it be?" The barman was cheery, small, and red-faced. His short, light brown hair was parted in the center.

"Rye, if you got it. Ice?"

"Got whatever you need friend, plenty of ice too." The man stepped down the bar for a bottle and poured a healthy shot over ice into a pickle-jar glass.

"Don't recognize your face. Imagine you're passin' through, though."

"Oh? Why do you say that?"

"The look of you. Guessin' you, do gun work."

"Sometimes. Actually here to meet my brother. Plan to silver prospect up to Nevada."

The barman smiled. "Nevady, ay? They findin' good ore up there?"

"So they say."

"Well, good luck to ya. Holler when you're dry."

Bass nodded and smiled back at the man as he turned and walked down to another customer not because of anything he'd said, but because he was the only person he'd met today that seemed to be happy at their work. Bass looked around the room. It was a typical saloon, long and narrow. A space not much good for anything but a saloon. Bar that ran nearly the length of the room. A few tables against the opposite wall. 'Mirror behind the bar and a few shelves here and there for bottles and glassware. Everyone seemed to be enjoying themselves. At least Bass heard no coarse words or drunken challenges. He finished his drink and signaled the bartender again.

"Another?"

"Yeah, please. Say, I got a question for you."

"Shoot." The bartender set a rye whiskey in a clean glass in front of Bass.

"What's your name, first of all?"

"Buddy Simms, like the sign says."

"Buddy, how come is it that you seem to be happy in what you do, but some of the rest of the folks I've met here seem downright sour?"

"Hah. Cause they gotta pay."

"They gotta pay?"

"Yup. You ever hear of Vicente Silva?"

"No, but I'm new in town. Who is he, a councilman or somethin'?"

"No, he ain't no councilman, but he runs this town just the same. Does a pretty good job of it, too, all things considered."

# Stolen

"So, you gotta pay him?"

"Not me. Not any of the saloon owners, neither. All we have to do is see to it that Mr. Silva's special guests drink free and win at cards. But some of the other businesses that have been here a while say they have to pay an insurance for protection. And they don't like it for spit."

"Insurance? What for?"

"Protection. If they didn't pay, they'd start seein their winders busted, and small fires started in storerooms—that kinda thing. You prob'ly haven't seen 'em out yet, too early, but Vicente Silva has a small army of 'collectors' if you take my meanin'. If you come up short with your weekly insurance, you'll get a visit from a couple of his collectors. I don't mean to make light of it. It's a bad situation."

"Sounds like it. But why don't you stand up to 'em?"

"Jason Wheatley, he owned the Adelaide Bar in the Plaza hotel, he wouldn't pay. 'Started walkin' about heeled. Big mistake. 'Makes you fair game for the collectors. Jason got it right on the front steps of the Hotel. 'Kind of an example for others. Since then, they pay, or they don't do business."

# Stolen

"Geeze, Buddy, why not just leave; start-up elsewhere?"

"Ain't that easy. Collectors keep you from sellin' out. And some folks like Herman Driscol who owns the Monte Suma Hotel, everything he has is in that place. But then the other side is there's no shortage of customers. The way Silva has things organized appeals to a lot of, well, gentlemen of a certain calling. Now, you gotta treat 'em carefully, but boy, howdy, they do spend their money. And fortunately for me, they all like to drink. What I thought you was when you came in. 'Probably why you got such a cold reception. You look like one of Silva's customers. The Mexicans call them Don Vicente's special friends."

"I take it you don't have any local law enforcement?"

"Sheriff? Oh, we have a sheriff, all right. 'Lefty' Belcher. Nice guy. Comes in all the time. 'Very impressive with his badge and his office. Hell, he's a wanted man in most of Texas. 'Course, he's in on the game, too."

"And the Territorial Marshals don't come by?"

"The Federales? Hah. Sure, one stops by now and then. Don Vicente treats him to a tour of the town and all the smiling faces. Sheriff Belcher tells him life is great.

# Stolen

Then he gets a free room with companionship at the hotel for a night or two, and he's on his way. Dumb as a bag of hammers. But hey, he paid a call."

"Sounds ideal for this Vicente fella."

"It's kind of become an accepted way of life here."

"What about families, farmers, ranchers, and the like?

"Only a couple 'farmers tried to make a go of it here. They quit after a couple years and sold out to Silva, pennies on the dollar. There is a rancher, though, name's Randall Keebler. 'Ranch is the Circle K. 'Bout nine miles north at the base of the mountains. This was before my time, but he was here before Vicente Silva. This is all hear-tell ya understand, but I guess Silva tried to hoorah ol' Randall into payin his share. You know, insurance against havin' his cattle rustled. But Randall had more men and gave Silva's boys better than he got. Now, they leave each other alone. Sorta coexist."

"What about his ranch, the cattle and supplies?"

"He drives his cows to Watrous about thirty miles away, railhead there. And they come into town for supplies, doctorin' and such. They always come with two wagons and fifteen riders. Quite a procession."

# Stolen

"I guess so. Well, that certainly explains a lot. But tell me, aren't you afraid talkin' like this to a stranger? All about Silva and his shakedown."

"Me? Hell no. I'm a favorite a his. Sides, it ain't a secret; everbody in town's in on it one end or the other. Oh, and one thing: don't ever call it a shakedown. That offends Silva."

Bass put two dollars on the bar.
"Well, thanks for the info and the explanation. Makes more sense now. I'll be back, gotta go track down my brother."

"Say, what's he look like, maybe I've seen him in here?"

But Bass was already out the door.

# Stolen

Chapter 23

*3:45 p.m., January 7, 1888*
*Dr. Morris Laske's Office*
*Las Vegas*
*New Mexico Territory*

"What seems to be the trouble, Mr. uh . . . Bass?" Doctor Morris Laske was reading from a note that was left on his office door.

"Well, Doc, I wanted to have you look at a wound I got a week or so ago. I got thrown from my horse and landed on a sharp rock. Cut me bad enough that I had to cauterize it myself."

"Okay. Lemme see." Bass opened his shirt and let the doctor remove the bandage.

"This was infected, right? Somebody used the bromide to treat the infection, I'm guessing."

"Yes, when I finally got to a doctor, he told me it was infected and poured something on it. Hurt real bad."

"I'll bet. Yeah, the bromide will kill the infection, but it also damages the skin around the infection. Who was the doctor?"

"A guy in Agua Negra Chiquita."

"Don't know anybody there. Well, the infection is gone, but I bet it's still sore. Eventually, the skin will repair itself, but you'll always have discoloration along with the scar."

"Yeah, okay, but you don't think the infection is back?"

"No, definitely not. Have you been having fever sweats?"

"No."

"Okay. I'm gonna put a Hawes Extract on it. 'Good for the skin and reduces inflammation. It's also a mild astringent, which never hurts, ha. Pardon my pun. I'll put a fresh bandage on, and you can go." The doctor went to a cabinet for a small jar, gauze, cotton, and tape.

"You get many injuries in here, Doc?"

"Some, of course, illnesses too. Why do you ask?"

"Eh. I'm supposed to meet my brother here, and he's late, thought you'd know if anybody's been hurt or sick lately that's not from around here. That's all."

"Well, there was a man in here last week. A wagon accident, broken arm. I've never seen him before."

"Do you remember his name?"

"Ah, it wasn't Bass, I know."

# Stolen

"Forgive me, Doc. Sometimes, we don't use our real names. I hope you understand."

The doctor stopped smiling and nodded. "Yes, yes. I understand. See if I can remember . . . something like Dawse—maybe Dawson."

"Ah, no, that isn't him. What do I owe you?"

"Are you a friend of Mr. Silva?"

"No, I don't know him."

"Then ten dollars."

"Whoa. That's a lot of money for rebandaging."

"Yes, it is. Ten dollars, please."

Bass paid the doctor and left his office thinking, *I'm gonna need more money for this place*. He'd already checked out two liveries, a hotel, and now one of the doctors in town. He was running out of ideas, so he decided to try a different saloon and talk with the bartender there.

This time, he walked down Lincoln Street, not far from his hotel, to a place appropriately called The Lincoln Street Saloon and Café. As he walked in, he was struck by the size of the place. The bar was on the left and curved around the corner of the saloon. There were tables and matching chairs scattered in the middle of the room. The café was to the right when you entered and had a separate door, presumably to keep out the noise of a bar and card

337

room. Bass stuck his head inside, and it looked fancier than any café he'd ever been in—red leather booths along the far wall with tables and chairs over the rest of the floor. White linen tablecloths stood out against the dark rugs that nearly covered the plank wood floor. There was no lunch counter, something Bass thought was commonplace for cafés. He went first to the bar and sat in his usual spot near the end by the door. After a few moments, a middle-aged man approached.

"What'll it be, mister?"

Bass judged his temperament by his posture and the tone of his voice. He decided that this was 'not a happy man.'

"Rye, please, over ice."

"Ain't got ice. You want it straight?"

"Sure. How come no ice?"

"Some people ain't happy with me these days, is all. Ice wagon's been passin' us by." The bartender walked around the length of the bar and brought back a bottle.

"'At's six bits."

Bass put a dollar on the bar and said, "Silva, huh?'

"How'd you know that? I wouldn't be talkin' like that too loud, mister. Might come back at ya, in a dark alley, say."

# Stolen

"Don't mean nothin' by it. Just heard stuff from other bars, is all."

"Yeah? Just what'd you hear 'bout my place?"

"This place here? Nothin. 'Heard a lot about Vicente Silva, though, and the shakedown he runs. Seems everybody does business in this town is involved."

"Everbody that wants to stay healthy and in the black. I was short last week. S'why I got no ice."

"Huh. I was told saloons didn't have to pay?"

"This is a restaurant, too."

"Silva sure has this town bound up. Gotta hand it to him, though. He's smart. He knows threatening folks when they're alone works. Not so when they're all armed and banded together as one, so to speak."

"Mister, Silva's got at least fifteen men, all hardened killers workin' for him. One of 'em, an older gunman named Chavez, keeps 'em all in line. Him and a big Mexican guy they call El Chalequero. I seen that giant once or twice around town. I can say I never want to see him again in life. Sometimes they call him 'the Ripper.'"

"I heard this Chavez guy was killed a few days ago south of here. Little Town on the Pecos. And this El

# Stolen

Chalequero? He's a man like any other. Bullets will work against him, friend. I guarantee it."

"I s'pose if you're good with a gun and got a lotta men with you, there might be a chance . . . shit, I don't know why I'm even talkin' this way with you, stranger an' all. Could get me another visit from a collector . . . or worse."

"Don't worry. I ain't the chatty sort. Gimme another whiskey, will ya?"

"Sure, on the house. Just remember, we never talked. Got it?"

"Got it." Bass nursed his whiskey while a plan began to hatch. It was risky, very risky, but it might solve a whole lotta problems for the decent people of Las Vegas, New Mexico.

# Stolen

*6:00 p.m., January 7, 1888*

*Plaza Hotel*

*Las Vegas, New Mexico Territory*

Bass walked back to the hotel and stopped along the way at the Las Vegas Sundries and Notions, where he bought a bar of Pear's soap, bandages, and tape. He also asked for a small bottle of witch hazel and a package of sterile cotton packing. When he got to the hotel, he inquired as to the bathing facilities. The bathhouse was connected to the hotel on the north side of the building.

"I musta walked past it coming back from the Lincoln Street Saloon," he told the desk clerk. Bass asked for twenty gallons of hot water and paid the two-dollar fee to have it brought to his bath. The hot water was free. The delivery cost two dollars. Bass then went to his room to pick up his kit and lock away his Remington-Smoot .38. He kept the Peacemaker and belt on and walked the long corridor to the bathhouse.

The tub room was similar to all the other facilities Bass had ever used. Plank wood construction, with cedar floors and a bench along two walls with hooks in the wall above. There was a hot stove in a corner. Towels were provided free of charge. There were four separate rooms,

# Stolen

each with a Standard Sanitary Co. five-foot cast iron tub.
Each had claw feet, was covered in porcelain, and faced the
door. Bass locked the door behind him and stripped down,
hanging his clothing on the hooks provided along the wall.
He removed the bandaging around his arm and middle and
eased into the hot water. At first, the burn on his stomach
didn't like the hot water and stung like a swarm of bees.
The wound on his arm was fine. He lathered himself up and
sat back against the high curved back of the tub, thinking of
possible ways to find Viligry and the workability of his
new plan.

By 7:00 p.m., Bass was rebandaged, shaved, and
dressed. He decided to postpone dinner and pay a visit to
yet another saloon. The one he wanted to check had been
recommended by the clerk as being the place where many
of Vicente Silva's guests frequented. It was in the Monte
Suma Hotel a few blocks south on Gonzales Street. Bass
had decided on his methods while shaving, noting how
such a simple act had changed his appearance from a few
days earlier. It gave him the completion of the plan he'd
been contemplating and the notion that it just might work.
Before he left the hotel, he stole a derby hat from a coat
rack next to the café where he'd eaten breakfast. He walked
the several blocks in weather that had stiffened somewhat.

# Stolen

The earlier gusts had steadied into a constant blow off the mountains, and Bass walked through snow flurries blown in swirls and eddies about the street. The lamplight was shrouded in the snow, but Bass could make out the entrance to the Monte Suma Hotel and assumed the Saloon would be accessible from the lobby.

The Monte Suma Hotel was a 'Gentlemen's Club' he discovered as he entered. The sign above the double doors in the foyer read: Only Gentlemen May Enter. Ladies Permitted by Invitation. The lobby was spartan in its decor, and the smell of cigars and the accompanying smoky haze was apparent. The tall lobby windows were closed against the weather, and the lone hearth in the small parlor off the lobby could not draw fast enough to clear the air. The parlor was to his left, the registration desk directly ahead, and the Adelaide Saloon was to his right.

Bass tilted the black derby slightly forward and to his right and began to assume the identity of Texas Ben Thompson, the most notorious and ruthless gunman of the day. And responsible for no less than twenty killings in and around the San Antonio, Texas, area. Bass was more than a little familiar with the killer's look and swagger, having arrested him twice only to see him escape justice on the grounds of self-defense. Bass knew Thompson to be tall

# Stolen

and clean-shaven and hoped he didn't run into any of Thompson's known associates.

Bass entered the bar, ordered a whiskey from the bartender, and after scanning the room, asked, "There a card game for men in this hall?"

"Mister, there's three games for high stakes in the back room. Gimme your name, and I'll see if I can get you a chair." Thompson was a well-known big-money gambler who always carried hundreds in cash. Bass could make about half that amount if need be.

"You tell 'em Ben Thompson wants in. And take a bottle for the table in with you." Bass was careful to let the bartender see his one hundred dollar note.

"Yes, sir, Mr. Thompson, see what I can do."

Bass leaned into the bar and sipped his whiskey, making a point of avoiding eye contact.
The bartender came back quickly and waved Bass to the door at the back of the room. As he walked through the saloon, he tried to imitate Thompson's sideling stride. He lit a cigar, opened the door, and walked in.

The room was larger than he expected. There were three round, green, felt-covered tables with between six to eight men holding cards at each one.

# Stolen

"Barkeep says one a' these tables needs a real card hawk. Which one is it?"

The dealer at the table farthest from the door waved him in. "Leave your hardware on the hook with the others, please. Sit here, Mr. Thompson, and welcome. This is a Stud poker table, sir, seven cards. I'm the dealer and house banker. My name is Andre Gillette."

The men then went round the table counterclockwise, introducing themselves, some smiling a welcome, some barely speaking. Bass was interested in two Mexican men who introduced themselves as Patricio Maes and Gabriel Sandoval. The three other men were all white. One was Bill Clay Forrester; he seemed too drunk to play but may have been spoofing. Then there was Henry Wyatt, the older man who seemed friendly enough, and finally, there was a well-dressed man who introduced himself as Arlo Singer. He did not look up from the table but was the only one who remembered to say thanks for the bottle.

"This is a table stakes game, Mr. Thompson. How much in chips can I dispense?"

"I'll start with a hundred." Bass tossed his bill to Andre and was given twenty white, five red, four blue, and one gray in chips.

# Stolen

Forrester, who was sitting next to him, poured him a tall whiskey, and the five-dollar ante went in. The first hand was dealt, and Bass was happy with his start. His hole cards were two eights, and his 'door' or open card was a red deuce. Bass was a passable card player, and Stud poker was his best game. He was not a regular gambler, however, and had to cover that fact with his play. His deuce began the betting, and he started with five dollars. He was seen around the table except for Forrester, who raised by five. Bass tossed in another red chip, and everyone called.

His fourth street and fifth street cards face up, were a four and a jack, respectively. Betting continued until the pot was nearing the two-hundred-dollar level. His sixth street card was another four, giving him a low pair showing. There were two tens up on the board in front of Arlo Singer, so he bet first. Bass called at the ten-dollar bet, and the river card was dealt. Bass drew another eight, giving him a full house, three eights, and two fours. Not a mighty hand, but a likely one. The final round of betting took another ten dollars, but at the showdown, his small full house won the pot. He had won nearly two hundred dollars after removing the sixty he bet.

Forrester dropped out after that; he was a loser, so no one seemed to mind. Bass won the next pot with a straight flush, three to the seven in clubs, and he collected another hundred-and-eighty dollars. After that, the other players began noticing his 'luck' and asking where he'd played before.

"You look familiar to me, gringo. Did I not see you once in Ciudad Juarez? The jail, maybe, or at Cantina Ortiz?" Maes asked.

"Never been there, my friend. What's your name, Patricia? 'Never been to Mexico, period. Too dangerous." The other men at the table laughed, but Gabriel Sandoval watched Bass's eyes. Maes was not amused.

"You think I am a girl, hombre? That my name is a big . . . *como se dice*—a joke?" Bass knew that Maes had been drinking for some time, and he wanted to antagonize the man into action.

"Look, Pepe, you got a Mexican name sounds like a white woman's name. Ain't my fault you're sensitive about it." Gabriel Sandoval stood up at that point, throwing his cigar to the floor, his hand on the hilt of his knife.

Andre Gillette spoke up. "I think it's time for a break, maybe some fresh air. If anyone wants to cash out now, the bank is open. He looked at Bass and said, "Sir?"

"Yeah, all right, cash me out. This game somehow has lost its charm."

# Stolen

Bass made a show of folding the bills and putting them in his hip pocket. He put the bowler on his head and picked up his pistol at the door. Before leaving, he turned to the room and sneered, "See ya round the campfire, boys." He spoke directly to the two Mexicans. "Adios, niñas." And he walked out the door, buckling his gun belt before he left. He'd won over three hundred dollars, which he knew wouldn't last long in a town as expensive as this.

As he hoped, the two Mexican men were incensed. That a gringo should question their manhood was unforgivable. Bass knew this and fully expected what happened as he walked back to his hotel. It was past 11:00 p.m. on a Saturday, and the streets were being darkened by the lamplighters. As Bass walked across an open alley off Gonzales Street, he heard a voice from the darkness say, "Señor. You look to be heavily weighted. Perhaps, it is all the silver you hold gringo, heh?"

"Which one of you niñitas is it, Maes or Sandoval?" Bass knew both men were probably drunk.

"This time, gringo, you must deal with us together."

"Hah, be the first time two Mexicans ever managed anything together, but come on, if you're comin'. Ain't got all night." With that, both men appeared in the light, smiling and speaking in Spanish to one another. Bass was just able to make out *elevas* and *piernas*, signaling a high and low assault strategy.

The first one, Maes, got too close to Bass and misjudged the taller man's reach. Bass threw a quick left fist into the man's nose, breaking it, crossing the man's eyes, and knocking him off balance.

Sandoval was not as clumsy, but Bass easily sidestepped the man's rush, allowing him to stumble to the dirt, slamming his head into the adobe wall of the building where Bass positioned himself. Maes, bleeding profusely from his nose, had pulled his knife and was standing in a low, crouched position, looking for an opening. Bass gave him none, standing sideways to him and keeping an eye on Sandoval at the same time.

Maes thrust his blade several times, but Bass, who was somewhat protected by his heavy clothing, was able to deflect the man's jab with his left arm. Sandoval was on his feet now and fumbling for his knife. Bass quickly grabbed Maes' right arm with his left hand pushing it aside and, at the same time, brought his own right fist upward into the Mexican's jaw. Maes crumbled to the ground unconscious.

Sandoval screamed in his frustration and rushed at Bass with his knife, but again, Bass sidestepped the man, tripping him as he passed sending him sprawling to the ground. Bass then walked to the dazed Sandoval, lifted his chin, and knocked him unconscious with his balled right fist. Bass looked at the two men lying in the alley, shook his head, and rubbed his right hand. He began whistling as he headed back to his hotel, satisfied that his plan was well underway.

# Stolen

Chapter 24

*7:15 a.m., January 8, 1888*
*Plaza Hotel*
*Las Vegas, New México Territory*

Bass woke up with a sore right hand and swollen knuckles. It took a moment for him to remember the events of last night but when he did, he smiled faintly. The two wounds he had suffered only a week ago were already starting to heal and bothered him only slightly. He noticed fresh blood on the bandage on his left arm and supposed it was due to the action last night. His stomach felt fine. The witch hazel was working on the burn.

He washed up at the basin. The hotel had provided clean towels, and then dressed and went down to the lobby. He picked up a copy of the Las Vegas Daily Optic, a nickel at the front desk, and walked into the café. This time, he waited to be seated. A young man with a dishtowel over his arm asked Bass to follow him and seated him at the table next to the one from yesterday.

"The councilman's special table, that one, right? Bass asked.

# Stolen

"Yes, sir, Councilman Roman is having breakfast with a guest this morning."

Maevis appeared shortly after the young man left and put a glass of water on the table.

"See if I remember: coffee, black; a large scramble, with a ham slice and a side a bacon. Right? Oh, and biscuits and gravy, huh?"

"Maevis, you remembered. How thoughtful."

"' Taint that so much, dearie, folks are buzzin' 'bout the hi-jinks you caused last night at Mr. Silva's game. 'Tween you and me, that's why he's eatin' here this mornin. Wanted you seated right there."

"Didn't know it was his game. Didn't see him there."

"Oh, he don't ever play, just sets up the game, you see. Let's others lose. Most a' the men know to let the Mexicans win a bit. It's a part a how they get paid."

"Nobody told me anything about it."

"Ah, you're new here, travelin' through. He prob'ly just wants to set you straight, is all. I'll be right back with your coffee."

Bass sat reading his paper and sipping the hot coffee Maevis brought. There was nothing unusual on the front pages, but toward the rear was an entry about the violent death of one Jose Chavez y Chavez in the small town of Agua Negra Chiquita, some fifty miles to the southeast. The article said:

> . . . *he died of terrible gunshot wounds suffered in a*
> *gunfight with an unknown assailant while*
> *protecting the lives of two school-age children.*

The article went on to say that,

> *Mr. Chavez y Chavez would receive a hero's burial*

*at the town's expen*se.

Of course, Bass knew the story had been sensationalized to sell news papers and may have been influenced by Silva's reputation.

Harry Roman and Vicente Silva walked into the café just as Bass was being served his breakfast. Harry Roman was a man of average height but ample girth. Bass pegged his age in the late forties. He was dressed in a blue worsted suit and silk vest with a white starched shirt and cellulose collar. Bass couldn't remember the last time he'd seen one of those. He hung his dark brown overcoat on the rack next to the door and took Silva's from him to do the same. Where Roman was nearly bald, Silva had a full head of thick, gray-white hair trimmed neatly around his ears and collar. He was dressed in a black frock coat similar to

Bass with light gray slacks. His shirt was blue pinstriped, and where Roman wore a top hat, Silva was bare-headed. Both men had enviable mustaches; Roman's joined his sideburns in a mutton chop, and Silva's was a fully waxed handlebar.

Silva sat in the chair adjacent to Bass, and Roman sat in the chair next to Silva rather than across from him. That way they could both share the view of the Plaza and National Avenue. As soon as Silva sat down, he turned to Bass and introduced himself.

"*Buenas dias, Señor*—ah, Thompson, is it?"

"That's right." Bass put his fork down, sat back, and folded his hands in his lap indicating he accepted being interrupted and was ready to listen.

"It is interesting to me that at your hotel you are signed in as Frederick Bass. Well, it is no matter. Names are such small things in my business, but occasionally, they do get in the way. Don't you agree, Señor?"

Bass just continued to watch and listen to Vicente Silva. The notion to shoot him in the head where he sat crossed his mind, but he knew someone else would just step in.

"My name is Vicente Silva. You may have heard my name about the town. I have heard that you, *como se*

# Stolen

*dice*, waylaid two of my men last night, Señor Maes and Señor Sandoval, I believe?"

"Well. Any 'waylaying' that was done was on their part. They stopped me on my way back to my hotel after the game and indicated that I had too much money. They wanted it and were willing to accept the consequences if I chose not to give it to them."

"I have seen those consequences, Señor. You have a violent streak, I believe."

"I've been told that, yes."

"And does your violent behavior include gun work?"

"It has. In the past."

"I am in a difficult position here, Señor Thompson. That card game you attended is an entertainment of mine. I provide, ah, how is it . . . sponsor, it is an entertainment I sponsor for some of my employees who have distinguished themselves in their work. Now, these two men, as I have noted, are not able to perform their duties. And probably not for some time to come."

"Well, gee whiz, Mr. Silva, I can't tell you how sorry I am to hear that. But I don't see how it affects me."

"That brings me to my point, Señor. Mr. Roman here is a city councilman. If I were to complain to him that

355

two of my best collectors have been ah…crippled by you, he would be compelled to have our sheriff arrest you. Is that not so, Harry?"

"Oh, I can practically guarantee that Vicente. And in our jail, why it's damn near impossible to know when a District Judge'll show up. 'Could be in a week, could be several months. How about that, Mr. Thompson? Can you afford to cool your heels in our jail for that long?"

Bass was silent, listening, giving nothing away. Silva began to wave his hand, "Now, now. Such talk of the jail and delays. I have, perhaps, a happy solution for you, Mr. Thompson. Why don't you come to work for me? As an ah—subs—ah, substitute for the two men you have broken down. I can use a man of violent actions. Such a man would be well paid."

Bass thought for a moment and answered, "Okay. Let me make sure I got this right. I come to work for you, fill in for your two 'minions totas' or Harry boy here flags down your lawman, locks me up, and tosses the key. That about right?"

"Si, Señor Thompson, and fine words too."

"Whew, lemme think while I finish my breakfast. How well paid? And for how long?"

# Stolen

"One hundred dollars a week to start. If you perform well with *iniciativa*, who knows? And only until Maes and Sandoval can work again. You think about it, eat. *Dasayunar*. But tell me before you leave this room, Señor, eh?"

Bass nodded and went back to his breakfast. As he took the last swallow of his coffee, he silently said to himself, *Bingo*.

Silva was back into his conversation with Harry Roman, and Bass stared at what was left of his breakfast. He had no intention of letting things continue for more than a day or two, and he felt certain that by then, he'd have at least a line on Gabe Viligry and his posse. He thought it would be likely that between them, they might topple Silva's web of extortion and fear. In the process, they might even restore control of the community to its decent members. Certainly, a few would object to a new ethic, some of the saloon keepers and brothel owners for the most part, but Bass figured after so much depravity, a little excess virtue might be in order. Bass put his coffee cup down and turned to Silva, interrupting the councilman's rhetoric.

"Okay, Silva, I'm in for the short-haul anyway. But my service is worth a lot more than a hundred a week."

# Stolen

Silva smiled at Bass and thought for a moment. "I believe you are right, Mr. Thompson. Walk with me back to my office across the Plaza, and we will talk further. I'm sure Councilman Roman will excuse us." Silva sent a firm glance at Harry Roman, and the councilman stood and walked away from the table. Silva then stood and retrieved his coat.

"Come Señor. Just across the Plaza, there." He pointed to a three-story building with a sign outside that read: Silva Freight and Shipping. "That is my business, Mr. Thompson. Everything that comes and goes from Las Vegas, Mr. Thompson, every bottle of liquor, every spool of thread, every barrel of flour or feed goes through me, for a fee, of course. Always for a fee."

"Sounds mighty prosperous."

"Oh, Señor, it is. Do you know we have no post office? Oh, we have a building that says post office on it, but all the correspondence that comes in or goes out must go through my office. It can be very useful to know the names and addresses of the people and offices one's enemies communicate with."

"I can see that but isn't that a, what is it called, a federal crime? Won't the Government find out? Shut you down?"

# Stolen

"Mr. Thompson, don't underestimate me. I have a long list of friends. The Honorable Antonio Joseph, for example, is a particular friend of mine. Please, come in and sit down."

Bass walked into Silva's office and was struck immediately with its stark, even spartan nature. A corner room on the first floor with a desk, two chairs in front of it, a small stove in the corner between two windows and a threadbare divan against the back wall next to the door. Pictures of western vistas on the walls, and one, behind the desk hung a picture of Mexican President Porfirio Diaz sitting horseback in full regalia. Silva noticed Bass's interest in the picture.

"Presidente Diaz. I have his picture to remind me that even a half-breed soldier can achieve success. Please sit."

Bass took a seat across the desk and asked, "So, tell me again how the process works and how I get paid."

Silva smiled. "You will be assigned the same two blocks of businesses that Maes and Sandoval worked. Each week, you will visit the business owner. I suggest Mondays when they are flush from the weekend. The terms are simple: each will pay you five dollars, Yankee. This assures them that evil mischance shall not befall them

# Stolen

throughout the week. Of the five dollars, you will pay me half and keep the other half for yourself. I assure you of freedom from interference by our sheriff or the town council. Simple, no? But know this. If you miss collecting or take your payment in service from a woman, say. You still owe me for that week."

Bass nodded. "As you say, simple. So how many collections do I make in a week?"

"There are twenty businesses in your sleeve, as I call them."

"That's only fifty bucks a week. You said a hundred!"

"Please relax, Mr. Thompson. Let me finish. I personally will pay you fifty dollars per week to keep my other collectors in line, much as you did with Maes and Sandoval. The position is open because the man who used to do it is no longer available. He disappeared after failing to complete a project I had entrusted to him. It is of no consequence to us now. There you have it. I assume you will begin tomorrow?"

Bass pretended to consider the offer for a moment and finally said, "Deal. Like you said, tomorrow's Monday, everyone should have money. Where do I start?"

"Come to the map, and I will show you."

# Stolen

Bass followed Silva to a large street map of Las Vegas with businesses and their owners written in pencil. Bass's 'route' was to be two, three-block sections of Sixth and Seventh streets starting at Grand Avenue near the railroad station. He was glad it would not include any of the saloons or liveries he'd already visited. The deal was closed on a handshake, and Bass left to go back to his hotel. His Elgin told him it was 10:15 a.m. He was hoping to receive answers to his telegrams from yesterday.

At the desk were the two messages he'd hoped for. The first from Sally read:

> *'About to explode. Feel Fine. Maggie and Elsie coming soon. 'Can't wait. Please be careful, Father—love always Sally.*

The second one from Avery read:

> *Viligry is my height, brown hair over collar, clean-shaven, 26yrs. With him are Patchelski, 40yrs; Boon, 48yrs; and Ramsfeld, 35. Maria seems happy. Avery*

361

# Stolen

Bass knew that Silva would be sure to see both messages, and after reading and rereading both, he could see nothing that might compromise his standing with his new boss. He folded both notes and put them in his coat pocket as he walked out the front door and down the street to the trolley stand for a ride back to the railroad area and his new clientele.

The trolley was a compact narrow-gauge ore train with a half-size steam engine and three enclosed coaches. It was certainly capable of carrying twenty or thirty people from the EP& SW Terminal to the hotels and businesses at the Plaza and those along the way. Bass wondered if Silva had a hand in its implementation. The trolley dropped him off at Grand Avenue and Douglas Street.

The weather was bright and sunny, and the winds calm, perfect for a walk around his new revenue source. He spotted two saloons, a hotel, and a general store all on one block. He found more of the same, including the newspaper office and a fire house on the second block. He decided to stop into a café on Sixth Street called the Dining Car and get a feel for ownership. *How tough could the owner of a café be?* He thought. The café was set up like a dining car on a train, with low booths along the three windows in the

# Stolen

front and counter seating that ran the width of the café. The
door was at one end of the café.

Bass entered and took a seat at the counter. There
was a menu card, handwritten, set in a stand in front. There
were also salt and pepper shakers, a covered bowl of sugar
cubes, and paper napkins. There were also containers of
Gulden's mustard and Heinz Ketchup, something Bass had
only sampled when back east. The menu was typical
breakfast and lunch fare, and Bass decided on his favorite
corned beef sandwich and fried potatoes. There was a
selection of bread offered, including white, rye, and brown
bread. At one time, they must have had sourdough bread,
but it was crossed off the card. A pretty young girl stopped
to take his order. Bass could never judge age, but she may
have been in her midteens, with long dark hair tied behind
her head, a green jumper outfit like the one Sally had, and a
yellow cotton apron. She said her name was Luella, but just
to call her Lu, and what would Bass like to order? Bass
asked for a grilled corned beef on rye and fried potatoes,
and a tall rye whiskey with ice.

"I'm sorry, sir, we don't serve whiskey, but I can
get you a beer if you like. We have two kinds on ice, one
from our Las Vegas Brewery over on Pacific Street and
Glorieta Beer from Southwestern Brewing in 'Burque."

# Stolen

"Well, then, I believe I'll try our local brew. 'Support your local businesses, I always say. Can I ask is the owner available?"

"I think so, I'll check. Pa! Customer wants to see ya!"

Bass smiled and looked down so he wouldn't embarrass the girl. A large man with long hair tied in back like his daughter's walked through a door that most likely led to the kitchen. He was dressed in an undershirt and trousers hidden by a long apron tied at the waist. He was easily three inches taller and thirty pounds heavier than Bass and looked perturbed at being called to the front. He was wiping his hands on a towel as he spoke.

"You're new. This ain't Monday. Go on, scat from here 'fore I break your head. Lu, you go in the back and watch the stove."

Bass wasn't expecting the rough treatment to begin so soon, but he played his role as best he could. "Whats your name, Buster?"

"Early Gates. An' you ain't welcome. Ain't due 'til Monday, anyhow . . . . Tell that thievin' Mexican he'll get his money tomorrow, and you get the hell outta my place now."

# Stolen

Bass instinctively liked the big man, knowing he was being swindled but resisting any way he could. He smiled and stood up, keeping eye contact as he did.

"Guess I'll have to wait 'til tomorrow for my beer, little man. Lookin forward to it."

Bass turned and walked out the door, hoping he'd acted tough enough to convince Early Gates of his complicity with Silva. Bass decided he'd remember the big man.

Bass walked on down to a friendly-looking saloon called The Mandarin Bar and stepped through the door. The room was eerily quiet and smelled of some kind of flowery incense. The room was dark, lit only by candles, one on each wooden table. And several down the highly polished wooden bar. There were eight stools positioned neatly in front of the bar, and each one had a small dragon carved into the backrest. Bass was the only one seated at the bar and had to wait for service. He noted business was slow. Only one other guy was sitting at a table staring at the candles flickering.

Afer a few moments, a very pretty Chinese woman appeared through beaded curtains and walked slowly down the bar toward Bass. She wore a tight red bodice dress that stopped mid-thigh and revealed fishnet stockings down to tall black leather boots. Her long hair was black and hung straight down to the middle of her back. Her eyes were like dark almonds, and her lips were full, slightly parted, and dark red.

"I hep you, sah?" she smiled as she spoke, not to be enticing but only to provide the customer's order. Bass had been in opium dens before but never one that appeared to be 'full service,' so to speak.

"Whiskey, please, rye if you have it with ice." Bass smiled politely, and she turned to the bar for a bottle and glass. She opened an insulated box and filled the demitasse with ice. Setting it in front of Bass, she looked into his eyes as she poured.

"Say when."

"That's fine there. Thanks."

"Now. What else can I get handsome man as you today? Maybe a needle or a pipe? One of our beauteous young ladies, so you enjoy a private room?"

Bass knew opium use had been popular for years. Some of the old timers like Hickock and Kit Carson preferred it to liquor. The Civil war was where many men first experienced opium dosed by doctors. It was the medicine of choice for all wounds and amputations. Even laudanum, the tincture of heroin mixed with alcohol, was

# Stolen

available for sale at most general stores and Sutlers. Bass remembered stories told by his Cavalry commanders about officers 'chasing the dragon' whenever they got leave, and he also knew that many women, and not just whores were regular opium eaters too. He knew that opium, like liquor, could eventually kill the user, either by overdosing or simply ignoring healthy food and liquids in favor of the drug. A good many marriages and businesses dissolved as a result of dependence on both alcohol and opium, but for him, the poppy flower was always the worst. More potent and denigrating, it seemed like there was no using opium in moderation. It always became the user's reason for living.

"Not today, sweetheart. I'm your new collector. I'll be by tomorrow."

The woman spit on the floor and turned away, walking back through the beaded curtain. Bass shrugged, finished his whiskey, left a dollar on the bar, and walked out.

The next place he came to was a barber shop two doors down passed a bank—a small storefront with red, blue, and white pole. Bass remembered hearing something about the pole representing the time when barbers did surgeries along with dental extractions, but he never fully saw the meaning. The gold paint on the front window read:

# Stolen

Sonny Turturo's Barber Styles. It was a Sunday, and Bass expected the place to be closed, but looking through the window, he saw a young man getting a haircut. The door was open, so he walked in.

"Eh? It's a Sunday, and you walk in like you own it." The voice came from a middle-aged man in a smock of some kind. He had thin black hair, dark brows, and mustache, and a long scar on the left side of his face.

"You, Sonny?"

"Yeah, don't tell me you're here for your 'honorarium.' What happened to the beaner 'at usually comes in? And this is still Sunday, *derecha*?"

"The ah, Mexican gentleman is ill. I'm filling in. And I know what day it is." Bass smiled and said, "I just wanted to say hello, and I hope you have a pleasant day."

The barber made some kind of gesture as Bass walked out, but he didn't care. If he could just find Viligry and his men, this whole thing could be over by Tuesday.

# Stolen

Chapter 25

*3:30 p.m., January 8, 1888*
*Jinks Hardware and Paint*
*Seventh Street, Las Vegas*
*New Mexico Territory*

The hardware store was another business Bass expected to be closed on Sunday, but the door was open, and there were customers at the counter. Bass walked down a couple of the aisles noting the merchandise was pretty much as advertised: hinges, locks, door hardware, hand tools, all the items you'd expect to find in a moderately sized hardware store. There were also household items like cast iron pans, ladles, and pot forks.

The clerk at the counter was an older man, fifty or more, with graying hair and a goatee. He wore a full cotton apron with large pockets and a leather tool belt around the outside of it. He was talking to a customer about a large folding knife, the kind you might use for skinning and dressing a large animal like a hog or a deer. The customer bore a striking resemblance to the description that Avery had sent for Gabe Viligry: mid-twenties, Avery's size, long brown hair, and clean-shaven. Bass decided to try something. He walked up behind the customer and began talking to the clerk.

"Sorry to interrupt, just looking for an oil can."

"Aisle three left-hand side," came the response.

Then Bass looked at the customer and said, "Gabe? Gabe, is that you? God, it's been a while, huh?"

The customer looked up at Bass, then dropped his eyes. "Sorry, mister. Wrong guy. My name's Rod, Rod Patchelski."

Bass smiled. "Oh, my mistake. Sorry to bother you." Bass walked over to aisle three and waited 'til the

customer left, certain and relieved that he'd found his man. He remembered that Patchelski was one of the other names in Avery's wire. Now, he had to think of a way to let Viligry know who he was. Viligry knew he'd been spotted, and he didn't know the man who approached him from a hole in the ground. Bass walked up to the clerk and looked the man straight in the eye.

"Maes and Sandoval are out, and I'm in. I'll be back tomorrow for your contribution. Have it ready." The clerk swallowed hard and nodded as Bass left the store.

Outside, Bass paused to look around the general area, but he'd have been surprised to see Viligry waiting for him. Viligry would make contact when he was ready.

# Stolen

He had to. He couldn't very well allow some yahoo to walk around town calling his name, looking for an out-of-place lawman. With all that on his mind, Bass walked down the opposite side of the street, stopping at a livery barn with a sign that said Hopkins Livery and Buggy Rents, and below that in someone's hand was written Sweet Tempered Saddle Ponys to Let To. Bass noticed the 'closed' sign hanging on the barn door but heard talking coming from inside. He couldn't make out what was being said, but it was near certain to be Viligry and his boys.

Bass walked around through the corral gate and into the barn through the paddock area. He saw four men talking and gesturing at a volume just short of a holler. He could make out several words now. Words like 'discovered' and 'deep shit.' The men were all armed and appeared as capable as one might expect. There was no panic in their tone or their movements and he felt he'd be comfortable being backed up by this bunch. Bass was hidden behind stacked hay bales and stepped out into the stable's center aisle.

"You men'd be the posse from Hartley, I'm guessin'?" Bass spoke in a normal tone, no threat to be perceived, but the men were obviously jumpy, and two of them reached for their pistols. Bass continued, "Hold on, hold on now. I don't mean no harm at all. But I'm right, ain't I. 'At's who you'd be?"

The man Bass took for Viligry spoke up, "Just who the hell are you, mister? How come you know 'bout us?"

"My name's Frank Bass, I'm a Deputy United States Marshal, and you're Gabe Viligry, Sheriff of Hartley, and these men are Patchelski, Boone, and Ramsfeld. Am I right?"

"Yeah. How'd—?"

"Avery Matlock. This is the wire he sent describing y'all." Bass held up the message. "I been walkin' the streets a' this town lookin for ya. First thing I wanna tell you . . . the little girls are home safe, and Avery got the money back."

All four men slumped noticeably as if a tremendous weight had been removed from their collective shoulders.

"My name's Boone Waverly, and how in God's name did you accomplish that?"

Bass grinned. "Boone, I didn't do it! The little girls escaped on their own, stole a horse, and found me out on the Llano recovering from a knife wound."

Viligry started, "How'd you get—?"

# Stolen

Bass held his hand up. "Long story. Right now, it's enough that the girls are home safe."

Alan Ramsfeld was next. "I'm the town minister, Alan Ramsfeld. You said Avery got the money back, too? How'd that work?"

"Well, 'at's another long story, gotta be for another time. I want to know how you boys feel about stickin' it to the man who masterminded the whole thing. Bring him and his whole opera to justice and leave Las Vegas a better place than we found it. I know you been away from Hartley a long time. No shame in wantin' to go home."

Everyone was quiet for a few moments, and then Mike Patchelski stepped forward. "Marshal, we all been here about a week hold up in this horse barn afraid to say boo. Hell yeah! Let's burn the bastard's house down round his pointy ears."

Everyone chuckled in agreement, and Bass smiled. "All right, listen up then. Vicente Silva runs this town by extorting money from all the local businesses. As long as the business pays the fee, no harm comes to him, his family, or his business. A couple nights ago, I—ah . . . disabled two of Silva's collectors. He has no idea who I really am, 'thinks I'm an outlaw named Ben Thompson.

373

# Stolen

Anyway, this mornin', he offered me the collectors' positions of both the men I laid up. It's a sizable number of folks. I paid a call on some of 'em today, and if the rest of my 'sleeve,' as he calls 'em, feel the same way, and I believe they do, then we'd have a formidable army to throw up against Silva's crew. The first thing we gotta do is take care of Silva and his stalwarts, the guys loyal to him no matter the odds. That'll be my job. You boys need to find and, well, like I said, disable as many of Silva's collectors as you can, either together or individually. 'Up to you.

My guess is that once they see Silva's out of the picture, and they ain't gonna get paid anymore, most'll high tail it for the hills anyway. Then, it'll be time for the good citizens of Las Vegas to hold a special election for a new town sheriff and city council. Sound like it's workable?"

There was general agreement the plan was sound, but Gabe Viligry asked, "Marshal, it's a fine plan, a sound idea, and God knows we're real familiar with this town. 'Been checkin' out every saloon, café, and gamblin room tryin' to get a line on where them children might be. We know this town well, so I like your plan, but we have no jurisdiction here, no authority to impose our will on the

# Stolen

people of Las Vegas, whether they be good citizens or evil. How do we deal with that?"

Bass thought about it for a minute. Viligry was right. In the end, the District Courts would have to condone and recognize the legality of their actions against Silva. It was a loophole that had worked for many wrongdoers in the past.

"Boys, I'm a Federal Deputy Marshal, assigned to the south west Texas District and eastern New Mexico Territory. But the man who hired me once explained jurisdiction like this. He said, *Frank, you're a Federal Marshal now. Your jurisdiction is pretty much wherever in this country you might happen to be standin'*, so I interpret that as being wherever the hell I happen to be. Now, you boys all still got the Texas star that Gabe here gave ya? Says Deputy on it?" They all agreed and fished them from their pockets.

"Good. Raise your right hand. Do you solemnly swear to uphold and defend the laws of the territory of New Mexico, *sine stipendium*?"

They all said "I Do," except Boone Waverly, who said 'Yup.'"

"Fine, now I suggest you all keep 'em stars under wraps unless a citizen calls for seein' one. Just visit every business you can and explain to the owner who you are and what we're doin'. Then try to take down as many of Silva's collectors as you can. My guess is they'll mostly be Mexicans and all well-healed. The first call I'm gonna make is on the sheriff, put him to rights, and deal with any deputies he may have. After that, we'll use the town's jail facility as a kinda holding pen for the rascals you bring in. Once that's underway, I'm goin' for Silva. Any questions?"

"Just to be clear, Marshal Bass, how far do we go in dealing with these collector fellas?" Ramsfeld asked.

"Do whatever it takes, Preacher. Remember, these men ain't known for their piety. So, tell me, where have you all been stayin?"

"Right here. We didn't come with enough money for a hotel, wasn't expectin' to need one. And I didn't want to give myself away by goin' to a bank to draw down on the Hartley Township Account. Lionel Graves, he owns the livery. I told him who we are, and he was happy to let us stay—' been here for a couple days now. I imagine he's hopin' we'll do him an' the town some good. Didn't have a workable plan 'til now, Marshal," Viligry answered.

"Next time you see him, ask him for his help. None a' this works, lest we have the townsfolk on our side. I got some money here, say fifty bucks."

# Stolen

Bass fished in his pocket for some bills. "Go buy grub, an' maybe give some to Lionel for his service. I'm headin' to the jail now. 'Stop back later on. You boys watch yourselves tonight; stay low as you can."

Bass went out the way he came in and took the trolley up Douglas Street to Twelfth. Lights were on in the jail side of the building and smoke was weaving up from the chimney flue. It was near 6:30 p.m., and the sun had sunk below the Sangre de Christos, dropping the town into near darkness. The ride on the little train had been chilly, and Bass blew on his hands to warm them. There was a small barn across the street where Bass stood for a few minutes watching the jail, looking for any movement that might indicate who all was inside.

After a few minutes, he decided it was too cold to wait any longer, and if there were more than just a couple guys inside, too bad for them. He got a decent look at the interior of the office as he passed a window and stopped at the front door. He'd seen a heavy, balding man with a thin mustache sitting at a desk. He withdrew his pistol and slid the door latch. The warmth of the room struck him as he stepped inside, and he leveled his Colt at the man sitting behind the desk wearing a star.

Bass spoke quietly. "What's your name, Sheriff?"

# Stolen

The sheriff was caught completely off guard, and he sat staring in wonder at the tall man with the pistol aimed at his middle. "What the God damn do you think you're doing, idiot. Do you know where you are?"

"I know I'm lookin' at a corrupt, boot-licking excuse for a lawman, buster. Now what's your damn name?" Bass stepped closer so the man knew his resolve.

"Harry Belcher, mister, an' you're makin' a big mistake. And who the devil are you, bustin' in like this?"

"Stand up, Belcher. My name's Frank Bass, US Deputy Marshal, and you're under arrest. Who else is here?" Belcher blanched at hearing Bass's name and slowly stood at his desk as instructed, eyes wide watching Bass.

"Who else is here!?"

"No-Nobody." There was a slight quaver in his voice, and beads of sweat began to pop out on his forehead.

"Drop your gun belt and step away from the desk." Belcher, again, did as he was told.

"Where's your jail?" Bass was moving to Belcher's side to get a better view of the back door he assumed led to the jail.

"Through there." Belcher pointed at the back door.

"The keys . . . now!"

# Stolen

Belcher reached into his pocket and produced a key ring with eight keys. As he did, Bass could see the door latch move. Belcher saw the latch move as well and called out, "He's got a gun on me, he's got a gun!"

The back door swung open, and a large Mexican holding two revolvers kicked open the door and fired both without aiming. The noise was deafening in the close quarters, but Bass fired back and hit the big man squarely in the chest. He fell backward, clanging a cell door shut, and lay motionless on the floor, dying. Bass went to Belcher and, without hesitating, pistol-whipped the sheriff into unconsciousness. He crumbled to the floor against his chair.

"Nobody else in here, huh?" Bass hated crooked lawmen.

Next, Bass took the jail keys and went into the jail room. There were eight cells along the back wall, iron bars, no windows, and no other way out. Fortunately, none of the cells were occupied. He discovered each cell had its own key, so he found the key for the last cell, opened it, and dragged the dead man in. Bass checked the man's pockets and found another set of keys. He pulled Belcher into the same cell, closed and locked the door, and went back out front. Thinking the sound of the shots might arouse some interest, he looked outside into the street. He saw no movement of any kind and then remembered it was Sunday night, and all the businesses were closed. If Belcher woke up and started calling for help, no one would hear him. He decided to head back to Lionel Graves's barn and caught the trolley heading east on Douglas Street.

Bass hopped off the trolley at Seventh and walked to the barn, again entering unseen through the corral. The four men were inside, huddled around a stove, eating what looked like stew from a large pot. They were also passing a bottle around among them.

"You boys, go light on that bottle. You're gonna need your wits about ya tomorrow. Won't be no cakewalk, I'll bet."

Waverly spoke up. "Don't worry, Marshall. We'll be there for ya."

"Take your word. 'Soon as you're done, head on up to the jail, spend the night there, an' make sure no one causes trouble in the morning." Bass threw a key ring to Viligry. "Anybody suspicious shows up, invite them into one of the cells."

Gabe Viligry asked, "We heard a couple of pops, sounded a ways off. That you?"

# Stolen

"Was. 'Sheriff had a trigger-happy jailer. He's laid out in the far cell along with the sheriff. The sheriff's all right, though he'll have a lump on his noggin when he wakes. Intend to see to it he stands trial. Crooked lawmen rankle me no end. I'm goin' back to the hotel like nothin' happened. All this effort has made me hungry anyway. I suggest you guys go one at a time up to the jail. 'Might be that four men traipsing about on a Sunday night could draw interest. I'll come by first thing tomorrow mornin', and like I said, go easy on the liquor."

Bass left the barn and got on the trolley once again. The trolley conductor, an older man who punched tickets, acknowledged Bass on his fourth trip of the evening. "It's Sunday night, mister. God-fearin' folk should be abed!"

"'At's where I'm headed, Pops. No one's more afraid of him than me."

The trolley crossed the bridge, and Bass jumped off in front of his hotel. He went inside and up to his room where he reloaded his Colt and washed up. Next, he went downstairs first to the front desk to check for messages and then to the café, where he took a seat at the counter. Much of the café was dark, being near closing for the evening, but there was a waitress behind the counter who took his order.

# Stolen

Bass checked his Elgin; it was 9:35 p.m. The girl came back and struck up a conversation.

"Hate workin' the Sunday late. Never any business, and I can't get by without the kindness of extras from the customers. How come you're out so late, mister?"

"Card game." Bass thought it was as good a reason as any.

"Oh . . . you're at Silva's game, playin' with outlaws."

Bass looked up with a hard glance. "Sorry, mister, don't mean nothin' by it. Them fellas is my best customers. What'd you do to get an invite?"

Bass looked at her for a moment. "Shot a sassy waitress in Santa Fe."

The girl raised her eyebrows and walked down the counter, leaving Bass to eat in peace. When he finished, she came back to clear his place setting. "Sorry again, mister, don't do for me to be offendin' customers. Got a baby to feed an' need all the help I can get."

Bass smiled at her comment and asked for a whiskey. She went to the bar and brought it to him, set it down on the counter, and walked back down to a wash pan to clean glassware. Bass thought of Sally and their baby and his place in El Paso. It all seemed pretty far away now.

382

# Stolen

He thought then about his plan to restore order to Las Vegas and figured it might take more than another day or two. But felt good again about his work and life in general. Bass finished his whiskey, paid his bill, and left five dollars for the sassy waitress with the baby.

# Stolen

Chapter 26

*6:45 a.m., January 9, 1888*
*Plaza Hotel*
*Las Vegas, New Mexico Territory*

Bass woke in a sweat, even though it was quite cold in his room. He recalled no disturbing dreams; his wounds were on the mend and causing little discomfort. Still, he couldn't explain the feeling of dread that swam inside him, his gut, and his chest. He tried shaking it off, thinking somehow it was a part of his plan for Silva, and for a while, that worked. Deciding he was better safe than sorry, he strapped on one of his Walker Colts and adjusted his belt for the heavier weight. He knew the Walker was powerful enough to offset most any shortcoming there might be in his plan. Somewhat reassured, he went down to the café and had coffee and a Naegelin's pastry before heading down to the jail.

The morning was cloudy and cold, with the threat of snow in the air. The Sangre de Cristos were shrouded in a white haze and barely visible though less than two miles away. The trolley was late making its first tour of the day, and Bass stood on the hotel steps waiting, trying to shake the unsettling feeling that he'd missed something. When the little train arrived, Bass jumped on but remained standing for the short trip. He was still rolling his plan over, trying to spot the weakness. He knew it was there he just couldn't find it. He hopped off the trolley on Douglas and walked the last block to Twelfth Street. As he approached the jail, all seemed well. He walked in to find Gabe eating bacon from a pan and Patchelski locking someone into a cell.

"Look who's here? Hey Marshall, come see what I found this morning at the diner down the street."

It seemed that Mike Patchelski was elected to fetch coffee this morning from a small breakfast place further down on Twelfth Street. When he got there, two half-drunk Mexicans were putting the squeeze on the owners trying to recoup money they'd lost in a card game. Patchelski knocked one on the head and held the other under his gun as he explained to the owner what was happening and would continue to happen all over town. The café owner, a Swede named Ahern, was so grateful he helped Patchelski get the men to the jail and didn't charge for the coffee.

Gabe took Bass to the cells, where Bass saw the two vaqueros asleep on top of each other, and while he was there, he looked in on Sheriff Belcher.

# Stolen

"Hey, Bass. How long do I gotta stay in the same cell with this stiff? He's gonna get ripe in a little while."

"If it bothers you that much, Belcher, we'll shut the stove off back here an' keep ya both on ice."

Bass left the cells and congratulated Mike Patchelski. He asked Viligry about Waverly and Ramsfeld and was told they were out walking the streets on 'collector patrol,' and he was about to leave himself. Bass clapped both men on the back and stepped back out into the street. It was time to pay a visit to Mr. Silva, and Bass decided he'd prefer to walk. He walked up Twelfth Street and turned left at National, crossing the little bridge over the Gallinas Creek. As he walked up the steps to the office of Silva Freight and Shipping, he felt comfortable once again in his plan and his work.

Bass opened Silva's office door, and the first thing he saw was what he thought might be the world's largest living human being. He had to be seven feet tall and weigh at least three hundred pounds. Bass's mouth fell open, and for a moment, he was speechless. Then he heard movement behind him and felt a blow to the back of his head. Momentarily dazed, he fell forward into Silva's office and the waiting arms of the giant that Silva seemed to control.

"Sit him down in that chair, Francisco."

# Stolen

Bass was picked up bodily by the brute and placed unceremoniously into a chair in front of Silva. As he shook the cobwebs from his head, he turned to see who'd clubbed him and chuckled, realizing he'd found the cause of his uneasiness.

"Miguel de Storano, by God, if you ain't the prodigal snake in the grass. Murder any old men lately?"

"You underestimated me, hombre." De Storano put his face close to Bass as he tightened the leather straps around Bass's wrists. "You should have killed me, gringo."

"Hah. Yeah, well, the day is young, prick."

"I am sorry for the old man on the train, but in the end, Señor, his death lies at your feet."

"Boy, nothin''s ever your fault, is it, Miguel? I won't make the same mistake again." Silva entered the conversation now, "It is too late for you now, Marshal Bass."

Vicente Silva sat behind his desk holding a short, barreled pistol that looked like a Remington Iroquois .22. It was pointed at Bass's middle.

"It seems that you have cost me a few of my most trusted men, including, I might add, my Segundo, Jose Chavez, y Chavez. A loyal man . . . and a friend." With that, Silva fired the little pistol.

# Stolen

Bass heard a small 'pop' and felt a sharp pain in his right knee below the joint. Because of the way Bass was sitting, the small caliber round caused not much more than a flesh wound.

"Ow, holy shit, that hurts." Bass doubled over, looking for a way to stop the bleeding and cursing at the pain. When he'd recovered enough, he looked back up at Silva, snarling, and said,

"Silva, I'm getting real tired of this businessman-outlaw-captain game you got goin' on here. You should know there's a flock of US Marshals on their way to your little kingdom, and they all mean to shut you down, try you, and hang you in the street like the cur dog you are."

Silva had a smug look on his face and smiled. "I am afraid you're mistaken on that, Marshal. I told you, I control all the news that goes in or out of my town, and no such wire, letter, or signal of any kind has left Las Vegas. No, Frank, there's only you."

"You're wrong there, Silva and your men outside are findin' that out right now. My posse's rounding up all your collectors. They're being locked away in the jail as we speak, along with Sheriff Belcher."

Silva's face turned white. This time, he believed Bass. He started to realize his time may be ending, and the rage of failure backed up in him like the bile that eventually chokes all evil men.

"Marshal Bass, you have gone too far. I promise you will not survive an interview with my friend here. Let me introduce Francisco Guerrero, or as his friends refer to him, El Chelequero."

Silva's monster had been standing in a corner, cracking his knuckles and watching the room. Now, he advanced slowly, never taking his eyes off Bass. He was dressed in a fine blue suit with a red satin vest, his namesake, over a white silk shirt. He had long, greasy black hair and a thick mustache that framed the wicked smile on his pock-marked face. He was grinning at Bass and showing his yellowed and missing teeth.

Bass, bleeding from his leg, could only think to say, "Howdy do there, amigo. Boy, I'd like to stand and greet you proper, but you see, your boss has just shot me."

Silva raised the gun again. "Enough of this foolishness." He fired once more, this time catching Bass in his left forearm.

Bass grimaced and growled through the new pain and willed himself to sit back up in the chair. Silva turned back to El Chelequero in a rage and said, "Francisco *hazlo rapido*."

# Stolen

The big man nodded and moved to pick up Bass by the collar. Just as El Chelequero reached for Bass, the office door flew open, and a shotgun blast tore through the giant, dropping him to his knees. He was thrown back over himself when the second barrel of the gun went off. Silva dropped his gun with the two explosions and was caught by the pattern of the birdshot that was fired. Several pellets entered his left arm and shoulder. He fell backward over his chair and sprawled against the wall.

Early Gates, the café owner who had kicked Bass out of his diner the day before, cut the leather bands that bound Bass's hands.

"Heard what you were doin' from one a' your men. They said you were coming to get Silva, so I thought I'd come help."

Just as Bass managed to stand, Silva rose with his pistol from behind his desk and fired a round that grazed Early Gates's left temple. Bass drew his Walker and fired at Silva. The oversized round nearly cut him in two. He lay crumpled on the floor, his eyes open in death, clothes smoking from the blast, and blood dripping from his mouth.

Bass turned to look for de Storano, who'd dashed out as Gates came in. Bass chased out of the building as best his wounds would allow. His right leg caused a pronounced limp, and his left arm dripped blood down his cuff. His right hand gripped the Walker Colt. His vision was hazy, but he glimpsed the older Mexican running toward a corral behind the court house. He wiped the sweat from his brow with his right sleeve and then tried to level the Colt at de Storano's legs as he was running. He fired, and the bullet severed de Storano's right foot. He fell hard, screaming in pain and clutching at the exposed bone and tendon that was once his ankle.

"*Bastardo. Diablo malvado!*"

Bass felt only relief as he walked toward Miguel de Storano. "You were right, amigo. I shoulda killed you when I had the chance."

De Storano was drooling in pain as he watched Bass, and finally, half crying, he spit at Bass's feet. "Yeah, well. Better late than never."

And Bass pulled the trigger.


Bass slumped in relief and limped to a bench next to the corral, nearly collapsing onto it. He stared at the body of Miguel de Storano and thought of the old porter, Clancy Mulacky. Gates helped Bass to the nearest doctor, a man named Petrie, who'd been an army surgeon until his

# Stolen

retirement. Now, his practice was limited, but he stayed current with the practices of the day. Doc Petrie was near sixty years old but still spry and quick-witted. Balding and a little heavy with round wire-rimmed glasses perched on his nose, he enjoyed talking with Bass as he examined him.

The wound on Gates's head was minor; Doc didn't even think it warranted stitches to close. He cleaned and bandaged it and sent Gates on his way, assuring him Bass would be 'fine as snuff' when he was through.

"I believe I'll go check on my daughter, then head on back to the jail, see if I can help out there. Might be a good idea to have someone who knows the bastards to lookin on 'em." Gates left, and Doc Petrie continued on Bass.

"Damn, what'd that ol' bandit use on you, a slingshot?"

"Little gun, thank God."

"Yeah, the one in your arm ain't a worry. I'll just patch that over. Gonna hurt for a while, though. The one in your leg is trickier, son. The lead's still in there. Gotta dig it out. You want somethin' for the pain?"

Bass thought for a moment, "No, just get to it, I guess."

# Stolen

Petrie positioned Bass's right knee over a rolled pillow facing up.

"I know it's just a wee little thing, but the bullet nicked what's called your medial collateral ligament. 'Missed the bone, I believe, but I'm gonna have to set your knee in pretty much this position for at least a couple weeks. If the ligament tears any more, you're talkin' big trouble. Means needin' a real fancy back east surgeon to fix it and walkin' funny the rest a your days. Lemme just have a look here." Doc Petrie did a shallow probe of the wound and then backed away. "I'm gonna have to put you under, Marshal. If you wince or move just a little, that ligament could tear further, maybe all the way."

"Okay, Doc. Do what ya gotta. You ever done this before?"

"Oh yeah, 'course. This should be a cake walk once you're under." The old man lied. "Just lay still now."

Petrie placed a sponge soaked in chloroform over a gauze-covered screen, set it over Bass's nose and mouth, and told him to breath normally. It only took a couple of breaths before Bass was asleep, and Doc Petrie quickly removed the sponge and screen. The bullet removal was a quick procedure: a shallow probe to locate the bullet and forceps to remove it carefully. Petrie placed the small

# Stolen

misshapen piece of metal in a dish and then turned a magnifying glass on the wound. Spreading the damaged muscle revealed the slight tear in the pale white ligament. Petrie decided to treat the wound as a sprain since he had no way to surgically fix the ligament. Even if he had the means, he decided, the surgical repair might be more dangerous and take longer to mend. The tear was small enough that, with care and rest, a good prognosis could be achieved.

He doused the area in antiseptic and sewed five stitches over the wound to close it. After bandaging, he used a section of stiff elastic, usually used by vets, to hold the joint in a fixed, immobile position while Bass slept. When he woke, Petrie would advise the patient of his diagnosis and use tape and plaster if need be.

As Bass slept, Gabe Viligry and his posse, along with an increasing number of townspeople, were gradually filling the jail with Vicente Silva's former collectors. Three councilmen, including Harry Roman, had been arrested as well. Bass's plan for the town had come off better than expected, notwithstanding gunshot wounds and several conspirators being too dead at this point to be prosecuted for their crimes.

# Stolen

Nevertheless, by 3:00 p.m., when Bass awoke, the town seemed secure from extortion and the violence of Vicente Silva's gang. Gabe Viligry still had concerns, however. He and his posse-men had spent several days earlier in the month observing the Silva Rancho and knew that a cadre of loyal fighters might possibly be preparing a counterattack on the town right now. His concern was real, echoed by his men, and would require a new plan to deal with the likely threat.

# Stolen

Chapter 27

*5:00 p.m., January 9, 1888*
*Plaza Hotel*
*Las Vegas, New Mexico Territory*

Bass had been helped back to his hotel by an appreciative throng of business owners and townsfolk. Many were already discussing names for the new city council, and Early Gates was the odds-on favorite for the position of sheriff. Bass used crutches and had difficulty climbing the steps to the front door, so several men—including the blacksmith Bass had met two mornings ago—lifted him and carried him to the top step before setting him down easily.

He thanked the small crowd that had followed him to the hotel and reminded them that Gabe Viligry and his posse deserved all the credit for locking up Silva's men and most of the city council. Several other members had been seen leaving town on horseback, heading in the general direction of Silva's rancho several miles to the north. Bass thanked all those present and said he'd stay 'til the job was done. He also reminded the gathering that what happened next in Las Vegas was up to them.

# Stolen

"Elect a mayor and council you know and trust. As to sheriff, men don't come with more sand than Early Gates, but that's up to you, too." This drew spontaneous cheers and whistles while Bass turned and walked into the hotel.

As he hobbled inside, he was met by a young man with a telegram. Bass glanced at it and recognized it was the answer to a question he'd sent to District Judge Clarence Hobart days ago. Bass took the wire and went into the bar, where he leaned his crutches against a stool and asked the bartender for a tall rye with plenty of ice. The man smiled big enough to be seen in Texas, and Bass had a free drink in almost no time. Still standing, he took a long swallow and let it slide down his throat, warming him as it went. The wire from Judge Hobart said simply:

> *District Justice L. Bradford Prince is your man.*
> *'Know him but little. Fine jurist and honest man.*
> *Solid reputation. 'Will send your precedent. –*
> *Hobart*

This was the name Bass needed to ensure the legality of all that was done. There was no question that good had triumphed over evil and that many wrongs had been righted, but Bass also knew that what was right and what was legal were not always the same thing. The example he always used was the gunfight in Tombstone some years back. Everyone knew the Earp brothers and Holiday were enforcing the law and in the right, but they still had to stand trial for murder and be acquitted by a court of law. Las Vegas was in a similar situation. Citizens were killed or injured, and only a court of law could proclaim the actions just. Hence his telegram to Clarence Hobart and his wire to be sent this evening to District Judge L. Bradford Prince at the Territorial Capitol in Santa Fe.

For Bass, the most pressing issue was his jurisdictional authority in the territory and, by extension, the arresting authority of the Texas sheriff and his posse. An unfavorable decision by the District Judge could see all the villains now in the city lockup, set free, not to mention charges against himself. And while it was true the 'head of the snake' one Vicente Silva was no more, it would be possible, even likely, that a subordinate might step up and recreate the same criminal environment all over again. Until that time, however, Bass's authority in the New Mexico Territory was undisputed, and additional arrests were likely. The next day, Bass would lead his peacekeeping army to the Silva Rancho north of Las Vegas,

# Stolen

where he would first interview Señora Silva and speak to her about the death of her husband. Then, he would ascertain the nature of the rancho's vaqueros and laborers. If their duties were legitimately a part of the workings of the rancho, then the status quo would remain. If on the other hand . . . there were certain individuals on the payroll that had shady or criminal backgrounds, or there were too many men with vague or indistinct job descriptions, then Bass would have to take steps.

And that's what concerned him. Starting a range war was not part of his plan. Before retiring to his room for the night, he wrote out a telegram to be sent to District Judge Prince. He asked Early Gates to take it to the telegraph office for him with strict instructions that no one else was to see the contents of the wire. Once Early had gone, Bass asked that a meal and a bottle be brought to his room, and he made his way, slowly and carefully, upstairs. He doubted he'd ever get used to using crutches and hated everything about them, even the name. Once in his room, he removed his gun belt and felt relief from the heavy weight of the larger gun.

He stripped down to his blood-stained drawers and lay back on the bed, his right leg resting on a pillow at the appropriate angle. A knock on the door meant his meal had arrived, and he called to the server to come in. It was the front desk clerk who carried the tray and set everything down on a small table that he moved to the bedside from the other side of the room. The man poured whiskey into a glass of ice and set it down within reach. He also handed Bass the day's newspaper. He wore a humble look on his face and stared at the floor most of the time.

"Mr. Bass, I'd like to say, on behalf of the hotel, how grateful we are for everything you and your deputies have done for us. Naturally, there will be no charge for your stay. I'd also like to apologize for my less-than-welcoming attitude the other day. If there is anything I can do for you in the meantime, please ring this bell. From experience, I know I will be able to hear it through the heating ducts."

"What's your name, sir?"

"Philip Stilton, sir."

"Well, Philip Stilton, apology accepted. I wasn't exactly a flower of civility either, as I recall. I guess we both better remember not to make too many assumptions about folks we don't actually know. Thanks for bringin' my supper."

# Stolen

The younger man smiled. "Of course, sir, when you're ready to have the tray picked up, just ring the bell. Good night."

Stilton left the room, and Bass took a swallow of the whiskey and a bite of his ham sandwich. He decided to save the pickle for dessert.

# Stolen

Bass woke to the same sound of the blacksmith's hammer, and this time, there was a rooster crowing somewhere close by as well. He decided that his older wounds were just a little sore, but the new ones, especially his knee, ached pretty bad, and maybe he should have taken the Doc up on the pain killers after all. He really wanted coffee and decided to roll himself out of bed, taking care of his knee as he did. It took a great deal longer to dress than usual, and Bass hoped that as time went by, it would get easier. He couldn't see how, though, and resigned himself to the notion that the knee wound would slow him down more than usual. He had no intention of ever using the damned bell, 'just couldn't picture himself sitting in bed like a 'Grand Poobah' ringing servants for their attention. It was considerate of Stilton, but just not Bass's style.

He made it downstairs by hopping from one step to another and sliding the crutches down before him. He finally made it to the café, and Maevis rushed up to take his order, smiling and bubbling on about how everything was on the house and was he comfortable or not. Bass smiled

402

and tried to act cheery. He ordered eggs, a pork chop and fried potatoes, coffee, and a biscuit. While he was waiting, Gabe Viligry walked in and sat next to him, signaling to Maevis for coffee.

"Mornin' Frank, how're you feelin'?"

"Not too bad, all things considered. Where'd you boys spend the night now that you don't have to hole up in the livery barn anymore?"

We all stayed at a place called the Monte Suma Hotel. Two hundred rooms and three stories tall it is. Got three saloons all to itself each with a separate card room. And a real elegant dining room too. We was sure outta place there, but my, the food was fine."

Bass smiled as he listened. It was a small reward for the discomfort the posse had endured over the last ten or twelve days.

"Well, I'm glad you and the others enjoyed it. Where are they now?"

"Outside waitin' on you. We got a horse for you from old man Hopkins, but if you ain't up to it, we can go ourselves. Several of the more able-looking townsfolk wanna come out there too."

"I plan to go, Gabe, 'just gotta take it a little easy. Not too spry with these damn sticks here. Why'nt ya have 'em all come inside outta the cold while I eat? Have a coffee."

"Sounds good. Be right back."

Bass could hear people coming in from the outdoors speaking loudly, but all in good humor. When he finished eating, he went out to the lobby to greet as many townspeople as he could. There were nearly fifteen men in the lobby, all armed and seemingly able-bodied. Bass hopped up on one of the steps and turned to the crowd.

"Ah, first, I wanna thank you all for coming out. As I hope you know, we're gonna be riding out to Silva's ranch this morning to talk with Mrs. Silva, of course, but also to check out the number of *vaqueros* and *pistoleros* that may be still hangin' on out there. My guess is the news has already reached them, and in my experience, a gun hand don't hang around too long when he finds out the boss is dead an' he ain't gonna be paid. Ya never know, though, so I want you all to be aware of what you're getting into. I see you're all armed, and that's good. But you keep your pistols, your rifles low. I don't want no accidents on this trip. You take your cue to action from me and me alone. Any questions?"

One hand went up in the back. "Are we deputies, Marshal?"

# Stolen

"No, I can't deputize you all. I believe, technically, you're a vigilante committee. 'Least that's what my report will say. Any others?" There was another voice from the back.

"Marshal?"

"Yes."

"Thank you."

Bass smiled and dropped his head.

"Well, you thank these four boys here in front. They done the hard part. And remember, once we're gone, it'll be up to you and the rest of the town to make the place decent again. Keep it that way. Oh, and it's Deputy Marshal, actually."

After a short laugh, Bass led the way to the Plaza, where the horses stood waiting. Once mounted, Bass was able to maintain his right leg at the proper angle for the short ride to Silva's ranch. The weather was clear and brisk, and the mountains behind the town created moving shadows and colors as the sun rose. The peppery smell of wood smoke was everywhere as people lit fires and stoves to warm their homes and businesses.

It only took twenty minutes or so for the column of vigilantes to reach the main gate of the rancho and a few minutes more to pull up in the front paddock next to the house. BooneWaverly had already seen a part of the inside of the place when he was looking for the girls, and he was visibly impressed with the size of the main house.

The structure covered the better part of an acre. Bass could see at least two atria and several verandas about the perimeter from his position on horseback. The construction was adobe and timber walls with a red clay tile roof. There were four chimneys visible and smaller chimineas on the verandas, and in the atria. There were two large wooden barns within several hundred feet of the house, a long low bunk house between the barns, and corrals around each barn. The entire compound stood on flat ground that had to measure at least five square acres, all backed up to the Sangre de Cristo Mountains.

As the final riders were coming into the yard, a middle-aged woman of old-world bearing appeared at the door. She was tall, Bass reckoned, with white hair that had been pulled back and wound on top of her head like a crown. She stood in perfect posture, her hands folded in front of her black dress and shawl. When she spoke, it was slowly and with great deliberation.

"I am Señora Telesfora Silva, gentlemen. How can I help you?"

# Stolen

Bass made eye contact with her. "Good morning to you, ma'am. I am US Deputy Marshal Frank Bass, and these gentlemen are the Las Vegas Vigilante Committee. We'd like to speak to you about your husband and his business practices in town, and his employees in particular, and anything else that you might be able to add from your own knowledge about this rancho. May we have your permission to interview your employees here at the ranch?"

"To what end, may I ask, Marshal?"

"Ma'am, it is possible, even likely, that a criminal element is present here. If so, it is our intention to bring them to justice. I am asking for your cooperation in the matter, ma'am, though, in all honesty, I don't really need it."

Señora Silva stiffened at the last remark but softened immediately, possibly recognizing that to refuse was pointless.

"Of course, Marshal. *Puedo*—that is, can I offer you a coffee? Tea, against the chill?"

"Well, thank you, ma'am. Most gracious."

Bass gave instructions to Gabe Viligry to break the group into four different parties, with him and his men leading, and then to search the entire grounds. They were to detain any armed men, of course, disarming them, but also any man who could not name and explain his duties on the ranch.

Bass carefully dismounted and, using his crutches, climbed the stairs to the wide veranda. He was led through a curved arch to a hallway that spanned the width of the house. There were decorative benches along the wall with paintings and large potted plants at regular intervals. He went through an arched double door that led to a large salon on the left and an open atrium on the right. The hearth in the salon was ablaze with candlelight, and the room was comfortably warm. The parlor was decorated in the Moorish style. Bass had seen pictures, and there were several heavy pieces of furniture intricately carved and stained or painted in dark colors. From the artwork on the wall to the Persian carpets on the floors, Bass thought it was the most impressive room he'd ever seen. He also knew he'd hate living in it.

"Please sit, Marshall. Let me ah—how is it said, fetch?—yes, fetch a stool for your leg. There, are you comfortable?"

"Yes, ma'am, thank you."

"Marshal, before you begin, let me say that I am fully aware that my husband was *delecuente*…a—a criminal. I also understand from men employed here that

# Stolen

you killed him. Is that right? Is that why you are wounded?"

"Yes, ma'am, on both counts. I need to explain, ma'am, it was self-defense."

"I have no doubt. I know exactly who and what Vicente was and that this day was coming, in fact overdue. I hope you are not in too much pain. Please ask any questions you wish; I will be completely open with you."

"Thank you, ma'am. All right, let's get to the hog killin' then."

"Pardon me?"

"I'm sorry, it's an expression, it means let's begin. I must ask you, Señora, were you aware of the kidnapping that your husband carried out?"

Genuine shock and then dismay shown on Telesfora's face. "Kidnapping? It means to steal someone, yes?"

"Yes, ma'am. In this case two young girls from a small town in Texas."

The older woman was pained at hearing this and began wringing her hands. "Oh no. *Ver a Dios*, no. Where are they now, the children? Please say they are not harmed."

# Stolen

"They are fine, Señora. They are home in Texas with their family."

Telesfora's shoulders sagged, and her face whitened. "I'm sorry, Marshal. I had no idea he was capable of such a thing. I must write to their parents, have you their address?"

"Yes, ma'am."

They both heard gunshots fired outside, and Bass jumped to his feet, hobbling to the door without his crutches. He saw men shouting and running in the direction of the bunkhouse and then heard several more shots and more shouting. Ignoring everything Doc Petrie had said, he ran as best he could after the crowd, fearful of what he might find. As he turned the corner at one of the barns, he saw two men lying in the dirt in front of the bunkhouse. Both were unmoving and appeared to be dead. One was a Mexican that Bass recognized as Patricio Maes. The other was Mike Patchelski, Gabe Viligry's good-natured deputy. Bass couldn't take his eyes off the scene, knowing it could erupt in a bloodbath.

"Mike was only standin' at the door, Marshal. The Mexican he just threw open the door and shot him." It was Boone Waverly speaking, choked up, with his eyes filing. "I did for the Mexican. There's still some in there."

# Stolen

Bass turned away and faced the bunkhouse. Señora Silva had run up to his side, tears on her cheeks. Bass signaled for her to stand behind him and spoke in a loud, clear voice, *"Este es acabo, comprende!?* It's over! Come out now, and no one will shoot. You men from town put your weapons away."

There was silence for a few moments as the events that had transpired sunk in. When no one appeared at the bunkhouse door to surrender, Señora Silva stepped up beside Bass.

*"Mi esposo esta muerto. No debe haber mas XXXatanzas! Rindete ahora. No seras dañado. Por favor.* No more killing!"

A few moments later, five men emerged from the bunkhouse, unarmed with their hands up. Bass recognized Sandoval but none of the others. He guessed they were all wanted somewhere, in the territory, or perhaps, in Mexico. Bass knew as well that many of the outlaws Silva employed or protected had fled as word of his death got around. They were not his concern any longer, but might be one day in the future.

Bass and Telesfora walked back to the hacienda together, and he thanked her for her courage at the bunkhouse. He was sure, he told her, that she saved lives. Still weeping, she went quietly inside.

Gabe Viligry was still shaken as he approached Bass. "Been talkin' with the others. 'General feeling is to bury Mike here. Preacher'll read over him. He got no kin that anybody knows of back in Texas." There was a pause as Viligry looked away, wiping his eyes. "Boy, I hate to bury a man. It's so damn permanent."

Bass put his arm around Gabe Viligry's shoulder. "You boys did a fine job, a fine job. Be proud to serve with ya'll again."

Viligry nodded and walked back to the bunkhouse to take care of moving Patchelski. Bass walked back behind him and called Early Gates over.

"Gates, I'm turnin' these five over to you for transport back to town. 'Probably need more lock-up space. Maybe one of the hotels or business'll let you use a storeroom for it. Keep 'em guarded, though. You've seen what can happen."

"Will do, Marshal. Awful sorry 'bout your man."

Bass just looked down and nodded. "Yeah, well . . . ." He climbed slowly onto the rented horse and headed

# Stolen

back to town alone. When he got to his hotel, someone was waiting for him.

"You must be US Marshal Frank Bass. I got your wire," said the well-dressed older man, extending his hand. "Judge L. Bradford Prince. How can I help you?"

Bass smiled at the man. He was dead tired, and it wasn't even noon yet. "It's Deputy Marshal, actually. And I'm gonna tell you a story."

# Stolen

Chapter 28

*6:15 p.m., January 12, 1888*
*En Route, EP & SW Station*
*El Paso, Texas*

The train was running forty minutes late getting from
'Burque to El Paso. Coal was short at Las Palomas, and a
second stop was necessary in Rincon. Other than that, the
trip from Las Vegas was uneventful. Bass couldn't
remember when he'd spent so much time traveling by train.
It certainly made the frontier smaller, and Bass knew it
would continue as new track was being laid every day.
Bigger and more powerful steam engines would be built,
coaches, diners, and sleeping cars would be more
comfortable. Innovation fuels the economy and lightens the
load on humanity. As he sat musing, the train lurched
violently, nearly throwing folks into the aisle and rattling
windows and nerves. A dip in the track or uneven roadbed,
most likely. He turned his thoughts to his own position in
the game and considered it akin to the role of referee,
ejecting the errant players while keeping the game alive for
the ticket holders.

# Stolen

The stop at Las Cruces returned his musings to the previous summer and how often he'd stopped at that station while seeking answers for Theo Treece. He was anxious to get home now and only a few miles away. Another hour to Sally and his home, his friends. The familiar day-to-day of ranch life and marshaling. His right leg ached, and he considered that he may have—what was the term, exacerbated?—made his injury worse. Those last days in Las Vegas were arduous, to say the least. But there was 'resolution, favorable in all regards. Judge Prince had ruled generously on the question of jurisdiction. The most violent remnants of Silva's White Hat Gang were incarcerated without bail and would stand trial in the new town that would build on the old. Lengthy terms in the Penitentiary at Yuma were all but guaranteed. The nonviolent rascals, the councilmen, and greedy businessmen would face stiff fines, which would pay for the things worthwhile communities need: schools, courts, and proper law enforcement. He was proud to have been a part of it and keeping the game alive. But now it was time to rest, to wait for his baby, and to heal-up. He needed to take his mind off the game for a while.

The train rolled to a stop at the passenger platform, and people began moving toward the coach's doors at either end. Bass assumed that many were coming to visit personnel at Fort Bliss, just north of El Paso. Then again, some were probably coming to visit Ciudad Juarez. Whatever the reason, there were more travelers milling about, looking for baggage or family and friends.

Bass was still trying to get used to the crutches he was told to use to protect his knee and waited to be the last off the car so he wouldn't hold anyone back. Once he'd hopped down the steps from the car to the platform, he started looking for someone who might've been sent for him. He'd wired his arrival time to Sally and figured she'd have someone here to meet him. He checked Franklin and St. Louis Streets but saw no one he recognized. As he was standing on Franklin Street, checking his Elgin, a dapper-looking fellow holding a notepad approached. Soon, another and then another arrived, each vying for Bass's attention. There was a bright flash followed by a shock of white smoke from somewhere in front. It took a moment, but Bass realized his picture had been taken and the men crowding around were reporters asking questions of him.

"Now, just hold on a damned minute, will ya? I'm just tryin' to get home to see my wife and friends."

# Stolen

"Marshal Bass, Marshal Bass, Edward Selkirk, New York Herald Tribune. How many gunmen did Silva employ in Las Vegas?

"What? I don't know, too many."

"Marshal Bass, Joe Pulitzer, St. Louis Post-Dispatch. How widespread was the political corruption in Las Vegas?"

"The top down, Joe. From the top down. 'Bout wide as you can get, I'd say. Now please fellas, leave me be, ok?" At a distance, Bass saw Paulo Armendez sitting in a buckboard on Franklin Street, laughing and clapping his hands.

"That there's my ride home, boys, thanks for meetin' the train. So long, now." Bass pushed through the reporters and the crowd of gawkers that had gathered and made his way to the wagon stand where Paulo waited.

"Well, by God, Chato, if you ain't just about the most famous thing ever? Takes my breath away, it does." He jumped down from the seat and helped Bass get his valise, gun belt, and rifle into the wagon.

"You need help getting in, your worship?"

"You just hush and drive."

Bass set his crutches in the back, hopped onto the step, and sat down. Paulo got up, released the brake, and clucked his team into motion, away from the crowd that still stood watching. In a few minutes they were passing the Chamizal and talking like the old friends they were.

"You hurt your knee?"

"Oh, that Silva fella shot me with his pop gun, just at the knee and in my left arm. Doc that took out the lead in my leg said I had a slight tear in my medium collar *liga-thingy*, and if I weren't careful, I could make it worse."

"So let's see then, on this little rodeo, you been shot three times and stabbed once bad enough that it took septic and you had to burn out the poison, that about right?"

"Yeah, yeah, Sally told the world, I imagine, but it really weren't as bad as it sounds. And them children are back with their parents, without handin' over the money. Pretty fair trade, I think."

"Doubt Sally's gonna see it that way, but 'case I forget, congratulations. 'Whole city's pretty proud of you. Those reporters been hangin' around for a couple a' days asking anyone who might know you personal questions about you. Say, what is your favorite color, anyway?"

"Anymore a' that, and you can walk. I ain't that crippled, you know."

"All right, all right. Just havin' some fun with ya. I know it must've been a grind on you, the last two weeks. I

# Stolen

can tell you Sally's 'bout bustin' her buttons over you. Just yesterday, some reporter came to the house wantin' to interview her. Sally said somethin' like, 'My husband is truly a fine man and the most competent man I've ever known at what he does. I shouldn't be surprised at his exploits anymore, but he still amazes me.'"

"My word, Paulo, that means the world, you know? I guess I'm in for a hero's welcome at home. Wait here for a bit, Vato. I'll come back for my stuff."

The wagon pulled into the yard in front of the house at TwainHeart Ranch, and Bass clambered down from the seat and hopped up the steps to the front porch. As he opened the door, he called out, "Sal? I'm ho—"

"Well, you certainly took your own good time about it. I'm sitting here two years pregnant, certain you won't be here for the birth of our child, and you're out in some far-flung terri—oh stars! What happened to your leg, my love? Please sit and tell me how badly you're hurt." Sally helped Bass to a chair by the hearth and stood behind him as he sat. She bent to hug him from behind and kissed his cheek and neck.

"Oh, it ain't much. Fella got me using a little pop gun, is all. I'll be fine by and by. But how are you, Sal? You must be in a way, I'm sure."

# Stolen

"Well, you can see I'm near to busting open. I can't sit for very long. 'Can't stand for long, either. I surely will love this baby, but by God, I'm ready for this part to be over with. Nesta and Marianna have been angels putting up with me." Sally caught herself seeing Bass with his knee bent and the crutches on the floor beside him. "I'm sorry, sweetheart, you've been gone so long doing wonderful, selfless things for others, and I'm rattling on about my cares."

"Well, Sal, nothin's more important than you and the baby." Bass hugged her as best he could. "Has Doc Spalding been out?"

"Every other day. He just keeps sayin' 'any time now, any time now.' And how about the stab wound that hurt you so?"

"Oh, it's fine. I had a doc look at it in Las Vegas, and he said it would be ok. Scar looks funny, though."

"And your knee. Please be truthful about it. If it's bad enough that you'd consent to use crutches, I'd like to know the whole story."

"You know me well, don't you, Sal?"

"Yes. And I love you too, Frederick, so tell me about the knee."

# Stolen

"All right. I was tied up, hands behind me, in Vicente Silva's office. He'd got the drop on me with the help of a Mexican outlaw and 'snuck up behind. Well, this Silva fella was awful mad at me cause of all I'd done to turn him out, and he used this little pistol on me. Shot me once in the arm, see?" Bass rolled up his sleeve to show Sally the bandage. "Then, a bit later, he popped me in the knee. He was real frustrated, see. Now this other doc says, and these were both fine doctors, mind, it slightly tore my medical continual liger-thing, and I'd better use these sticks for a while is all. He said it was as if I'd sprained somethin'. I'm fine to walk around—"

Sally suddenly looked startled and concerned. "Sweetheart, hold that thought. I believe my water broke. Yes...yes, I'm making a mess, all right. Let me lie down on the divan here, dear, and maybe I'll be able to get up to my bed in a bit."

Bass jumped from the chair to help Sally lie down and did his best to make her comfortable. He then went out to the porch and called to Paulo, who'd been waiting patiently. "Paulo, I believe it's her time! Would you please fetch Nesta and then maybe see about finding Doc Spalding?"

# Stolen

Paulo said nothing as he threw some pebbles at his team to wake them. He cracked his buggy whip over their ears and was off as fast as the wheels could turn. Bass went back inside and pulled the footstool over to the divan.

"Can I get you anything, sweetheart? A cold towel, maybe?"

"I'd dearly love a tall sherry, Frederick, if you please?" Bass went to the kitchen cupboard for a pickle-jar glass and filled it nearly to halfway.

From the front room, he heard Sally. "And perhaps a towel or two, please, Frederick?"

Bass hobbled as quickly as he could, dropping off the sherry wine and then heading to the linen closet. He returned with two of their fancy terrycloth towels which he helped her to position. It was then that Sally started to feel the initial contractions of early labor.

"Spalding says that when these begin, dear, it sometimes helps to get up and walk a bit, so if you'll help me up, I believe I'll go upstairs."

"Yes, yes, of course, Sal. Here we go, upsy daisy."

As it turned out, Bass was the one who needed the most help climbing the stairs. He grabbed the railing and hopped each step, holding Sally for balance. Eventually,

# Stolen

Sally was comfortably in her bed with the pillows fixed just so.

"Frederick? Would you please—oh dear God!" Sally groaned and took several deep breaths. "Give me my hand mirror and the large bru—Jesus Christ Almighty!" She moaned. "My word. Ah, thank you, dear." Sally's eyes were wide, and her face pale and damp.

Bass was dumbfounded. He'd never seen anyone handle pain so matter-of-factly before.

"I sent Paulo home to get Nesta. She'll be here pretty soon, and then he's gonna go find Doc Spalding."

Bass sat on the bed holding Sally's hands. Several small contractions came moments apart and left fingernail gouge marks on the backs of Bass's hands.

"Would you like another sherry wine, sweetheart?"

Sally was perspiring now, even though the bedroom stove had been cold for some time.

"Oh yes, dear, please, yes."

Bass hobbled carefully downstairs and refilled Sally's glass. Going back upstairs, he threw caution to the wind and put some weight on his right leg. It seemed fine, so he continued. When he entered their bedroom, Sally was brushing her hair and occasionally dabbing at the moisture on her brow.

# Stolen

"Thank you dear, this will calm me—!" Her words trailed on. "Agh, Christ Good God in Heaven!"

Bass nearly slipped off the bed. This was all new to him, but then he realized it was just as new to Sally as well. His first baby was born years ago by a young Indian maid name Moon in Winter Sky. When that happened, Moon just walked to the river with a birth helper and appeared the next morning with a baby boy. Both had died of typhus months later, but this was the only close exposure to childbirth that Bass had ever had.

They both heard sounds downstairs and then Nesta's voice as she entered the room. "Paulo has gone for the doctor, Marshal. And welcome home, too. We're all very proud of you. I will stay with her if you wish to go downstairs and wait."

"Yes. Do that, please, Frederick."

Bass nodded quickly and leaned in to kiss his wife, but as he did, another contraction hit her, and she lurched forward, splitting his lip with her forehead. Bass patted her back and limped from the room.

Once downstairs, Bass poured a tall whiskey and did not bother to visit the ice box before swallowing it down. He checked his Elgin, it was 9:45 p.m. Paulo had gone to find Doc Spalding, and at this hour, he would most probably be at his home behind his office. He reasoned it would take at least an hour, to an hour and a half, for him to get there and then back here, and after all, women had been giving birth since time began, and Nesta, who had delivered twins but was younger than Sally was upstairs, he figured she would be just fine if he had another whiskey.

At about that time, Theo and Marianna Treece knocked on the door. Paulo had told him that he was picking Bass up at the station, so Theo and Marianna decided to come by. Marianna had made enchiladas that needed warming, and Bass took them with his thank yous and set them on the dining table. At that point, Sally could be heard commenting to Jesus the Lord God, and Marianna dashed upstairs, leaving Theo and Bass in charge of the decanter. After filling Theo's glass and refilling his own, both men took the small cigars that Bass preferred out to the porch.

The night was clear and cold with a waning crescent moon that shown directly over the Rio, reflecting up to the porch. There was little wind at that hour, and they could smell the woodsmoke from the hearth inside. Theo still had his heavy sheepskin jacket on, but Bass wore only the frock coat and light vest he'd worn on the train. It mattered little to him. By this time, the whiskey was doing its work.

# Stolen

"How long has she been in labor, Frank?"

"'Bout an hour, I guess . . . maybe a bit longer."

"Huh. Did she have any pains at all beforehand?"

"Didn't seem to, why?"

"Well, obviously, she's in active labor now, which may mean a shorter-than-expected delivery. This is her first, though, so that kind of works against the short labor period."

"Theo?"

"Yeah, Frank?"

"Have another drink, will ya?"

"Oh. Sure, Frank. Say, you know you're quite a celebrity around here now." Theo talked through the open front door. "Had two reporters at the feed lot yesterday wantin' to know 'bout you, how you cleaned up Las Vegas, and had you ever done it before?"

"What'd you tell 'em?"

"Told 'em I didn't know, but if anyone could do it twice, it'd be you."

"Huh. Thanks, Theo. They kinda mobbed me at the train station, too. 'Told 'em I'd talk to 'em later. Sure is quiet upstairs now. God, I hope everything's ok."

# Stolen

"I'm sure it's—"

From a distance, both men heard. "Holy Jesus, Lord Mother of God."

Both men looked at each other, and half smiled, not at Sally's pain but the indication that things were progressing normally. A few minutes later, Marianna poked her head outside.

"Señor Frank, where is Sally's sherry wine?"

"Oh, it's on the chest by the dining table, Marianna. The one that's half gone."

Marianna hurried back upstairs, and Bass and Theo continued talking. Bass talked mostly about the posse-men from Hartley and the young Sheriff Gabe Viligry.

"They're the real heroes of Las Vegas, you know. They tracked the kidnappers clean across the Llano, four days in trying weather, and then another couple watchin' the ranch from a distant rise. When it came time to round up Silva's henchmen, those boys were right there—arrested and jailed everyone. One of 'em lost his life on the second day tryin' to arrest the remaining outlaws that were out at Silva's ranch. Yessir, those boys did fine, just fine. Damn proud to know 'em, too. Work with them again, anytime."

# Stolen

"Well then, I guess you'll have the chance to speak up for 'em when those reporter types start showin' up, huh?"

As Theo was speaking, Bass caught a glimpse of torchlight heading his way down the river road. Doc Spalding, in his buggy, led the way with Paulo behind in the buckboard. Doc pulled up and didn't even take time to tie off his gelding; 'just dropped the reins on the buggy seat, grabbed his bag, and dashed inside. Bass called after him that Sally was upstairs, and without breaking stride or even offering a good evening, he was up the stairs to care for his patient.

Paulo followed him and tied off Doc's rig after seeing to his own. Then, he joined Bass and Theo on the porch.

"So? Where's my cigar? My whiskey? C'mon, Cisco. Havin' a baby is one thing, but a man left without his whiskey? Damn near intolerable."

Bass limped inside and brought out a fresh bottle, a glass, and the box of small cigars. There— along with his two friends—he spent the next three hours on the porch in the dead of winter, solving the world's problems.

The sound of a newborn's wail is unmistakable to expectant fathers, and at the first cry, Bass was through the

# Stolen

front door, hopping up the stairs and into the bedroom to hold his child. At exactly 1:55 a.m., according to his trustee Elgin, his daughter was born healthy, loud, and complete. Sally was exhausted but well, and Doc proclaimed the whole thing a roaring success.

Bass could not remember being happier in his life, even when his son was born more than two years ago. Nesta agreed to stay the night, mostly to keep Sally company and provide relief when Sally needed sleep. Bass said goodnight to Doc with as much gratitude as he could muster and asked Theo, Marianna, and Paulo to come back the next day for a real celebration. Once they were safely on their way, he laid down on the divan and drifted off, trying out girls' names to see how they fit with a simple surname like Bass.

# Stolen

*7:15 a.m., January 13, 1888*

*TwainHeart Ranch*

*El Paso, Texas*

Bass was awake before anyone else and first went into the
kitchen to light off the stove and make coffee. As he
measured the grounds, he heard the baby upstairs in a high-
pitched, quickly-paced cry, which must've meant she was
hungry. Her complaining didn't last long, and Bass took
that to mean that Sally was awake and on duty. He left the
coffee to percolate and, eschewing the crutches by the
divan, climbed the stairs as carefully as his desire to see his
family would allow.

In the bedroom, Bass could not have imagined a
more perfect scene. Sally was sitting up, her auburn hair
brushed and framing her beautiful face, smiling at the small
being at her breast. She looked up at Bass, fairly glowing
with misty eyes but the same full smile.

"Frederick, look what we made."

Bass approached the bed, and Nesta took her cue to
give them some privacy.

"I know, love. I met her last night. How do you
feel?"

430

# Stolen

"Surprisingly, well, much better than I thought I would. A bit sore and tired, of course, but look at her. She's absolutely perfect. I don't think I shall ever put her down. But sweetheart, you so hoped for a son. Are you terribly disappointed?"

"Dear God, no, my love. As you say, she's perfect. But I'm wondering about a name, dear. I've been thinking some, last night and this morning, but I can't come up with anything I like."

"Well, I've thought about it for some time. I wasn't as sure as you that we were going to have a son. Anyway, if it's all right with you, I'd like to name her after my grandmother. Her name was Lillian."

"Lillian. Hm. Lillian. Lilly . . . Lil. Oh, I like it, Sal. Lillian is kinda regal sounding, and Lil is a name for the frontier where she'll grow. Done! Lillian Bass. Oh, wait. What about a middle name? Shouldn't she have a middle name too?

"Yes, yes, of course. How about your mother's name?"

Bass thought for a moment, "No, I don't think so. Don't get me wrong, I loved my mother, but her memory is clouded for me because of what she became. I don't blame her, you understand. She did what she had to do to feed her children. Still, it's not a name I want for Lil."

Both were quiet for some time, and finally, Sally offered, "Frederick, please tell me if you think I'm out of line, but I remember your story of the Crow Woman who cared for you and healed you when you were younger. She showed you your totem spirit, and you said once you cared for her like a mother. Do you know her birth name?"

Bass was touched that Sally remembered how important Crow Woman was in his life.

"You know, I only remember her saying her Cheyenne name once. She talked of her lover, Owl, often but only said her name the one time that I recall. In Cheyenne, it was Henoe Exooe. It means 'Meadow Blossom.'" Bass continued to think and then offered, "The Cheyenne term for Medicine Woman is 'Nova Vae.'"

Sally looked up at Bass, "Hm. I like Meadow Blossom very much, but I also like Nova Vae."

Bass was not a very emotional man, but he was visibly touched. Sally looked at the baby, and tears filled her eyes.

"I'll leave that choice up to you, dear. Whatever you like best."

# Stolen

Bass thought for a long moment. He had never called the old woman Meadow Blossom, and it was only in passing that she told him her birth name. He had always known her as Crow Woman. The 'Crow' totem was a symbol of her healing power. Her medicine.

"I believe I like the term for Medicine Woman best. In the end, that's what she was for me. So, 'Nova Vae.' Okay?"

Sally smiled immediately, thinking of the words. Together, they sounded poetic and even celestial.

"Oh, yes. I like it, Frederick. Very much."

"Lillian Nova Vae Bass."

Sally rolled it around in her thoughts for a moment, "Just as you said, dear. Done!"

# Stolen

Chapter 29

*8:45 a.m. January 16, 1888*
*TwainHeart Ranch*
*El Paso, Texas*

Bass sat at the kitchen table, drinking coffee and eating a leftover biscuit from dinner the previous night. Sally was still asleep, recovering from several nighttime feedings that Lilly demanded. At 10:00 p.m., she began crying to be fed nearly every hour. Sal called these 'cluster feedings.' Bass had another name. After nursing, Lilly slept nearly four hours before requiring Sally again. Bass was perfectly happy to get up each time and walk the baby, gently swaying, until Sal was ready.

Being a new father at thirty-four years was something of a mystery for Bass. He loved sitting at the fire after dinner, holding her and watching her make faces. And he made them back of course, along with some funny noises and gurgles. Sally got a kick out of watching this big man who'd busted heads all over the territory, being so gentle with his baby girl. And he didn't shy away from the changing table either, though there were times he needed a whiskey directly after.

# Stolen

Lilly slept in her cradle next to Sally's side of the bed. Silas Pratt had put the finishing touches on Lilly's room now that he knew it would be for a girl, and Sally was ordering furniture. Soon, Lilly would make the journey to a crib in her own room.

As Bass daydreamed, there was a knock at the front door. He put his cup down and swallowed the last of the biscuit. He pulled the suspenders from his pants up over his shoulders and tucked in the long-sleeved drawers he was wearing. He padded to the door, barefoot, and opened it to find Johnny Cojar, one of the youngsters who delivered telegrams.

"Damn, Johnny, what brings you out so early? What time is it anyway?"

"8:00 a.m. when I left the office. Don't know now. Got two telegrams for you, Marshal, and a 'notice of delivery' from the railroad." The boy handed three slips of paper to Bass. "Didn't say I should wait. You want me to?"

Bass took the notes and fumbled in his pocket for a bill. He handed Johnny a dollar note.

"Maybe. Hang on a minute." Bass read the first one. It was from Sally's sister Maggie, advising that she and her daughter, Elsie, would be arriving today at 4:00 p.m. Bass nodded his head. She had originally been due on the twelfth, but she got delayed by business at her ranch in Torrington, Wyoming. Bass could take only so much of Maggie, but he really looked forward to seeing Elsie. Bass and the girl had developed a special bond after she'd been raped and brutalized, a crime Bass had discovered was organized by the girl's stepfather, now deceased, thanks to Sally.

The second message was from Avery Matlock in Hartley.

*Dear Frank, warmest regards from all the Matlocks, a family again, thanks to you. This note will advise you of a gift of appreciation from XIT Ranch. I imagine it's waiting for you on the loading dock at the train station. – Avery*

The third note was a bill of lading stipulating the freight company's approximate weight and delivery location. Bass read the weight. "Twenty-three hundred pounds? What in God's creation weighs twenty-three hundred pounds? Johnny, you know what it is?"

"No, sir. It was still on the train when I left. You got any answer for the others?"

"Huh? No, no, you go on now."

# Stolen

"Okay, thanks for the dollar, Marshal." Johnny turned back to the small plug he rode for deliveries and headed down the path and back to town. Bass stood on the porch scratching his head when Sally walked out with the baby. Sally was recovering quickly, and aside from slight fatigue due to the disruption in her sleep schedule, she was nearly back to her normal weight and disposition.

"Who was that dear?"

"Hm? Oh, telegrams. Your sister arrives today at four o'clock."

"Wonderful. Perfect timing. What were the others?"

"Huh?"

"The others. You said *telegrams*."

"Oh, well, one was from Avery thanking us again and saying that his ranch had sent a 'gift of appreciation.' It's waiting at the train station and weighs twenty-three hundred pounds!"

"Oh, my goodness. What in the world . . . ? Well, I'm sure it's lovely, whatever it may be."

"Twenty-three hundred pounds, Sal. What weighs twenty-three hundred pounds? Oh, and how're we gonna move it?"

Sally had already walked back inside and was seated in a chair by the fire, feeding Lilly.

# Stolen

"Seriously Sal. What could it be?"

"I hear those new Benz motor cars can weigh a lot, though I don't think twenty-three hundred pounds. And anyway, of what use could one possibly be on a cattle ranch?"

"A plow, a good heavy, iron plow. I'll bet that's it. Say, and we can use one, too, as much planting as I plan for this spring. Yeah, that's it. Thoughtful and useful, too."

"I'm sure you're right, love. Now, we have to make ready the third bedroom upstairs. We can move in Lilly's dresser. It's small but should serve. I'll need to put sheets on the bed, shake out the curtains and such. Will you bring up a supply of wood for the stove? That corner of the house gets the wind, you know. I'll make a list of things we'll need so you can go to town early to buy groceries and things for their visit. We'll certainly need towels, for example. Oh, this will be fun, don't you think, dear?"

"Yup, yup, lotsa fun indeed. I gotta stop by the feedlot anyway. "Want me to invite Theo and Marianna over?"

"Of course. Maybe for tomorrow, though. Maggie and Elsie will be tired after their trip. I want them to meet Paulo and Nesta, too. Oh, and speaking of Nesta, I'll need to ask her help with Lillian this afternoon while I do the house."

"I'll do it. I'm gonna ride over and ask Paulo to help unload the plow once I get it back here. The freighters at the rail yard will help load it. 'Might have to use one of our hay wagons at the feedlot to haul it back. 'Leave our buggy at the office."

"I'd like for you to leave in an hour or so. Give you plenty of time to shop before meeting the train."

"Uh-huh, yeah. Okay then, I'll ride over to Paulo's now. Back 'quick as I can."

Bass finished his coffee and stopped to put on his boots and heavy jacket. He strapped on his Colt and went to the barn to saddle his tall mare, Emma, for the short ride to the Armendez house. The weather was cold, and scattered snow flurries swirled in the gusts off the Rio.

When he got there, Paulo was in the barn feeding his animals. Bass walked in and went directly to the oversized stall that housed Willy, the Shire horse Bass planned to breed one day. Willy had come as a bonus when Bass bought the Puholz Ranch that was adjacent to his. Paulo, Nesta and their girls were homesteading the place, doing repairs, and living in the house. The extra acreage he and Paulo used to graze cattle they owned jointly.

# Stolen

"Hey Paulo, how're you this mornin'?"

"Ugh. Feel something; comin' on Cisco, cold likely, don't come too close. Get one every year . . . only question's when. My ma calls it Catarrh. Whatever it's called, I don't like it. Slows me down too much." Paulo continued pitching hay from the loft into the corral as they spoke.

"Yeah, Paps back in the Rangers always said he had a cure for colds."

"He did? Well, tell me, please."

"He'd say 'rub bacon grease mixed with garlic on your chest day and night and drink a whiskey every two hours. In ten days to two weeks, you'll be good as new.'"

"Hah, thanks a lot. Sounds like Paps, though, surely it does. What brings you over?" At this point, Paulo had a lengthy sneezing fit and held up his hand till he felt he was finished.

"Two things. First, Sally asks if Nesta can help with the baby for a couple of hours this afternoon. Sally's sister arrives at four o'clock, and she needs to make the house ready."

"Lucky you. Yeah, Nesta's in with the twins; go on, ask her."

# Stolen

"Will do. I also need your help. Avery Matlock's ranch sent me a thank you gift, and I may need your help unloadin' it."

"Really? What is it?"

"Don't know for sure, but I believe it's a heavy iron plow. The freighter says it weighs twenty-three hundred pounds."

"Too heavy for one. Could be two, sure enough, or some other farming equipment." Bass patted Willy's muzzle and reached up to scratch his ears.

"How's Willy been?"

"Oh, he's fine as can be. Eats enough for three horses, though. Be glad when you move him over."

"Well, been plannin' to take some time off with the baby an' all. I'll come for him in a week or so. 'Guess I'll go ask Nesta for help this afternoon. Oh, and Sally plans to invite you two and Theo and Marianna over maybe tomorrow to meet her sister and niece, but if you're ailin', don't worry about it."

"Okay, see ya later then. Come fetch me if you need help."

Bass gave Little Willy's forehead a pat and walked to the house. He stopped at the back door and could hear Nesta talking to her two girls in the kitchen.

441

# Stolen

"Mornin', Nesta. Miss Isidra, good morning to you as well."

"Well, howdy, Marshal. You havin' a good day so far?"

"Isidra Armendez! Is that how a lady speaks to a gentleman?" Chinesta scolded her daughter.

"But Ma, it's Marshal Bass. He's not a gentleman."

"Isidra!"

Immediately, Isidra realized what she'd said and covered her mouth with her hand, embarrassed. "I am sorry, Señor Marshal, I didn't mean you're not a gentleman. I only meant that we know you."

Nesta looked chagrinned. "Chica, you'd better stop right now. You're only making it worse. Find your sister and look for something worthwhile to do."

"*Sí*, Mama—I mean—yes, Mother." Isidra left the kitchen, watching both her mother and Bass.

"She's not too far off the truth of it, Nesta. I ain't no gentleman. Usually, anyway. Say, I came to ask if you'd help with Lilly this afternoon. Sally's sister and niece are comin' in on the 4:00 p.m. train, and she's got a slew a chores to make ready. She also wants to have you all over tomorrow to meet them."

# Stolen

"Oh of course, any chance I get to hold the baby, I take it. And whenever she wants us, we'll be there. What time does she need me today?"

"'Bout an hour, I guess. You want me to come pick you up?"

"No, no. The girls and I will ride over. Paulo has a sickness, so he mustn't come. We'll be there."

"Okay, good deal. See you then."

Bass left the house and headed toward the rail where Emma was tied. He climbed aboard, being careful of his knee, and rode to the barn door.

"Hope you feel better, bucket head!"

Paulo turned from the bale he was opening, "Yeah, me too. Say, don't you get this sickness and give it to Lilly. Nesta'll bust me proper if you do."

"Eh, I'm healthy as a horse."

"Yeah, one that's just been stabbed once and shot three times. Or was it four?"

Bass shook his head. "See ya around the hay baler, hard case." Bass clucked up Emma to the gate and galloped her across the flats to his barn.

As he walked inside, Sally and the baby waited in the kitchen at the counter. Evidently, Sally had just changed the baby, as she was using Doctor Springdale's Persian Talcum powder on her bottom to dry her quickly.

"That looks like fun. Think I might like to try it."

"Oh? Have you been wetting your drawers lately, Frederick?"

"No, but it looks like fun after a bath. Wanna give it a try?" Bass winked, and Sally gave him a wicked smile back.

"Maybe, conditions being right, if you take my meaning." Bass hugged her from behind, nuzzling her neck as she pinned up the diaper.

"I generally do. Ain't Lillian the proof?" Sally turned and kissed him quickly, signaling that playtime would have to wait. "I have some things for you to pick up from Mr. Hoffer, and then at Beckham's General, we need four more of those terry cloth towels and any light blue, extra-large, square, linen tablecloth they may have. I'll get my list. We still have a full root cellar, but fresh greens at Derby Market on St. Louis Street would be a treat. Oh, I need to add sugar for baking. Elsie and I always used to bake ginger cookies. So let me add that, and dear, anything else that you can think of. You're good at that."

Bass stood in his stocking feet, nodding and saying yes whenever the cue was issued. He took the list and his daughter for some "Papa time" before he left. Sally went to take an inventory of the root cellar now that she'd pronounced it well stocked.

Bass sat in the rocker he'd bought for this type of occasion near the fire and watched his daughter's face with a slight smile of wonder on his own.

"I smell of coffee and horses, don't I, sweetheart? And soon, I'm gonna smell of whiskey, too. But that ain't so bad. 'Fact is, there are some pretty good smells to get used to around here. I'm gonna be gone for a while this afternoon, and when I get back, you're gonna have some more family to meet. One day, we'll go see my sister, but she lives too far away for us to go now."

The baby looked directly into Bass's heart, the way only babies seem able to do. Then she yawned and slowly closed her eyes and slept. Bass rocked without moving her until Sally returned and traded the baby for the shopping list.

Bass wanted to wear clean clothes, meeting his sister-in-law for the first time in nearly a year. So, after changing and cleaning his teeth, he went into the barn and buckled his draft horses, Butch and Melody, up to the buckboard and snapped the whip for the Rio Road and El Paso.

# Stolen

# Stolen

Epilogue

*12:30 p.m. January 16, 1888*
*Hoffer's Butcher Shop, Overland St.*
*El Paso, Texas*


Fritz Hoffer's Butcher Shop was two doors down from the icehouse near the freight terminal and around the corner from Joseph Bilger's meat packing house. Hoffer kept a large ice closet in his shop, and he and his son, Hymen, broke down the sides of beef and pork they bought from Bilger's into usable portions and displayed them on ice each morning except Sunday.

Bass stopped there first, knowing it would take some time to fill and wrap the order, and he would call for it on his way out of town. The little bell above the door jingled as Bass entered the shop. Fritz came from the back room, wearing his butcher's cowl and bloody apron and wiping his hands on a towel. He was an older man in his sixties but still active and sharp as his knives, he would say.

"Marshal Frank, welcome back from your journey. You're limping, was you hurt out der?"

"Oh, tussled a bit, Fritz, just a bit. 'Good as new in a week or so. Say, Sally's got an order here, can you fill it?" Bass handed the slip to the butcher over one of the display cases. Hoffer reviewed it.

"Ach *ja*, Frau Ausfall. She has the baby?' The old man's round face smiled broadly.

"Yes, yes, a little girl. We named her Lillian."

"*Eine kleines madchen, wunderbar*. They are both good, yes?"

"Yes, they're both fine, just fine."

"Ach, *das ist gut*." Fritz continued smiling and nodding his head.

"Yes, yes. Ah, the order, Fritz?"

"*Ja, ja,* de order." Fritz looked at the paper again. "'Dis is much bacon, *ja*? *Und braten und schweinefleisch*?"

"We have company coming."

Fritz Hoffer nodded again, understanding the need for such a large order. "*Ja, Herr Marshal. Zwei*—ah—two hours, yes?"

"Yes, Thanks Fritz. See you then." Fritz waved as Bass left the shop and returned to his wagon.

Bass headed next to Beckham's General Merchandise, west of Hoffer's on Overland at Stanton. It was a three-story shopping venue that offered a selection for everyone. Beckham's sold hardware, toiletries, ammunition, condiments, linens, and usually the freshest green vegetables available in town. Bass pulled up near the loading dock and walked in through the back door. Heidi Beckham, the daughter of the owner and one-time flame of Marshal Frank Bass, met him.

"Hello, Frank. My, you still look good enough to eat. Even with that limp. My goodness, whole towns's just agog with your latest exploits out to the west." She watched him move as he walked to her. "You all right, honey?"

Heidi Beckham was a tall, dark-haired beauty who'd been the object of most eligible men's desire since she was sixteen. She was near thirty now, never wed, but not too anxious about it either. She and Bass had a moment or two when they were younger, but he was usually off Rangering, or Scouting for the army, and the two never managed to be available when the other was. Then, Bass settled down with Moon in Winter, and Heidi decided to focus on her father's retail business. She'd been the general manager of the store for six years, and it had grown substantially under her guidance. Still, there was a very small spark between them that would probably always be there.

"Oh no, I'm fine Heid, just a small holdover from my time in New Mexico. You look mighty fetchin' yourself."

# Stolen

"Mighty fetching? God, that dates us a bit. Nobody says 'fetching' anymore. Today, they say a girl is 'charming' or 'enchanting,' and men are 'sharp' or 'nifty.' 'All means the same thing. Anyway, welcome back, and thanks for bringin' all those newspaper types with you. They spend like crazy in here."

"Glad *some* good comes of it, lotta nonsense if you ask me. Say, can you help me out? Sally gave me a list. Her sister and niece are coming in this afternoon, and we need a few things for their stay."

"Sure, of course. How is Sally? 'Last time I saw her, she was like to burst she was so pregnant."

"Well, she did, kinda. We have a daughter, as of a few days ago, Lillian."

"Oh, Frank. That is wonderful. Mother and baby, okay?"

"Yeah, they're fine. That's why I'm doin' this. Sal must stay with the baby, naturally.

"Yeah, I got ya. Let me see. Sheets, towels, tissue . . . yeah, a' course, I'll box it up for you. 'Have it all ready in an hour or so."

"Oh hey, thanks, Heid. That's a big help. I ain't much good at that sorta thing."

# Stolen

"No problem, you go on about your business, and I'll see ya after a while."

Bass walked back out to the buckboard and checked his Elgin. 2:00 p.m. Still, time to pick up the plow and get back to Hoffer's and Beckham's. But first, maybe a little celebration with the crowd at Paddy Hannigan's Saloon. 'Wouldn't take long after all, and it was in the general direction of the EP & SW passenger station. Bass headed his team back down Overland St. to St. Louis and turned to the left. Paddy's place was halfway down the block. Once again, he pulled his team into the alley beside the building, set the brake, and eased himself down from the seat.

Strange faces and loud talking filled Paddy Hannigan's Irish Clover Saloon to bursting. He made his way to the bar and had to elbow himself into the railing. Hannigan stood fifteen feet down the bar, whistling and yelling himself red in the face. Bass tried to get his attention, but Paddy was involved with a customer and not looking anywhere but into the customer's face. Bass put his elbows on the bar to hold his position and looked around at the people standing about, drinking beer, smoking those little cigarettes, and talking loud enough to be heard across the street and down the block.

# Stolen

Finally, Paddy spotted him and called out, "There he is boys, the very same come down to Paddy's for a wee dram." As soon as he finished, newspaper people surrounded him, waving pencils and papers at him and peppering the air with questions. Paddy realized what he had unwittingly done and rushed down the bar to escort Bass behind it and into Paddy's office. Once inside, Paddy closed the door and seated Bass on the one chair in the room. He sat on his desk.

"Ach, boyo, I should be caged and put on display I should. I'm sorry indeed, Marshal. Let me pour you a glass of heather and give you some quiet." Paddy reached into a desk drawer and produced a bottle of Kilbeggan Parliament whiskey. He poured Bass a generous taste and one for himself.

"Thank you, Paddy. My that's fine sippin' liquor. Could make me rethink my Overholt Rye."

"Tis the water of life, it is lad. Now, tell me of your experience in the nether lands."

Bass relayed a quick version of his time with the girls and in Las Vegas: how he'd been shot and stabbed, how the little girls escaped on their own and found him by chance on the Llano Estacado. Paddy was duly impressed and then offered an idea for evading the swarm outside.

# Stolen

Bass agreed and slipped out the back through the storeroom, and Paddy went back to the bar, where he made his announcement.

"Gentlemen of the press. Your attention, please. I have just spoken with our hero himself, and I can tell ye meself his is a story you'll want to hear. So, the Marshal has agreed to meet you all tomorrow afternoon at two o clock, me darlins', at his office on Mesa Street, at which time he will take your questions in an orderly manner. Orderly, do ya hear? Now, to show you the kind of man he is, he's asked to buy you each a drink, so step forward, and I'll fill your drams."

There ensued the expected confusion, and Bass was able to back his team out to the street and head directly to the freight office to establish how to get his gift from XIT Ranch out to TwainHeart.

Bass arrived at three o'clock and presented the clerk at the freight counter the telegram he'd received that morning. Once the clerk had finished congratulating him and welcoming the Marshal home, he led the way to the farthest warehouse from the street there was. Upon entering, Bass's eyes went directly to his gift. Before him was a beautifully conformed snow-white Shire Mare standing at least nineteen hands and obviously weighing in

453

# Stolen

at about twenty-three hundred pounds. Bass was completely at a loss to know how Avery would remember. They had only talked of Shires once and only in passing at that. Still, here she was, Goddess-like, serene and quiet. Bass approached, slowly taking sugar cubes from his pocket and presenting them to her slowly, even reverently. She sniffed first and then carefully licked the cubes from Bass's hand. Then she turned her massive neck and perfect head to the front to look directly at Bass.

"Oh my. Sally and her sister will have quite a time naming you."

The clerk handed Bass an envelope which the clerk advised held the bill of sale, the bill of lading. And the pedigree of the horse. Bass read briefly that she was 'Angel Heart' out of broodmare Chelsea Wit. By Dunehaven's Crow Wing, the Sire.

Bass was dumbfounded but suitably impressed at the effort that had to have been put into bringing this wonderful animal to El Paso. He thanked the clerk several times and asked if he could leave her there until he collected his guests and supplies. The clerk, of course, agreed and Bass went back out to his buckboard and started his team back to Hoffer's Butcher Shop.

# Stolen

Following that, he stopped at Beckham's, where Heidi had completed his order and was waiting on the loading dock. After several thank yous and a friendly peck on his cheek, Bass headed back to the warehouse and his gift. The big horse seemed very mild-mannered and didn't balk at all to being tied at the back of the buckboard and waiting in front of the station, where she was gawked at and fawned over by everyone who saw her.

"Maggie, hello, you look wonderful. And Elsie, do you remember me?"

Elsie—who had been traumatized by her ordeal in Wyoming—remembered Bass and ran to him, hugged him, burying her face in his chest.

"Thank you for meeting us, Frederick. We're so anxious to see Sally and your new daughter. I imagine she's just lovely. And I must say I've heard an awful lot about your exploits in Las Vegas. Even on the train coming down people getting on in Denver and then Albuquerque; that's all they could talk about. And I never even heard of Las Vegas. I can't wait to hear the whole thing firsthand. And who is this fantastic creature attached to the back of our wagon? She is just lovely and very, very big."

"Yes, she is that. She's what's called a Shire horse. The breed's from England. When I bought the ranch next to

# Stolen

ours an inky black Shire horse I call Willy came with the deal. I happened to mention to Avery Matlock my plan to breed him one day. As a thank you, his ranch, XIT, gave me this. Her papers say her name is Angel Heart. For now, I'll just call her Angel. And she seems just as sweet as her namesake."

When they pulled up the path to the front of the house, Sally came out carrying the baby.
She stopped dead in her tracks when she saw the big white horse. After the hugs and kisses were finished, Sally went to Bass.

"This is our plow?"

"I know! Ain't she just fine? Just fine as fine can be?"

"She is beautiful, dear, but may I ask where you'll put her?"

"I thought about that. For now, I can put her in Butch and Melody's stalls. Open the gate between 'em. The draft horses can double up with Susie and Emma. Those stalls are oversized as it is, and they get along well anyway. 'Gonna have to talk with Paulo about getting' them together. He knows more 'n I do about such things. I 'been callin' her Angel but we can come up with another name if you like."

# Stolen

"She does seem sweet. Quiet and alert. Maybe 'Angel' fits. Come in as soon as you can. Lots to talk about."

"Yeah, yeah, right. Lots. Elsie looks good, doesn't she?"

"She does, Frederick. See you inside, dear."

Bass took the wagon down to the barn and put Butch and Melody away in the oversized stalls with Emma and the mule Susie. He covered both with blankets and filled the troughs in both stalls. He walked Angel around to the separate stalls, and Frank led her in opening the gate between the two enclosures. He had to use two blankets to cover her and double-strapped them under her chest. Finally, he filled the troughs with alfalfa and oat hay and made sure the water tub wasn't frozen. By this time, his knee was beginning to ache, so he went back up the rear porch steps and into the mudroom just off the kitchen. All three women were putting away groceries and fighting over who got to hold the baby next, so Bass excused himself to the dining room and the whiskey decanter on the tray. He lit a small cigar and sat by the fire in one of the big comfortable chairs and thought about everything that had happened over the last three weeks. He also thought about

# Stolen

what he would say to the reporters who were due to show up at his office tomorrow.

Outside, it began snowing. Through the front windows, he saw wind gusts wafting the snowflakes in the lantern light from the porch. The sun had set, and it looked cold outside. He'd had plenty of experience dealing with being cold lately, too. He thought about all the people in Las Vegas, New Mexico, and Hartley, Texas, whose lives he'd touched and, hopefully, had made better. But all the lives that mattered most to him now were safe and warm here at TwainHeart.

The fire felt good, and the whiskey was working. He thought he might have enough time for a short nap before dinner.


The End

# Stolen

*Vicente Silva's White Caps and the City of Las Vegas, New Mexico Territory*

Vicente Silva formed the Sociedad de Bandidos, also known as the White Caps or sometimes The Forty Bandits, in Las Vegas, New Mexico Territory, in 1879. At the time, Las Vegas, New Mexico, was the largest city between Independence, Missouri, and San Francisco, California. The White Caps got its name from the white hoods with eyehole cutouts the gang members wore when robbing banks, holding up stagecoaches, or committing the many murder-for-hire assassinations they did. The Gang became known for its vicious and ruthless treatment of its victims. Major crimes were commonplace. The White Caps should not be confused with the Ku Klux Klan, as racism had nothing to do with their villainy. They preyed upon businessmen, ranchers, and farmers of all races.

Vicente Silva was, for all outward appearances, an upstanding citizen and businessman in Las Vegas. Hardly one to expect as a promoter of murder and robbery.

The Gang operated in a Mafia style, often forcing landowners from their property, stealing livestock, and

# Stolen

burning crops. Wealthy citizens would often 'disappear' when carrying large sums of money, and Silva saw to it that the local Pueblo Indians got the blame by inferring to authorities that the Indians were getting revenge on the whites.

In 1893, Silva's wife became suspicious of a murder within the gang itself, and Vicente decided to have her killed. He paid several of his gang members to do the job, but each refused, so he committed the gruesome killing himself. As he was about to bury the woman's body, his gangmen decided he had gone too far and turned on him, killing him and burying his body along with that of his wife. Without Silva, the White Caps gang began to fade in prominence, and law enforcement officers rounded up and hanged the remaining members.

# Stolen

*Las Vegas, New Mexico*

The city of Las Vegas, New Mexico Territory, was established by a Mexican land grant to a group of settlers in 1835. By 1846, the town was thriving largely due to its location on the Santa Fe trail. In 1879, with the arrival of the railroad, new businesses and residents began arriving. However, along with a respectable citizenry came gunmen, gamblers, murderers, and thieves as well. Among the many new residents were the likes of Doc Holiday and Big Nose Kate, Dave Rudabaugh, Billy the Kid, Jesse James, Mysterious Dave Mather, and Hoodoo Brown. According to one historian, ". . . there was no town that harbored a more disreputable bunch of outlaws and desperados than Las Vegas."

Today, Las Vegas is known as a college town and tourist center. New Mexico Highlands University is downtown, and Luna Community College is located in North Las Vegas. The United World College is located nearby in Montezuma, which serves as a venue for teacher training in the United States. The Las Vegas Carnegie Library is the only Carnegie Library surviving in New Mexico.

# Stolen

Acknowledgments

And

Appreciations

I must always thank my wife, Sheri, for her patience and understanding. She is the first to see my scribbles and catch my many errors. She continues to be way smarter than me.

And to my Editor, C.E. Costa, She has taken the lines I've written and somehow made them coherent. I am in awe of her skills and so very grateful for her participation.

To my writing support group: Pam, Peter, Francis, Annie, and Colleen. Most of the many blunders I commit are caught by these wonderful, patient people.

Made in United States
Orlando, FL
25 July 2024

49553988R00252